The Gospel in Isaiah

a Christ focused walk through the Scriptures

By

Stuart L. Brogden

2021

The Gospel in Isaiah

a Christ focused walk through the Scriptures

by Stuart L. Brogden

Printed in the United States of America

ISBN 978-0-9986559-4-9

Table of Contents

Endorsements

Mike Ratliff - Possessing the Treasure

https://mikeratliff.wordpress.com/

I grew up going to church. The churches I attended until I was past middle-aged held to Dispensationalism as their basis for how to interpret Scripture that pertained to Eschatology. During my adult years I probably owned over 50 books about the End Times. Why? I desperately wanted to know about the Rapture of the Church and I kept my eyes on the News seeking everything I could find that pertained to what was going on in the Middle East because all those prophecy "experts" kept telling us that the "End Times" could begin with the next war Israel had with Egypt or Syria or Irag, etc.

However, as God matured me I found that Dispensationalism was relatively new in the history of the Church. So I began studying the various Millennial doctrinal positions and soon found that walking away from Dispensationalism was indeed a great freedom. Why? I found that I no longer had to use the Old Testament to interpret prophecies made in the New Testament because that is not how the Bible "works." In the Old Testament God used visions, poetry, prophecies, etc. as types and shadows of what would be clearly fulfilled in the New Testament. In other words the New Testament interprets the Old Testament.

In *The Gospel in Isaiah* Stuart does a wonderful job of showing from the New Testament what God was showing Isaiah in his prophecies. Yes, without Dispensationalism clouding our interpretation of scripture we can clearly see parallel passages in Isaiah and the New Testament as Stuart shows us over and over again through his excellent exegetical study of each chapter. Stuart does a careful examination of the key passages though Isaiah and combines thorough exegesis, readability, and clear argumentation so that the reader can take up their Bible, study Isaiah for themselves with fresh insight that they probably would never have had without first reading this book.

Mark Escalera
Pastor & Former Church-planting Missionary
Author of *From Scam Into Blessing* and *Heroes of Courage*

Many available commentaries are written on New Testament books, but rarely seen are Old Testament books, especially major books like Isaiah. While Brogden's commentary is not exhaustive, it does look at the book of Isaiah from a New Covenant Perspective.

Walking through each chapter a few verses at a time, Brogden points directly to the risen Christ and the hope of mankind's future. Isaiah has long been one of my favorite books to read, and this volume brought out aspects that I had not previously considered.

It was my privilege to be able to read through this new commentary and to write a brief review. In Brogden's new work, I found plenty to draw from both for the new student of the Scriptures as well as for those who are called to exposit the infallible Word of God. A person that would be concerned about falling asleep in the middle of a tedious tome will find this to be precise and worthy of reading again and gleaning from its pages.

Sam Hughey

https://www.reformedreader.org/index.html

Stuart Brogden's *The Gospel in Isaiah* presents the Gospel of Salvation, Forgiveness of sin, and Redemption from God's divinely inspired prophet. The work in this book is a refreshing and enlightening look into the Holy Spirit's revelation of the work of the Christ for our Redemption, which will not leave the reader confused with archaic terminology. Stuart's simple approach is precisely what New Covenant members need to understand the work of Christ throughout the entirety of Scripture.

For new and young believers, anxious to understand the full scope of the work of Redemption, The Gospel in Isaiah will bring satisfaction and thoroughness of understanding of the work of God throughout the entire canon of Scripture. For more mature believers, this is a work which will remind you that our Lord's prophetic ministry of His work on the cross began hundreds of years prior, which leads to the fulfillment of the purpose of our election by the Father, sealed by the Holy Spirit and received in Christ.

Forward

I take great joy to introduce Brother Stuart Brogden's work on the book of Isaiah. Brother Stuart is a precious brother in the Lord to me. I have been enriched by his messages, conversations, writings, and re-publishing of great works written by our forefathers of the faith that would have slipped into obscurity without his tedious efforts. I spent the vast majority of my ministry blinded by the hermeneutics of a dispensational fundamentalist. The hardest thing I faced was removing those lenses and presuppositions of the past. I am thankful our paths providentially crossed, and for his patience to guide and encourage a younger brother from an entirely different background.

Brother Stuart is gifted with the ability to help us see the Scriptures with fresh eyes and cast away the residue that clouds Christ's glory in obscurity. The title *The Gospel in Isaiah* is perfect! This is what we clearly see without ambiguity. It truly is a Christ focused walk through the Scriptures. We see the glories of YHWH. We see His attributes declared. His sovereignty indisputable. The promises of YHWH unshakeable. His redemption complete. God's words sure, and His wisdom extolled. Brother Stuart walks us not only through this exposition as an academic experience, but leads us into worship. I often felt like I was on the edge of my seat thinking of Christ's glorious conquest and longing for His triumphant return.

This study is pastoral in its affections. He is able to transcend time to make the book of Isaiah applicable and timely for our generation. He exhorts us with warnings and encouragement to see the YHWH of Isaiah as the same God today. Many stand aghast at the concept of a sovereign God, but Brother Stuart helps us to stand reverential awe. This work shines a spotlight on the beauty of sovereign grace.

The uniqueness of this endeavor through Isaiah is multifaceted:

1. His hermeneutics are solid. He understands the gravity and seriousness of properly interpreting the Scriptures. Brother Brogden tells us, "Isaiah is a vision given to the son of Amoz. This gives us a clue about the nature of this book - similar to John's Apocalypse, wherein he was shown a vision and told to write what he saw. So as you read Isaiah, bear in mind that visions tend towards the symbolic, often using common vernacular to paint a word picture of something else." Isaiah is challenging and many fail the test by making the symbolic literal, and the literal symbolic. Many Bible teachers insist we must interpret the Bible literally. If they mean we should take our method of interpreting the Bible very serious, I agree. If by literal you mean it is inspired, supernatural, and the Word of God, then Brother Stuart certainly does this. But, if you mean we must take books like Isaiah, Ezekiel, and Revelation as always literal, and never or rarely symbolic, I disagree.

He understands the shadows of the Old Testament do not shine light on the New Testament. He reaches forward to the substance and reality of Christ that we may see the glories of YWHW in Isaiah. He is faithful to use the analogy of faith. Scriptures truly unlock scripture. He makes the interpreting of the clear teaching of Scriptures a priority before the difficult. He interprets the plain before the symbolic. He makes sure to look at what the Bible has clearly and undisputedly stated first, then moves to the difficult and disputed passages. He accepts the clear and plain parts of scripture as a foundation to shed light on the book of Isaiah.

2. His simplicity is refreshing. Many approach books like Isaiah by giving numerous perspectives and then suggest one they most agree with. This often leaves me with more questions than clarity. You do not have to be an academic to be edified by this work. Reading this book will not be an exercise of parsing the Hebrew language and understanding

their syntactic roles. He is gifted in allowing the Bible to speak for itself. What is amazing to me is this work is scholarly, but is yet a study guide to Isaiah for the common man. Many have made prophetic books like this nearly impossible to understand and comprehend, but not so here. Perhaps, it is his approach to seeing Christ as the hermeneutical key to all the Scriptures. He is precise without longevity. It is true that brevity is the soul of wit.

3. He has a precise understanding and distinctiveness of the text. Brother Stuart demonstrates numerous times how Isaiah points to New Covenant fulfillment and that the blessedness of the New Covenant is a reality for us today. It is a glorious study when we are not hampered by presuppositions of dispensationalism, or being wedded to limitations of our religious traditions. To have clarity of the "In that Day" statements enables us to see the majesty of triumph and judgment of the Great Day of the Lord. You will find doxology in the promises made to Abraham fulfilled "On THAT Day" as the redeemed from every tribe, nation, and tongue join in and worship as the true "Israel of God".

4. He provides a constant reminder of where our citizenship is. We shouldn't be overwhelmed with elections, political unrest, nor the success of our political party. These things will not last nor will our troubles. God has not vacated His throne, nor will He ever forget His children. We should see our ultimate allegiance is not to the nation of our nativity, but to the one true King and Kingdom that shall not end.

This book is a must-have for the ministerial student of the Bible, as well as the person who has had no formal theological training and who desires to understand the book of Isaiah. It is not intimidating, but powerful with substance for the more earnest student. It is warm and encouraging with practical application. It is Christ centered. You will see the majesty of Christ and want to break out in praise to our great God. It clearly and precisely reveals how the promises of the

Old Covenant is a reality for us in the New Covenant. It is encouraging to see *The Gospel in Isaiah*.

Grant Hardwick

Pastor of the Mount Hebron Baptist Church, Lancaster KY.

President of the New Covenant College, Lexington KY.

Introduction.

Isaiah is a vision given to the son of Amoz. This gives us a clue about the nature of this book - similar to John's Apocalypse, wherein he was shown a vision and told to write what he saw. So as you read Isaiah, bear in mind that visions tend towards the symbolic, often using common vernacular to paint a word picture of something else. Isaiah brings a four-fold message to the reader: a.) Accusing God's covenant people of sin, rebelling against the God Who made them; b.) Sinners are instructed to repent and reform; c.) Announcing God's judgment on people because of their sin; and d.) Revealing the redemption of His people.

This book is not a commentary on Isaiah, filled with word studies and detailed exegesis of the text; although it does have a few word studies and some exegesis of the text. It's not a devotional, full of personal application exhortations; although it does have some personal application and exhortations.

This book, the Gospel in Isaiah, is a thematic walk through Isaiah, focusing on the dual vision of God's punishment and redemption of His earthly, time-bound covenant people and the contrast with the persecution by the world and God's redemption of His spiritual, eternal covenant people provided by the promised seed, the Lord Jesus. While not every phrase in the Bible is about Jesus, the whole Bible is. May we seek to see Him more clearly.

In most chapters, all the verses are included with commentary. In some, I summarize a block that has one message, without including every verse.

It is my prayer that this walk through Isaiah will be edifying to the reader, to provoke you to see Christ more clearly as He is presented in the Scriptures as the apostles saw Him. The Lord Jesus is more glorious than we can picture in our feeble minds; He is worth our efforts to see Him for Who He is and treasure Him and His Word - for we find Christ therein! May the Spirit of the living God give wisdom to His people for their edification so we will glorify Him in our lives as we serve one another.

I. Rebuke and Promise from YHWH

Isaiah 1 - Rebellion, Judgment, and Grace.

We find out who Isaiah is by the content of his vision. Isaiah 1:1 "The vision concerning Judah and Jerusalem that Isaiah son of Amoz saw during the reigns of Uzziah, Jotham, Ahaz, and Hezekiah, kings of Judah." Isaiah served God during the reign of several kings, from 783 B.C. through 686 B.C.; beginning in the last year of Uzziah's reign, 742 B.C.

Isaiah 1:2-4 *Listen, heavens, and pay attention, earth, for the LORD has spoken: "I have raised children and brought them up, but they have rebelled against Me. The ox knows its owner, and the donkey its master's feeding trough, [but] Israel does not know; My people do not understand." Oh sinful nation, people weighed down with iniquity, brood of evildoers, depraved children! They have abandoned the LORD; they have despised the Holy One of Israel; they have turned their backs [on Him].*

Immediately, YHWH brings a charge against Judah, reminding me of Paul's opening to Galatians. He calls heaven and earth as witnesses, reminding His covenant people that He raised them and they have rebelled, turned their backs to Him; weighed down with sin, full of wickedness. We will find this cycle of rebuke and judgment contrasted with redemption and salvation repeated countless times throughout this book.

Isaiah 1:9-11 *If the LORD of Hosts had not left us a few survivors, we would be like Sodom, we would resemble Gomorrah. Hear the word of the LORD, you rulers of Sodom! Listen to the instruction of our God, you people of Gomorrah! "What are all your sacrifices to Me?" asks the LORD. "I have had enough of burnt offerings and rams and the fat of well-fed cattle; I have no desire for the blood of bulls, lambs, or male goats.*

7

How often did Israel lament that if YHWH had not acted, they would be like Sodom and Gomorrah! Isaiah then addresses Israel as Sodom and Gomorrah and tells them He's fed up with their hypocritical religion. This image of God in this context cannot be written off as merely an Old Testament characterization. This is the same message Jesus had for the religious self-righteous of His day, calling them a brood of vipers and an evil and adulterous generation (Matt 12).

Isaiah 1:13-15 *Stop bringing useless offerings. [Your] incense is detestable to Me. New Moons and Sabbaths, and the calling of solemn assemblies— I cannot stand iniquity with a festival. I hate your New Moons and prescribed festivals. They have become a burden to Me; I am tired of putting up with [them]. When you lift up your hands [in prayer], I will refuse to look at you; even if you offer countless prayers, I will not listen. Your hands are covered with blood.*

When unrepentant sinners do religious rites, they are detestable, burdensome, hated, and YHWH will not pay attention to them. If your religion is mere formalism, it is detestable to God. If you and I are not repentant and humble, thankful and in awe at being in Christ, we are tiresome to God.

Isaiah 1:16-17 *Wash yourselves. Cleanse yourselves. Remove your evil deeds from My sight. Stop doing evil. Learn to do what is good. Seek justice. Correct the oppressor. Defend the rights of the fatherless. Plead the widow's cause.*

Israel had a long record of abusing widows and orphans, waiting for their Sabbath to be over so they could cheat people with unbalanced scales. They were called to repent and make good on those they had taken advantage of. Then we read, in verse 18, "*Come, let us reason together ...*" And then:

Isaiah 1:19-20 *If you are willing and obedient, you will eat the good things of the land. But if you refuse and rebel, you will be devoured by the sword." For the mouth of the LORD has spoken.*

This is the constant refrain in Scripture: those who do not repent will suffer the wrath of God - for the mouth of YHWH has spoken it (cue Handel!) What is spoken by YHWH is authoritative and cannot be overthrown or withstood.

In verses 21-23 Israel is judged as guilty - doing all the same things He noted earlier in this chapter. The rulers were corrupt and vile. Yet in verses 24-31 God promises to punish His enemies, remove the dross from Israel, make the remnant righteous, a faithful city. A peek into the new earth wherein righteousness dwells (2 Peter 3:13).

Isaiah 1:27-28 *Zion will be redeemed by justice, her repentant ones by righteousness. But both rebels and sinners will be destroyed, and those who abandon the LORD will perish. Here is the repeating contrast, repentant people redeemed by justice are made righteous. Rebels and sinners will be destroyed.*

Be not deceived - God is not mocked, is not ignorant of our sin. Foolish are we if we think we can wink at sin or, hiding it from other humans, thinking He doesn't see either. Let us agree with God - everything good is from Him; we can add only sin. By His Spirit we are given the will and the ability to do good (Phil 2:13).

Isaiah 2 - That Great and Terrible Day!

Isaiah chapter 2 is full of warning and rebuke, foretelling of that great and terrible day when Christ returns to judge the nations. National Israel is warned that their long record of rebellion against YHWH and friendship with the world will bring judgment upon them. God has turned His back on them.

Isaiah 2:6 *"For You have abandoned Your people, the house of Jacob, because they are full of [divination] from the East and of fortune-tellers like the Philistines. They are in league with foreigners."*

Here the prophet speaks of YHWH, how He has abandoned the house of Jacob. They were in league with foreigners. Verses 7 & 8 describe these foreigners: rich, self-satisfied, idolaters. Verse 9 brings the first of three declarations that man will be brought low on that Day. Isaiah 2:9 *"So humanity is brought low, and man is humbled. Do not forgive them!"* There will be no forgiveness when the Lord makes His second advent (Heb 9:28).

Those who have not been reconciled to God will seek a hiding place: Isaiah 2:10 *"Go into the rocks and hide in the dust from the terror of the LORD and from His majestic splendor."* But creation cannot hide creatures from the Creator!

Isaiah 2:11-12 *"Human pride will be humbled, and the loftiness of men will be brought low; the LORD alone will be exalted on that day. For a day belonging to the LORD of Hosts is [coming] against all that is proud and lofty, against all that is lifted up—it will be humbled"* This is the second time we read of humanity being brought low. For when the Lord of glory returns, ALL will kneel before Him, some in worship and adoration; others in terror beyond human description. On that day, there is no opportunity for forgiveness or refuge for those who are not called His people.

Verses 14-16 describe the symbols and signs of the worldly riches that will crumble on that Day. And the third time of man's undoing is seen in Isaiah 2:17-18 *"So human pride will be brought low, and the loftiness of men will be humbled; the LORD alone will be exalted on that day. The idols will vanish completely."*

Those who have not been reconciled to God will in vain seek a hiding place: Isaiah 2:19 *"People will go into caves in the rocks and holes in the ground, away from the terror of the LORD and from His majestic splendor, when He rises to terrify the earth."* But creation cannot hide creatures from the Creator!

Isaiah 2:21 *"They will go into the caves of the rocks and the crevices in the cliffs, away from the terror of the LORD and from His majestic splendor, when He rises to terrify the earth."* This verse and verse 10, above, ought to bring to your mind the scene in Revelation 6, when the sixth seal is opened:

Revelation 6:12-17 *"Then I saw Him open the sixth seal. A violent earthquake occurred; the sun turned black like sackcloth made of goat hair; the entire moon became like blood; the stars of heaven fell to the earth as a fig tree drops its unripe figs when shaken by a high wind; the sky separated like a scroll being rolled up; and every mountain and island was moved from its place. Then the kings of the earth, the nobles, the military commanders, the rich, the powerful, and every slave and free person hid in the caves and among the rocks of the mountains. And they said to the mountains and to the rocks, "Fall on us and hide us from the face of the One seated on the throne and from the wrath of the Lamb, because the great day of Their wrath has come! And who is able to stand?""*

Carnal man will not willingly surrender to Christ on that Day, for the day of salvation has passed. Jesus will return when the last spiritual stone has been mined from the earth and placed in the celestial city of New Jerusalem. And then comes judgment.

What is the bottom line? Isaiah 2:22 *"Put no more trust in man, who has only the breath in his nostrils. What is he really worth?"*

There is only One in whom we can find safety on that great and terrible day. Christ Jesus is a strong tower of refuge, and advocate for all who are in Him. If you hear His voice, do not harden your heart, for the day of salvation will not last forever. He is coming back. To judge the nations, gather His people, and make all things new.

Isaiah 3 - Judgment Begins Here.

Because of the thematic content of the latter verses in chapter 3, I am including them in chapter 4.

In chapter 3, Isaiah brings God's judgment and charges against His covenant people, national Israel. In the same fashion for His New Covenant people, judgment begins within the household of God. Note his charges - a common one of abusing the poor and weak within their community. Note His judgment - lack of order and chaos as the community is set up-side down. AS was Israel, so it is in the USA.

Isaiah 3:4-5 *"I will make youths their leaders, and the unstable will govern them." The people will oppress one another, man against man, neighbor against neighbor; the youth will act arrogantly toward the elder, and the worthless toward the honorable."*

Isaiah 3:8-9 *"For Jerusalem has stumbled and Judah has fallen because they have spoken and acted against the LORD, defying His glorious presence. The look on their faces testifies against them, and like Sodom, they flaunt their sin. They do not conceal it. Woe to them, for they have brought evil on themselves."*

See who is responsible for this judgment? Those who rebelled against YHWH, spoken and acted against Him. They flaunt their sin and brought evil upon themselves. Whenever you see "gay pride," ANTIFA riots, or celebration of murdering babies you see those who flaunt their sin and bring evil upon themselves.

Isaiah 3:13-15 *"The LORD rises to argue the case and stands to judge the people. The LORD brings [this] charge against the elders and leaders of His people: "You have devastated the vineyard. The plunder from the poor is in your houses. Why do you crush My people and grind the faces of the poor?" [This is] the declaration of the Lord GOD of Hosts."*

Again, we see that there is no escape from God's view, His judgment. Our charge is to proclaim the glorious gospel of Jesus Christ and plead with the nation to restore order for the sake of the poor and weak. We must walk as children of the light and be consistent in pointing saint and reprobate to Christ.

Isaiah 4 - On That Day!

Chapter 3 ends with a rebuke to the women of Jerusalem (verses 16 & 17), and verse 18 begins the judgment that will be poured out, beginning with the phrase "On that day." Through the end of chapter 3, all the wealth and signs of wealth will be stripped away from them with this result:

Isaiah 3:25-26 *"Your men will fall by the sword, your warriors in battle. Then her gates will lament and mourn; deserted, she will sit on the ground."*

This judgment on the women continues in what we call chapter 4, beginning with the phrase "On that day;" as seven seek one man to provide for them and take away their disgrace. The number often symbolizes completion or fullness in Scripture. Here is represents the complete number of Hebrew women.

Then we read, Isaiah 4:2-6 *"On that day the Branch of the LORD will be beautiful and glorious, and the fruit of the land will be the pride and glory of Israel's survivors. Whoever remains in Zion and whoever is left in Jerusalem will be called holy—all in Jerusalem who are destined to live— when the Lord has washed away the filth of the daughters of Zion and cleansed the bloodguilt from the heart of Jerusalem by a spirit of judgment and a spirit of burning. Then the LORD will create a cloud of smoke by day and a glowing flame of fire by night over the entire site of Mount Zion and over its assemblies. For there will be a canopy over all the glory, and there will be a booth for shade from heat by day, and a refuge and shelter from storm and rain."*

"On that day" promises are fulfilled and Isaiah uses familiar language to communicate to the Hebrew people how glorious it will be when the Lord washes away their filth and cleanses them of the bloodguilt of their wretched hearts. The familiar signs of a cloud of smoke and flame by night hearken back to the wilderness; the booth for shade reminds me of the end of Jonah's account. Isaiah is pointing the Hebrews forward to the age-to-come, where the survivors of Israel (a remnant, Paul would say) are forgiven and live with YHWH in fellowship, using language familiar to his kinsmen of the flesh.

Isaiah 5 - Woe to Those ...

The first part of chapter 5 of Isaiah is about a vineyard planted and tended by YHWH which did not produce good fruit. In His parable about a vineyard (Matt 21:33-46), wicked servants stole the fruit and were punished. In this chapter, slothful workers fail to produce good fruit and are punished. In both cases, the thieving and slothful workers are national Israel and God is the owner of the vineyard.

Isaiah 5:1-2 *"I will sing about the one I love, a song about my loved one's vineyard: The one I love had a vineyard on a very fertile hill. He broke up the soil, cleared it of stones, and planted it with the finest vines. He built a tower in the middle of it and even dug out a winepress there. He expected it to yield good grapes, but it yielded worthless grapes."*

This is God speaking; the One He loves is the Son Who did the work. In verses 3 & 4 the residents of Jerusalem and Judah are identified as witnesses of what is happening.

Isaiah 5:3-4 *"So now, residents of Jerusalem and men of Judah, please judge between Me and My vineyard. What more could I have done for My vineyard than I did? Why, when I expected a yield of good grapes, did it yield worthless grapes?"*

In the next two verses the judgment of God is revealed. He will reduce the vineyard to wasteland, just as He cursed the fig tree that did not bear fruit (Matt 21:18-22).

Isaiah 5:5-6 *"Now I will tell you what I am about to do to My vineyard: I will remove its hedge, and it will be consumed; I will tear down its wall, and it will be trampled. I will make it a wasteland. It will not be pruned or weeded; thorns and briers will grow up. I will also give orders to the clouds that rain should not fall on it."*

The end of this passage testifies to the power and authority of the One created all things and judges all things. And it reveals who is represented by the vineyard.

Isaiah 5:7 *"For the vineyard of the LORD of Hosts is the house of Israel, and the men of Judah, the plant He delighted in. He looked for justice but saw injustice, for righteousness, but heard cries of wretchedness."*

YHWH owns the vineyard which is national Israel (north and south kingdoms mentioned). They do injustice and are wretched and judgment will fall on them. This is the nature of the law covenant: temporal blessedness for obedience; judgment and punishment (often at the hands of pagan nations) for disobedience.

Contra is the New Covenant, wherein every branch will abide in the Root and bear good fruit (Matt 21:43). Note this: in Matt 21, Jesus has been telling many things to the leaders of national Israel and to His disciples, telling them of the disobedience of Israel and the judgement to come. This last reference, verse 43, is a critical passage, for we see here that ethnic Israel was a temporary people, just as the Mosaic Covenant was a temporary covenant. These things served their purposes as shadows and types. But in due season, the kingdom was revealed as spiritual and eternal and it was

15

taken from the temporary, temporal "guardian" of ethnic Israel and given to the eternal, spiritual heirs of spiritual Israel.

Verses 8-17 depict the first 2 woes pronounced upon apostate Israel.

Isaiah 5:8 *"Woe to those who add house to house and join field to field until there is no more room and you alone are left in the land."*

This "woe" must be seen in its context. YHWH had given His covenant people land, tribe by tribe, with a provision for the Levites. In this way, no child of Abraham (according to the flesh) would be homeless. But sinful men who accumulated power began to take advantage of the poor. This was a common charge of God against national Israel. This one comment in verse 8 may be reflective of King Ahab's taking of Naboth's land as recorded in 1 Kings 21.

The prophet Isaiah then records: *"I heard the LORD of Hosts say: Indeed, many houses will become desolate, grand and lovely ones without inhabitants. For a ten-acre vineyard will yield only six gallons, and 10 bushels of seed will yield only [one] bushel."* (Isaiah 5:9-10)

Judgment from God comes upon those who put their trust in things of this world. Recall how He would not allow Gideon to win the battle with many men, so all would know it was YHWH who had won the day. Recall how the children of Israel declared *"some trust in horses and chariots but we trust in the name of our God!"* Yet like so many of us, they grew comfortable and, like the farmer in the parable who went to sleep planning to build bigger barns, the Hebrew nation would find out their crops could not be depended upon if the Lord of the harvest did not bring in the produce.

Isaiah 5:11-12 *"Woe to those who rise early in the morning in pursuit of beer, who linger into the evening, inflamed by wine. At their feasts they have lyre, harp, tambourine, flute, and wine. They do not perceive the LORD's actions, and they do not see the work of His hands."*

The second "woe" - revealing another way in which the Hebrews had betrayed their God. They had grown comfortable living for today, engaging their fleshly senses with all sorts of stimuli. In the midst of so much luxury, they had forgotten Who had made all this possible, they had lost sight of their Creator.

Isaiah 5:13-15 *"Therefore My people will go into exile because they lack knowledge; her dignitaries are starving, and her masses are parched with thirst. Therefore Sheol enlarges its throat and opens wide its enormous jaws, and down go Zion's dignitaries, her masses, her crowds, and those who carouse in her! Humanity is brought low, man is humbled, and haughty eyes are humbled."*

Because of their rebellion in seeking security in their possessions, God would send them into exile. The grave would eventually consume all who sought satisfaction in goods. And we see the same refrain from chapter 2 - man is humbled, humanity is brought low. Prideful flesh cannot stand before God.

Isaiah 5:16-17 *"But the LORD of Hosts is exalted by His justice, and the holy God is distinguished by righteousness. Lambs will graze as [if in] their own pastures, and strangers will eat [among] the ruins of the rich."*

Contrary to sinful man, who seeks assurance from other men, YHWH is above all and is exalted and glorified by His justice and righteousness! Lambs (perhaps those Hebrews who had not gone the way of the flesh) will graze in peace and strangers - Gentiles - will be satisfied with what has been left behind. God will comfort and provide for His own and they will be satisfied.

Verses 18-22 reveal the final four "Woes" pronounced upon national Israel, wherein we see why the Lord will bring judgment on His covenant people. Note this: In the law covenant, failure to comply brought punishment. The biblical history of national Israel shows this cycle repeated countless times. In the New Covenant, which is a grace covenant, all the punishment for our rebellion and sinful neglect were laid upon the Lord Jesus. Because we are in Him, all that He has been given is ours and will be realized in the world to come.

While we sojourn in these fleshly tabernacles, let us learn from ethnic Israel's failures and let us be humbly awed at being brought into spiritual Israel and given true rest by the Son of Man.

Isaiah 5:18-19 *Woe to those who drag wickedness with cords of deceit and [pull] sin along with cart ropes, to those who say: "Let Him hurry up and do His work quickly so that we can see it! Let the plan of the Holy One of Israel take place so that we can know it!"*

These people mentioned in this woe are wicked, trying to deceive others and drag them along. They are kin to the folks who demanded a sign from Christ Jesus; not believing in God unless He does what they expect and can see with eyes of flesh. Woe on those who demand a sign! It is a wicked and evil generation - whether in the days of the Old Covenant or now. We can see and believe on Him only with spiritual eyes, which He must give us.

Isaiah 5:20 *Woe to those who call evil good and good evil, who substitute darkness for light and light for darkness, who substitute bitter for sweet and sweet for bitter.*

Is this not commentary on natural man's condition in every generation and nation? Natural man cannot help but suppress his knowledge of the truth by his own personal unrighteousness. People in our day call abortion and homosexuality good; they call law and order evil. They work hard to snuff out the light of truth on every news and social platform, because their deeds are evil and their depraved consciences accuse and excuse them.

Isaiah 5:21 *Woe to those who are wise in their own opinion and clever in their own sight.*

Here we see another common affliction of natural man. These people think they can hide their sin by their cleverness. From tax cheats to porn addicts to lying politicians - woe!

Isaiah 5:22-23 *Woe to those who are heroes at drinking wine, who are fearless at mixing beer, who acquit the guilty for a bribe and deprive the innocent of justice.*

This final (for this passage) woe is pronounced on those who live to satisfy their fleshly desires and pervert justice for their own gain.

All of these behaviors in this passage that provoked these woes are common among natural man - and, at times, among the redeemed. Let us who claim Christ see this clearly and repent of what we know to be sin and plead for the grace to walk as children of the light day-by-day.

The last section of Isaiah chapter 5 pronounces the judgments in response to the woes of the preceding section. Two long verses begin with "Therefore" and go on to reveal YHWH's judgment for disobedience.

Isaiah 5:24-25 *Therefore, as a tongue of fire consumes straw and as dry grass shrivels in the flame, so their roots will become like something rotten and their blossoms will blow away like dust, for they have rejected the instruction of the LORD of Hosts, and they have despised the word of the Holy One of Israel. Therefore the LORD's anger burns against His people. He raised His hand against them and struck them; the mountains quaked, and their corpses were like garbage in the streets. In all this, His anger is not removed, and His hand is still raised [to strike].*

Verse 24 shows us that these people who had the oracles of God and advantages no other nation did, rejected His instructions and despised His holy Word. Recall the scene when young Josiah was exposed to the Scriptures (2 Chron

34) - national Israel had suffered under countless worthless kings and the book of the law had been lost! It was found when Josiah was a young man and his response was remarkable, for he did what we would expect any leader of God's people to do. But he was the exception, not the rule.

And the Lord's anger burned against national Israel and He struck them so that their corpses were like overturned garbage cans in the street. When Isaiah wrote this, the hand of God was still raised against them. This is a stark contrast to the picture of YHWH leading them out of Egypt by His strong arm. Now that arm was against them and they were unable to stand.

Then we see that God turns His attention to the Gentiles: Isaiah 5:26 *He raises a signal flag for the distant nations and whistles for them from the ends of the earth. Look—how quickly and swiftly they come!*

When those who have been given ears to hear are called, they come! From before the foundation of the world, people from every nation, tribe, and tongue were chosen to be among the redeemed. Isaiah was one of several prophets who shed light on this. This is the Lord's doing and it is marvelous in our eyes!

The rest of this chapter describes the true covenant people of God. Isaiah 5:27-29 *None of them grows weary or stumbles; no one slumbers or sleeps. No belt is loose and no sandal strap broken. Their arrows are sharpened, and all their bows strung. Their horses' hooves are like flint; their [chariot] wheels are like a whirlwind. Their roaring is like a lion's; they roar like young lions; they growl and seize their prey and carry [it] off, and no one can rescue [it].*

His people don't grow weary, etc. because He holds them up and causes them to walk in His ways. Our obedience is not our doing, no flesh can satisfy YHWH's demands. And the gates of hell cannot defeat us!

Isaiah 5:30 *On that day they will roar over it, like the roaring of the sea. When one looks at the land, there will be darkness and distress; light will be obscured by clouds.*

On the day when Christ returns, victory will be ours. The people of the world will be in distress. The only hope for man is in the God-man, Christ Jesus. He came to save sinners - but when He comes the second time, it will not be to deal with sin. No second chances. He is coming. Are you ready?

Chapter 6 - Holy, Holy, Holy!

This is a familiar scene, filled with awe as Isaiah reveals a scene from heaven, where the glory of God is overwhelming; Isaiah struggles with words to portray what he has seen. The three-times holy reinforces the unbroachable gap between Creator and creature. Holy refers to being set apart from something. Natural man cannot approach God any more than a fish can approach an eagle. The eagle can swoop low and snatch up a fish; so God in Christ was brought low in order to snatch up sinners.

A side note: in verse 1 we read that the robe of God filled the temple. The Hebrew word is "seam" - as in the seam of His robe fills the temple. Again, I see this as indicating God is simply beyond our comprehension. We can understand Him in part, but full knowledge of Him is beyond us.

Isaiah 6:4 *"The foundations of the doorways shook at the sound of their voices."* I think the author of Hebrews was pondering this when the Spirit gave him this: Hebrews 12:25-29 *"Make sure that you do not reject the One who speaks. For if they did not escape when they rejected Him who warned them on earth, even less will we if we turn away from Him who warns us from heaven. His voice shook the earth at that time, but now He has promised, Yet once more I will shake not only the earth but also heaven. This expression, "Yet once more," indicates the removal of what can be shaken—that is, created things—so that what is not shaken might remain. Therefore, since we are receiving a kingdom that cannot be shaken, let us hold on to grace. By it, we may serve God acceptably, with reverence and awe, for our God is a consuming fire."*

Isaiah was undone, ruined, because he was *"a man of unclean lips in a nation of unclean lips."* A Scripture reference to this is Exodus 6:12 & 30, where Moses tries to excuse himself from service to God in speaking to Israel (verse 12) and to Pharaoh (verse 30) because he is a man of uncircumcised lips. The remedy for Moses and the nation of Israel was not for the males to be circumcised in the flesh, but for them all to be circumcised of the heart (Deut 10:16), which would be done by God. The remedy for Isaiah was to have his lips cleansed with fire - both of these point to the regeneration by the Spirit, wherein we are cleansed from sin by the imputed righteousness of God and circumcised without human hands.

Isaiah, called of God, agrees to serve Him - no excuses. Here we read of encouragement to gospel preachers.

Isaiah 6:9-10 *"And He replied: Go! Say to these people: Keep listening, but do not understand; keep looking, but do not perceive. Dull the minds of these people; deafen their ears and blind their eyes; otherwise they might see with their eyes and hear with their ears, understand with their minds, turn back, and be healed."*

Contrary to the disciples of Osteen, Hybels, Warren, the SBC leadership, and all man-pleasers, those who proclaim the gospel of Christ are not to be concerned with the opinions and responses of sinful man; we are to be faithful to the One Who called us. Salvation is of the Lord and Christ Jesus will have the full reward for His work.

Isaiah didn't shrink back but did ask, *"for how long, Lord?"* Isaiah 6:11-12 *"And He replied: Until cities lie in ruins without inhabitants, houses are without people, the land is ruined and desolate, and the LORD drives the people far away, leaving great emptiness in the land."*

YHWH will drive the people out, leaving the land empty and the house of Israel desolate. We are to be consistent and faithful in preaching His Word, even if people are driven away and the temporal signs of wealth fall away; even when countless gather to hear false teachers who tickle their ears.

Isaiah 6:13 *Though a tenth will remain in the land, it will be burned again. Like the terebinth or the oak that leaves a stump when felled, the holy seed is the stump.*

A tenth (remnant) will still be in the land, as Paul wrote: Romans 11:5 *"In the same way, then, there is also at the present time a remnant chosen by grace."* But though a remnant remains, *"the land it will be burned again"* - the judgment of God will consume all, as when He returns to judge the nations and make all things new.

Peter agrees: 2 Peter 3:10-13 *"But the Day of the Lord will come like a thief; on that [day] the heavens will pass away with a loud noise, the elements will burn and be dissolved, and the earth and the works on it will be disclosed. Since all these things are to be destroyed in this way, [it is clear] what sort of people you should be in holy conduct and godliness as you wait for and earnestly desire the coming of the day of God. The heavens will be on fire and be dissolved because of it, and the elements will melt with the heat. But based on His promise, we wait for the new heavens and a new earth, where righteousness will dwell."*

No matter what goes on in this age, on this earth, our call is to be fixed in Christ, focused on Christ, holy in conduct (not like the world) and godliness (like Christ) as we wait for and EARNESTLY desire His return.

1 Thessalonians 4:18 *"Therefore encourage one another with these words."*

II. The Promise of Immanuel

II. The Promise of Immanuel

Isaiah 7 - The Fear of Man.

Chapter 7 opens with a message to king Ahaz. In Israel at this time, as in most times, there was war and rumors of war. Ahaz's heart was troubled, for he feared the loss of his power and wealth.

Isaiah 7:1-2 This took place during the reign of Ahaz (2 Kings 15 & 16), son of Jotham (Judges 9), son of Uzziah king of Judah: Rezin king of Aram, along with Pekah, son of Remaliah, king of Israel, waged war against Jerusalem, but he could not succeed. When it became known to the house of David that Aram had occupied Ephraim, the heart of Ahaz and the hearts of his people trembled like trees of a forest shaking in the wind.

The pagan king of Aram and his ally, the king of the northern kingdom of Israel took Ephraim but were unable to conquer Jerusalem. When Ahaz heard that Ephraim had fallen, "the heart of Ahaz and the hearts of his people trembled like trees of a forest shaking in the wind." What a word picture we have, especially this time of year (late Fall), when the wind blows and the trees shake, and the leaves fall. In this world, we will have trouble, but fear not - Christ has overcome the world! Our flesh may shake in fear, but we belong to a kingdom that cannot be shaken: Hebrews 12:27-29 *"This expression, "Yet once more," indicates the removal of what can be shaken—that is, created things—so that what is not shaken might remain. Therefore, since we are receiving a kingdom that cannot be shaken, let us hold on to grace. By it, we may serve God acceptably, with reverence and awe, for our God is a consuming fire."*

Beginning in verse 3, YHWH tells Isaiah what to say to Ahaz. Isaiah 7:4-6 *Say to him: Calm down and be quiet. Don't be afraid or cowardly because of these two smoldering stubs of firebrands, the fierce anger of Rezin and Aram, and the son of Remaliah. For Aram, along with Ephraim and the son of Remaliah, has plotted harm against you. They say, 'Let us go up against Judah, terrorize it, and conquer it for ourselves. Then we can install Tabeel's son as king in it.'"*

God, Who is Lord of all, tells weak-in-knees Ahaz to not fear these raging kings that wage war against him; comparing them to "smoldering stubs of firebrands." What a contrast with God Himself, Who is a consuming fire! YHWH reveals what was planned - terrorize the southern kingdom, conquer it, and install their stooge as king. If your kingdom is of this world, madmen such as these will come and steal and destroy and you should fear. If your kingdom is in Christ, these madmen may kill the body but they cannot kill the soul - you are secure in Christ Jesus!

Isaiah 7:7-9 *This is what the Lord GOD says: It will not happen; it will not occur. The head of Aram is Damascus, the head of Damascus is Rezin (within 65 years Ephraim will be too shattered to be a people), the head of Ephraim is Samaria, and the head of Samaria is the son of Remaliah. If you do not stand firm in your faith, then you will not stand at all.*

See what YHWH tells Ahaz - these raging madmen will fail. Judah will not fall. He also reveals that the king of the northern kingdom is connected to the pagan nations, not connected to Him. In the light of this enormous conspiracy against Judah, YHWH tells Ahaz that he will fail if he is not firm in his faith. In other words, trust in God and not in chariots and horses. So it for us - the Lord our God is our strong tower of refuge, the ruler of the kingdom that cannot be shaken.

When your world is shaking, look to Christ!

The second part of chapter 7 of Isaiah brings more bad news for national Israel. Earlier we saw that YHWH had told Ahaz he would fall if he was not firm in his faith. Like Peter sinking into the waves when took his focus off Christ and fixed his eyes on the storm; he was not firm in his faith. So Ahaz, with disastrous results.

Our passage opens with God speaking to Ahaz. Isaiah 7:10-11 *Then the LORD spoke again to Ahaz: "Ask for a sign from the LORD your God—from the depths of Sheol to the heights of heaven." Ahaz put on false humility: Isaiah 7:12 But Ahaz replied, "I will not ask. I will not test the LORD." Note this: obedience to what God has commanded does NOT put God to the test; it puts man to the test. The Creator is not pleased with this creature's attitude. His prophet replies.*

Isaiah 7:13 *Isaiah said, "Listen, house of David! Is it not enough for you to try the patience of men? Will you also try the patience of my God?"* God's patience was tried by the creature's disobedience. By addressing Ahaz by his covenant identity, YHWH is reminding him that he (and the house of David) have been blessed by God unlike any other nation; and now he is rebelling against the One Who has been their provision.

Isaiah 7:14-17 *Therefore, the Lord Himself will give you a sign: The virgin will conceive, have a son, and name him Immanuel. By the time he learns to reject what is bad and choose what is good, he will be eating butter and honey. For before the boy knows to reject what is bad and choose what is good, the land of the two kings you dread will be abandoned. The LORD will bring on you, your people, and the house of your father, such a time as has never been since Ephraim separated from Judah—the king of Assyria [is coming]."*

This well-known prophecy, "a virgin will conceive and her son will be named Immanuel - God with us!" is couched in the middle of bad news for national Israel. We see this son will learn obedience (Heb 5:8) and will be poor (eating butter - or sour milk - and honey was a sign of poverty). While He is growing into manhood (we speak of His human nature)

27

both north and south Israel will be left destitute - YHWH will send Assyria to punish them for continued disobedience. Rome would rule Israel by the time Jesus walked its streets.

The closing passage on this chapter talks about the judgment that will come on national Israel, using the phrase, "On that day," four times in announcing bad news.

Isaiah 7:18-19 *On that day the LORD will whistle to the fly that is at the farthest streams of the Nile and to the bee that is in the land of Assyria. All of them will come and settle in the steep ravines, in the clefts of the rocks, in all the thornbushes, and in all the water holes.*

The Creator is sovereign over all creation - even bugs. He sent flies and bees to swarm over the entire kingdom that had been given to the people He had created. "Mother Nature" is the fabrication of unrighteous men who suppress their knowledge of truth.

Isaiah 7:20 *On that day the Lord will use a razor hired from beyond the Euphrates River—the king of Assyria—to shave the head, the hair on the legs, and to remove the beard as well.*

To be shaved clean was a mark of shame in that day. YHWH sends Assyria to bring shame to national Israel. This was merely one more step in God's redemptive plan, moving from the shadows to the substance. This was culminated by Christ when He told national Israel their house had been left to them desolate (Matt 23:38) and the kingdom had been taken from them and given to a nation bearing fruit (Matt 21:43).

Isaiah 7:21-22 *On that day a man will raise a young cow and two sheep, and from the abundant milk they give he will eat butter, for every survivor in the land will eat butter and honey.*

National Israel will be thrown into poverty; those who survive will have sour milk and honey; hallmarks of lack rather than abundance. This aligns with New Covenant teaching that we should be content with what we have been given, not lusting after riches. *For the kingdom of God is not eating and drinking, but righteousness, peace, and joy in the Holy Spirit.* Romans 14:17

Isaiah 7:23-25 *And **on that day** every place where there were 1,000 vines, worth 1,000 pieces of silver, will become thorns and briers. A man will go there with bow and arrows because the whole land will be thorns and briers. You will not go to all the hills that were once tilled with a hoe, for fear of the thorns and briers. [Those hills] will be places for oxen to graze and for sheep to trample.*

On that day, what was once bright and valuable will be as weeds and goat heads. Hunters will find nothing, farmers' work will yield nothing. Oxen will graze there and sheep will trample everything. The lost sheep of Israel, waiting for their Shepherd.

There is One Shepherd, one sheepfold. The everlasting kingdom is not your country, it's not of this world. His kingdom is spiritual and will be fulfilled on the new earth when He returns, not to deal with sin but to gather those who eagerly await Him. Are you looking for Him, being faithful with what He's given you? Are you grumbling because you don't have enough stuff? Someone more mighty and awesome than the king of Assyria is coming. Do you know Him? Are you ready?

Isaiah 8 - The Assyrians are Coming!

Chapter 8 of Isaiah is easily seen as two parts. The first part builds on the prophesied judgment on national Israel by YHWH's use of Assyria. He speaks to Isaiah: Isaiah 8:1-2 *Then the LORD said to me, "Take a large piece of parchment and write on it with an ordinary pen: Maher-shalal-hash-baz. I have appointed trustworthy witnesses—Uriah the priest and Zechariah son of Jeberechiah."* The phrase

"Maher-shalal-hash-baz" means "speeding to the plunder, hurrying to the spoil." That is the message to be proclaimed to national Israel. Assyria will hurry to spoil Israel, they will make speed to plunder that land. This message was one Israel did not want to hear - much as people in our day don't want to hear the gospel: abandon your self-righteousness and cry out for mercy in true humility.

Isaiah 8:3-4 *I was then intimate with the prophetess, and she conceived and gave birth to a son. The LORD said to me, "Name him Maher-shalal-hash-baz, for before the boy knows how to call out father or mother, the wealth of Damascus and the spoils of Samaria will be carried off to the king of Assyria."* Does this not remind of Hosea, who was told to take a woman as his wife and she gave birth to children with names that foretold what Jesus said in Matthew 21:43 *the kingdom of God shall be taken from you, and it shall be given to a nation that produces the fruits of it.* Isaiah's child had the name which was the same as the message of doom to national Israel; a precursor to the kingdom being taken from them by God.

Verses 5 - 8 are YHWH speaking judgment on Israel in colorful word pictures, flowing waters that were meant to fertilize were rejected so God brings judgment with rushing waters, which are identified as the king of Assyria. His exploitation of Israel overflow the banks - it will be total. The flood will overwhelm both north and south kingdoms, with Judah being identified in verse 8 as the one to be ruined. The end of verse 8 calls Judah "Immanuel" - for it was from that land that the promised One would come.

Verse 9 brings a change in tone - as YHWH pronounces doom on those who attack Judah: Isaiah 8:9-10 *Band together, peoples, and be broken; pay attention, all you distant lands; prepare for war, and be broken; prepare for war, and be broken. Devise a plan; it will fail. Make a prediction; it will not happen. For God is with us.*

The kings of Assyria and the northern kingdom of Israel would band together and be broken - three times, showing completeness. They will plan and prepare and predict their overthrow of Judah, the land called Immanuel, but they will not be able to succeed for YHWH tells His people "God is with us" - Immanuel!

Just as sure as the seed of the woman would crush the head of the seed of the serpent, so that seed would be born as a human in Judah and He would be Immanuel - God with us! This is the Lord's doing and it is marvelous in our eyes!

The second part of Isaiah 8 presents the only refuge, the only sanctuary that can save those who are otherwise doomed to His wrath. It begins with Isaiah's preface, calling what follows that which was told him to keep him from going the way of national Israel. Isaiah 8:11 *For this is what the LORD said to me with great power, to keep me from going the way of this people.*

It should bring great comfort to those who know Christ as king to know He will do what is needed to protect us, even from our own inclinations. That's what this message is.

Isaiah 8:12-13 *Do not call everything an alliance these people say is an alliance. Do not fear what they fear; do not be terrified. You are to regard only the LORD of Hosts as holy. Only He should be feared; only He should be held in awe.*

So often humans do what seems right to them because they want to prosper, to be safe. So they will team up with people who are naturally their enemies; fearing man more than they trust God. Rather than fear man or what terrifies him, we who call on YHWH as Father should rightly fear Him. He is totally separate (thrice holy!) from the creation. All that is from this earth will betray and crumble. God is - alone - above all and sovereign over all.

Isaiah 8:14-15 *He will be a sanctuary; but for the two houses of Israel, He will be a stone to stumble over and a rock to trip over, and a trap and a snare to the inhabitants of Jerusalem. Many will stumble over these; they will fall and be broken; they will be snared and captured.*

YHWH will be a safe haven - a sanctuary - but not for the two kingdoms of Israel. It's Jesus being referenced here, for He was a stumbling stone of offense to the Jews of His day. All who do not see Him as the promised One will fall and be broken, caught in a snare and captured - by Satan. All whom the Father chose will find refuge in Christ. No one else can; they will find Him to be offensive and they will stumble and be crushed under the Chief Cornerstone.

Isaiah 8:16 *Bind up the testimony. Seal up the instruction among my disciples.*

Note this: "Seal up the instruction AMONG my disciples." Progressive revelation - Daniel was told to seal the words (Dan 12:4); Isaiah was told to bind up the testimony but keep it among the disciples of God. In Revelation 5 Jesus begins to open the scroll and make it known to all.

Isaiah 8:17 *I will wait for the LORD, who is hiding His face from the house of Jacob. I will wait for Him.*

The servant of YHWH says he will wait for Him, the Creator and judge of things Who is hiding His face from Jacob (another reference to national Israel). He will make Himself known to those He has called.

Isaiah 8:18-22 *Here I am with the children the LORD has given me to be signs and wonders in Israel from the LORD of Hosts who dwells on Mount Zion. When they say to you, "Consult the spirits of the dead and the spiritists who chirp and mutter," shouldn't a people consult their God? [Should they consult] the dead on behalf of the living? To the law and to the testimony! If they do not speak according to this word, there will be no dawn for them. They will wander through the land, dejected and hungry. When they are famished, they will become enraged, and, looking upward, will curse their king and their God. They will look toward the earth and see only distress, darkness, and the gloom of affliction, and they will be driven into thick darkness.*

Jesus quotes the first part of verse 18 in Heb 2:13. Though it appears Isaiah is still speaking and refers to his children (signs and wonders), Christ Jesus is Immanuel, son of a virgin, given by God the Father, for the deliverance of His people and a sign to them!

Isaiah tells the leaders of Israel and Judah Who the real king is, the LORD of hosts who dwells on Mt. Zion; and he goes on to tell them not to continue following the ways of the pagan nations that have consistently infiltrated their community and culture. All who have not Christ will never be filled by things of this world - it can only bring distress, darkness, and affliction.

Turn to Christ while ye yet have breath! He - ALONE - is a refuge from the certain wrath of God that will eternally consume those who are NOT in His Book of Life.

Isaiah 9 - Peace and Repentance.

The first part of Isaiah 9 brings us a well-known poem of the birth of Christ. The introduction to this poem and the first few stanzas may be read over without much study, as they are not as clear to our way of thinking.

Isaiah 9:1 *Nevertheless, the gloom of the distressed land will not be like that of the former times when He humbled the land of Zebulun and the land of Naphtali. But in the future He will bring honor to the Way of the Sea, to the land east of the Jordan, and to Galilee of the nations.*

Zebulun and Naphtali were northern tribes that were decimated by the Assyrian invasion; whose king established three provinces in the northern kingdom: Magiddo (Galilee), Du'Ru (the Way of the See), and Gal'aza (the land east of the Jordan). Knowing this makes the opening verse more clear: the northern kingdom was reeling under the heavy boot of Assyria and YHWH was promising a future of victory over them. Was this a temporal victory to reclaim dirt, or was Isaiah revealing something spiritual about the eternal kingdom?

Isaiah 9:2-3 *The people walking in darkness have seen a great light; a light has dawned on those living in the land of darkness. You have enlarged the nation and increased its joy. [The people] have rejoiced before You as they rejoice at harvest time and as they rejoice when dividing spoils.*

Here the Spirit reveals what is termed "prophetic perfect", when that which is future is presented as present, now. Assyria had brought darkness to Israel, just as sin had brought darkness to the whole earth. A light has dawned - John wrote of this:

John 1:1-5 *In the beginning was the Word, and the Word was with God, and the Word was God. He was with God in the beginning. All things were created through Him, and apart from Him not one thing was created that has been created. Life was in Him, and that life was the light of men. That light shines in the darkness, yet the darkness did not overcome it.*

The light that overcomes the darkness is Christ Jesus. The nation that is enlarged is the body of Christ, wherein all who believe are one in Him. In Christ is unending joy that is firmly fixed on the Lord Jesus and not circumstances. This brings rejoicing at harvest time (when the harvest of souls is complete) when the rewards of labor are realized. We can understand while ethnic Israel saw renewed prosperity in the land as the fulfillment of this prophecy, but the references to Christ throughout tell us who are indwelt by the Spirit that something greater than Moses is here!

II. The Promise of Immanuel

Isaiah 9:4-5 *For You have shattered their oppressive yoke and the rod on their shoulders, the staff of their oppressor, just as [You did] on the day of Midian. For the trampling boot of battle and the bloodied garments of war will be burned as fuel for the fire.*

This references the victory over the Middianites when God worked through Gideon (Judges 6). But it also speaks of the breaking of the yoke of sin when one is brought to new life in Christ, as He gives victory over sin that cannot be overturned. How do I know this? Because of what comes next.

Isaiah 9:6-7 *For a child will be born for us, a son will be given to us, and the government will be on His shoulders. He will be named Wonderful Counselor, Mighty God, Eternal Father, Prince of Peace. The dominion will be vast, and its prosperity will never end. He will reign on the throne of David and over his kingdom, to establish and sustain it with justice and righteousness from now on and forever. The zeal of the LORD of Hosts will accomplish this.*

While some have said that Hezekiah or Josiah are the one herein prophesied, none but Jesus fulfills all of these superlative descriptions. Not the government of ethnic Israel, but of the whole of creation will be on His shoulders (ALL authority in heaven and earth has been given to me, Jesus announced, Matt 28:18). Who but Jesus is Wonderful Counselor, Mighty God, Eternal Father, and Prince of Peace? As Wonderful Counselor, Jesus is identified as perfect wisdom. Mighty God shows Him to the Son of David. Eternal Father reflects His unity with God the Father and eternal nature as God. And no one brings peace with God to wretched sinners but Jesus. *Come to me, all who are weak and weary, and I will give you rest! Peace I give, my peace; not as the world knows it. I have said these things to you so you may have peace. In this world you will have tribulation, but take heart - I have overcome the world!*

This the breaking of the heavy yoke, the giving of the light yoke. This is peace with God that the world can never provide nor understand. If you do not have peace, turn from those who promise peace, peace where there is no peace (politics, wealth, ease) and turn to the One Who, alone, can reconcile wretched sinners to God and bring unsurpassed peace to your soul.

The middle portion of Isaiah 9, beginning with verse 8, brings a shift in focus. From the exceedingly good news of Christ as the Son of God to Jesus as Lord who will bring chastisement upon ethnic Israel for their continued rebellion.

Isaiah 9:8-9 *The Lord sent a message against Jacob; it came against Israel. All the people— Ephraim and the inhabitants of Samaria—will know it.*

YHWH brought a message against Jacob and Israel - both the south and northern kingdoms; nobody in the Mosaic Covenant community escapes. Everyone - from a lesser tribe of Israel to the "mixed breed" people - will know this, that the God of Israel brings judgement against His people. At the end of the age, when Christ Jesus comes the second time, bringing judgment to the world, everyone on the planet will know it. Only none of the saints will suffer that judgment, for He will gather the sheep to Himself.

Isaiah 9:9-10 *They will say with pride and arrogance: "The bricks have fallen, but we will rebuild with cut stones; the sycamores have been cut down, but we will replace them with cedars."*

This short passage reveals the underlying problem that plagued ethnic Israel. They declared, many generations before, that some may trust in horses and chariots but they, the people of Israel, trusted in the name of YHWH! Yet they generally lived in mostly open rebellion against Him, trusting in wealth and seeking approval of pagan nations. They boasted in their ability to rebuild what had been torn down - as if God dwelt in houses made of stone.

Isaiah 9:11-12 *The LORD has raised up Rezin's adversaries against him and stirred up his enemies. Aram from the east and Philistia from the west have consumed Israel with open mouths. In all this, His anger is not removed, and His hand is still raised [to strike].*

Rezin was king of Assyria; YHWH raised up adversaries against him, stirring up enemies who also consumed Israel. Many times God had raised up pagan nations to punish national Israel for their rebellion. Sin against the Creator is not a light thing and His anger is not removed by cries of anguish and false tears of contrition; He will mete out His wrath on those who do not repent and embrace the Son.

Isaiah 9:13-16 *The people did not turn to Him who struck them; they did not seek the LORD of Hosts. So the LORD cut off Israel's head and tail, palm branch and reed in a single day. The head is the elder, the honored one; the tail is the prophet, the lying teacher. The leaders of the people mislead [them], and those they mislead are swallowed up.*

Chastisement of His people is intended to remind them of the promises He made and His faithfulness; just as discipline in the New Covenant congregation is intended to bring about repentance. Yet Jacob and Israel did not repent, did not turn back and seek their God. So their God "cut off Israel's head and tail" - a picture of complete destruction. We learn that head and tail are leaders who led people astray, and those who were misled were swallowed up. Be careful who you follow, test all things in light of Scripture - else you and I could be swallowed up in the error of our leaders. Guard your heart - we who are in Christ have the Spirit and He equips us to do what is pleasing to Him; those in national Israel did not. Their disobedience demonstrates the impossible task of unregenerate people being pleasing to God.

Isaiah 9:17 *Therefore the Lord does not rejoice over Israel's young men and has no compassion on its fatherless and widows, for everyone is a godless evildoer, and every mouth speaks folly. In all this, His anger is not removed, and His hand is still raised [to strike].*

This last verse is one of the saddest in Scripture. YHWH will not rejoice over the young men nor have compassion on the fatherless and widows amongst His law-covenant people. Because EVERYONE is a godless evildoer and every mouth speaks folly. Without union with Christ, being born from above and indwelt by the Spirit, we would each and everyone be godless evildoers, speaking folly. For all who are apart from Christ, God's anger is not removed, His hand is still raised to strike.

Judgment Day is coming. Are you trusting in your stuff or are you trusting in Christ Jesus and His completed work of redemption? What happened to ethnic Israel was for us, that we would not sin as they did (Rom 15:4, 1 Cor 10:11). While ye yet have breath, cry out to God, pleading with Him for mercy and new life in Christ. He is coming again. Not to deal with sin, but to gather those who eagerly await Him.

Chapter 9 of Isaiah ends with more gloom and doom. It's no wonder why the prophets of God were hated by ethnic Israel. Much as in our day when the faithful preachers of the Word are despised and those who declare "peace! peace!" where there is no peace are heralded and beloved by the world.

Isaiah 9:18 *For wickedness burns like a fire that consumes thorns and briers and kindles the forest thickets so that they go up in a column of smoke.*

Verse 17 reminded the Hebrews that YHWH's hand was raised to strike. Verse 18 continues the thought - His hand is ready for judgment because the wickedness of His covenant people is out of control, like a California wild fire. And it does not consume only those - it had spread to other nations. When God's covenant people disregard His will for them, everyone is affected and everyone suffers. Does not the last 50 years of our history in the USA resemble this?

Isaiah 9:19 *The land is scorched by the wrath of the LORD of Hosts, and the people are like fuel for the fire. No one has compassion on his brother.*

One would think the rampaging fires described would scorch the land, but we see here that these fires are symbolic of spiritual rebellion as the scorching is by the hand of God - that hand that was raised up to strike has landed a blow. The wickedness of the people is like fuel for the judgment - it is what has brought His hand down heavy on them. That same strong hand and arm that led them from slavery in Egypt. And those being punished do not have compassion for each other - for they are self-interested; this is the condition of natural man.

Isaiah 9:20 *They carve [meat] on the right, but they are [still] hungry; they have eaten on the left, but they are [still] not satisfied. Each one eats the flesh of his own arm.*

They have plenty but are not satisfied. The ancient preacher said the eye never tires of seeing something new, the ear never tires of hearing something new. He might have also said that the tongue never tires of tasting something new - for these who had plenty as the world sees it, were not satisfied. And so they ate their own flesh.

This is the same depravity of which Paul wrote in Romans 1:21-24 *For though they knew God, they did not glorify Him as God or show gratitude. Instead, their thinking became nonsense, and their senseless minds were darkened. Claiming to be wise, they became fools and exchanged the glory of the immortal God for images resembling mortal man, birds, four-footed animals, and reptiles. Therefore God delivered them over in the cravings of their hearts to sexual impurity, so that their bodies were degraded among themselves.*

Isaiah 9:21 *Manasseh is with Ephraim, and Ephraim with Manasseh; together, both are against Judah. In all this, His anger is not removed, and His hand is still raised [to strike].*

A few of the tribes rallied to strengthen each other; they came together to conquer the southern kingdom, Judah. This is not pleasing to YHWH and His hand is still raised to strike. Unity apart from the authority and compliance with the will of God is continued rebellion against Him. So in our day, when some religious leaders tell us we must develop a social conscience, see the gospel in a new light that the social rebels approve of. This is false unity, opposed to God and is not pleasing - for what has light to do with darkness?

Let each of us examine himself, to test everything in light of Scripture. Let us love one another in the truth of the Word in the power of the Spirit. For this is pleasing to God.

Isaiah 10 - The Light of Israel.

In chapter 10, attention shifts back to Assyria. Israel had a tendency to think too highly of themselves and lamented like a teenager when YHWH used a pagan nation to recompense Israel for their sin. Unregenerate folk are inclined to sin and when used by God as He did Assyria - and Judas - He is not the author of their sin, but He uses it and them to work out history as He has determined it.

Right off the bat we see it's going to be bad news for Assyria: Isaiah 10:1-2 *Woe to those enacting crooked statutes and writing oppressive laws to keep the poor from getting a fair trial and to deprive the afflicted among my people of justice, so that widows can be their spoil and they can plunder the fatherless.*

You may recall that Israel was often rebuked for unbalanced scales and taking advantage of widows and orphans - same things Assyria is accused of. Same things that happen in our time, as the US government enacts crooked laws that enrich the powerful and insulates them from justice. Nothing escapes the notice of the Creator Who will judge the nations when He comes the second time. Let us who claim Christ live with this knowledge and walk humbly with one another.

Isaiah 10:3-4 *What will you do on the day of punishment when devastation comes from far away? Who will you run to for help? Where will you leave your wealth? [There will be nothing to do] except crouch among the prisoners or fall among the slain. In all this, His anger is not removed, and His hand is still raised [to strike].*

And the next point is just that - the day of punishment is coming, where there will no refuge in the mountains or caves; the ONLY refuge is found in the Judge! For those who do not repent, do not cry out for mercy; all who trust in their wealth - EVERYONE not in Christ will be exposed. And His hand is still raised up to strike.

Isaiah 10:5-6 *Woe to Assyria, the rod of My anger— the staff in their hands is My wrath. I will send him against a godless nation; I will command him [to go] against a people destined for My rage, to take spoils, to plunder, and to trample them down like clay in the streets.*

Woe to Assyria! They were a godless nation. Assyria was the rod of God's anger used to work out His wrath on another godless nation - apostate Israel! While there was a remnant in ethnic Israel that were truly His people, the nation as a whole was godless and destined for YHWH's rage. He will plunder them and trample them like rubbish on the street. None of us should presume we are "OK with God" for self-deception is the easiest to fall victim to. This is just one of the reasons genuine fellowship with other saints is necessary!

Isaiah 10:7-11 *But this is not what he intends; this is not what he plans. It is his intent to destroy and to cut off many nations. For he says, "Aren't all my commanders kings? Isn't Calno like Carchemish? Isn't Hamath like Arpad? Isn't Samaria like Damascus? As my hand seized the idolatrous kingdoms, whose idols exceeded those of Jerusalem and Samaria, and as I did to Samaria and its idols will I not also do to Jerusalem and its idols?"*

The king of Assyria doesn't think He is the rod of God's anger; he has his own agenda that he thinks he is working out. The puny king of Assyria wants to conquer many peoples and has great confidence in his commanders and their realms. He has a high opinion of the strength of his hand, bragging on his conquests, condescending towards those who have different gods than he. And he has it in his heart to seizes and destroy Jerusalem and her idols. But God sits in the heavens and laughs! The nations are like dust in YHWH's scales!

Isaiah 10:12 *But when the Lord finishes all His work against Mount Zion and Jerusalem, [He will say,] "I will punish the king of Assyria for his arrogant acts and the proud look in his eyes."*

When God finishes using Assyria as His rod of anger against Israel He will punish the king of Assyria for his arrogance and pride. Verses 13 - 15 are what the king of Assyria said: I am proud and clever, having done all this with my own strength! As a man reaching into a nest for eggs, I gathered the WHOLE EARTH to myself! The ax does not boast - he who uses it gets to brag!

Isaiah 10:16 *Therefore the Lord GOD of Hosts will inflict an emaciating disease on the well-fed of Assyria, and He will kindle a burning fire under its glory.*

This type of pride brings judgment from God. Assyria will be brought low.

Isaiah 10:17-19 *Israel's Light will become a fire, and its Holy One, a flame. In one day it will burn up Assyria's thorns and thistles. He will completely destroy the glory of its forests and orchards as a sickness consumes a person. The remaining trees of its forest will be so few in number that a child could count them.*

Israel's light, a holy flame, will burn off Assyria's might. John's gospel tells Who this light is - the One Who is judge will destroy Assyria completely. And not just Assyria - every nation and person who is not in Christ will be destroyed with eternal fire.

Revelation 6:15-17 (ESV) *Then the kings of the earth and the great ones and the generals and the rich and the powerful, and everyone, slave and free, hid themselves in the caves and among the rocks of the mountains, calling to the mountains and rocks, "Fall on us and hide us from the face of him who is seated on the throne, and from the wrath of the Lamb, for the great day of their wrath has come, and who can stand?"*

No refuge apart from Christ. No boasting except in Him. 2 Corinthians 13:5 *Test yourselves [to see] if you are in the faith. Examine yourselves. Or do you yourselves not recognize that Jesus Christ is in you?—unless you fail the test.*

The next part of Isaiah 10 shifts gears - again. In our previous study we read how YHWH had judged Assyria such that there was so little left a child could count the trees. I was reminded of an old Peanuts comic strip, Lucy and Linus were outside on a dark night looking at the sky. Lucy wondered aloud how many stars there were. Linus, looking up, said, "more than ten." That's about the limit of a small child counting. Assyria fell from a powerhouse kingdom that ruled a good bit of the world. This is nothing in the hands of Creator God.

Now we see a focus on "that day" - which was seen as near term by most in Israel but is mostly eschatological. Isaiah 10:20 *On that day the remnant of Israel and the survivors of the house of Jacob will no longer depend on the one who struck them, but they will faithfully depend on the LORD, the Holy One of Israel.*

Jews saw the two kingdoms becoming self-sufficient again. Isaiah is telling us all who are in YHWH's true kingdom (the

REMNANT) will no longer fear man but will rightly fear God and trust Him. We know from the biblical record that ethnic Israel never turned back to YHWH as described here.

Isaiah 10:21-23 *The remnant will return, the remnant of Jacob, to the Mighty God. Israel, even if your people were as numerous as the sand of the sea, [only] a remnant of them will return. Destruction has been decreed; justice overflows. For throughout the land the Lord GOD of Hosts is carrying out a destruction that was decreed.*

Note again - only a remnant will return, only a remnant will be saved (see Romans 11:5-7). When Jesus comes the second time, He will judge the nations, eternal destruction will consume them. This is what He has decreed.

Isaiah 10:24-26 *Therefore, the Lord GOD of Hosts says this: "My people who dwell in Zion, do not fear Assyria, though he strikes you with a rod and raises his staff over you as the Egyptians did. In just a little while My wrath will be spent and My anger will turn to their destruction." And the LORD of Hosts will brandish a whip against him as [He did when He] struck Midian at the rock of Oreb; and He will raise His staff over the sea as [He did] in Egypt.*

YHWH's people who dwell in Zion - the mountain of peace with God, not to be confused with Sinai, the place of unbearable law-giving - will not fear man. Man can only kill the body - we who are on Zion are secure. God tells Israel that even if Assyria decimates them as did Egypt God will ultimately turn His wrath to them and bring sure destruction to Assyria - just as He did at Oreb (see Judges 7:25) and Egypt when He destroyed them in the see.

Brothers - Christ is our sure rock of refuge. Our world is certainly growing more crazy each week - showing us AGAIN not to put our trust therein. We who are in Christ sit with Him in the heavenlies (Eph 2:4-7), dwelling on the Mount of peace, Zion. This world is not our home, so we ought to weep when it is ravaged by those who belong to it.

We must be on guard that we don't see our wealth as barns (Luke 12:13-21). Be not anxious for what you will eat or wear, for your Father in heaven knows you need these things. Seek His kingdom - proclaim the gospel to every creature - and He will provide all your needs. For most of us, he provides work. So work and provide for your own and the household of God.

We come now to the end of chapter 10 of Isaiah. This is another judgment on Assyria - but with a difference.

Isaiah 10:27 On that day his burden will fall from your shoulders, and his yoke from your neck. The yoke will be broken because of fatness.

"On that day" - should draw our attention to the end of days, when the final judgment comes on the nations. The previous section speaks of the paradise we'll have in Jesus; this section builds on that. The burden will from the shoulders of God's covenant people, the heavy yoke will be removed, broken "because of fatness." There is a lack of consensus as to what the Hebrew word behind "fatness" means; it shows up as prosperity, anointing, and fat. Is the yoke broken because God's people are "fat" - rich? Is this wealth temporal or spiritual? Yet those who inherit the kingdom are poor in spirit.

We DO know, the heavy yoke is removed and broken. Jesus said His yoke was easy and His burden light (Matt 11:30) - both of these, burden and yoke, are mentioned in Isaiah 10:7. The apostles said the Mosaic Law was a heavy yoke that no man could bear (Acts 15:5 & 10). In Christ, the heavy yoke is broken and the burden thereof removed; we take His yoke which is light, as is His burden. This is the change between the Old and New Covenants.

Isaiah 10:28-32 Assyria has come to Aiath and has gone through Migron, storing his equipment at Michmash. They crossed over at the ford, saying, "We will spend the night at Geba." The people of Ramah are trembling; those at Gibeah of Saul have fled. Cry aloud, daughter of Gallim! Listen, Laishah! Anathoth is miserable. Madmenah has fled. The inhabitants of Gebim have sought refuge. Today he will stand at Nob, shaking his fist at the mountain of Daughter Zion, the hill of Jerusalem.

Historians tell us Assyria never took this route in battle; that it actually represents the route "as the crow flies." It seems this describes the spiritual battle waged against the people of God, typified by ethnic Israel's arch enemy. The list of small villages along this route include Jeremiah's home town of Anathoth and Nob is northeast of Jerusalem, where Saul took out revenge on the priests (1 Sam 22:11-23) for aiding David (1 Sam 21:1-9). This is where, Isaiah said, Assyria will stand, shaking his fist at Jerusalem. This typifies the enemy of the saints, who shakes his fist at the temple of God - His saints. For we are the New Jerusalem that will come down to the new earth on that day.

Isaiah 10:33-34 *Look, the Lord GOD of Hosts will chop off the branches with terrifying power, and the tall [trees] will be cut down, the high [trees] felled. He is clearing the thickets of the forest with an ax, and Lebanon with its majesty will fall.*

I will give you a scene from the gospel. Matthew 3:1-2 & 7-10 *In those days John the Baptist came, preaching in the Wilderness of Judea and saying, "Repent, because the kingdom of heaven has come near!" ... When he saw many of the Pharisees and Sadducees coming to the place of his baptism, he said to them, "Brood of vipers! Who warned you to flee from the coming wrath? Therefore produce fruit consistent with repentance. And don't presume to say to yourselves, 'We have Abraham as our father.' For I tell you that God is able to raise up children for Abraham from these stones! Even now the ax is ready to strike the root of the trees! Therefore, every tree that doesn't produce good fruit will be cut down and thrown into the fire.*

In Isaiah we see the Lord ready to cut down tall trees and clear the thickets with His ax. John picks up on this and tells the self-righteous Jews that they have no basis for boasting, for God has the ax in His raised hand, ready to cut down the tall trees at the root. And every tree that does not bear good fruit will be cut down and burned.

So it will be on that day, when the Lord Jesus returns with shout and the sound of the trumpet. Are you built on the Rock or do you yet stand on the sand of your own righteousness? There remains only one sure refuge on that day. Christ Jesus - it is He!

Isaiah 11 - The Shoot of Jesse.

Isaiah 11 is in two parts; part 1 is a revelation of the Son of David, part 2 is a revelation of the kingdom of God, typified by the two kingdoms of ethnic Israel.

Isaiah 11:1 *Then a shoot will grow from the stump of Jesse, and a branch from his roots will bear fruit.*

This reference to the stump of Jesse establishes David in history by referring to his father and shows that new life will come from David's loins. The branch will bear fruit. Having the complete Scriptures in our hands and minds, we ought to be drawn to Matthew 21:43, wherein Jesus told the leaders of ethnic Israel, "*Therefore I tell you, the kingdom of God will be taken away from you and given to a nation producing its fruit.*" Good fruit is a characteristic of those who are united with Christ.

Isaiah 11:2 *The Spirit of the LORD will rest on Him— a Spirit of wisdom and understanding, a Spirit of counsel and strength, a Spirit of knowledge and of the fear of the LORD.*

When Jesus was baptized by John, the heavens opened, the Father announced His approval of His Son, and the Spirit descended upon Him. This was just before His temptation, where He rebuked Satan with Scripture - displaying the right fear of Himself and what He had spoken. All wisdom and knowledge is summed up in Christ, the ultimate example of everything truly good.

Isaiah 11:3-5 *His delight will be in the fear of the LORD. He will not judge by what He sees with His eyes, He will not execute justice by what He hears with His ears, but He will judge the poor righteously and execute justice for the oppressed of the land. He will strike the land with discipline from His mouth, and He will kill the wicked with a command from His lips. Righteousness will be a belt around His loins; faithfulness will be a belt around His waist.*

Recall the scene in 1 Samuel 16 where the next king of Israel is being selected. YHWH tells His prophet not to look on the outward appearance - tall men make good kings and nearly always win US presidential elections - because that's how men measure one another. God looks on the inner man, his soul. Jesus doesn't judge using human senses, sight and hearing; He judges using righteousness that He has by His divine nature. While the ancient preacher said (Ecclesiastes 8:11) *Because the sentence against a criminal act is not carried out quickly, the heart of people is filled [with the desire] to commit crime*; Christ Jesus executes justice on time, perfectly. Striking the land with discipline from His mouth ought to remind us of Rev 19:16 *A sharp sword came from His mouth, so that He might strike the nations with it. He will shepherd them with an iron scepter. He will also trample the winepress of the fierce anger of God, the Almighty.* The wicked, self-righteous, carnal people will not escape the justice of YHWH. His belt of righteousness signifies His royal standing, hinting at the New Covenant that will come from this shoot of Jesse.

Isaiah 11:6-9 *The wolf will live with the lamb, and the leopard will lie down with the goat. The calf, the young lion, and the fatling will be together, and a child will lead them. The cow and the bear will graze, their young ones will lie down together, and the lion will eat straw like the ox. An infant will play beside the cobra's pit, and a toddler will put his hand into a snake's den. None will harm or destroy [another] on My entire holy mountain, for the land will be as full of the knowledge of the LORD as the sea is filled with water.*

This scene is the new earth, not a half-baked temporal millennium. As it was before the Fall, there will no killing. But it will be better - there will be no Fall. Now we are taught to keep on growing in the grace and knowledge of Christ Jesus; that will not end but we will grow deeper then and it will be like seas as deep as the mountains. Nobody brings this kind of peace, this depth of knowledge except the One Who came from the Father to redeem those He created.

Do you have this peace? Do you desire this knowledge? Cry out to God for the mercy to believe on Him. He really did come to save sinners.

Part two of Isaiah 11 reveals the ingathering of Gentiles and the remnant of Israel into the kingdom of God. There are those who claim this is merely the return of ethnic Israel to the land they inhabited. We shall see.

Isaiah 11:10-12 *On that day the root of Jesse will stand as a banner for the peoples. The nations will seek Him, and His resting place will be glorious. On that day the Lord will [extend] His hand a second time to recover—from Assyria, Egypt, Pathros, Cush, Elam, Shinar, Hamath, and the coasts and islands of the west—the remnant of His people who survive. He will lift up a banner for the nations and gather the dispersed of Israel; He will collect the scattered of Judah from the four corners of the earth.*

We see this phrase, "On that day," which repeatedly brings very good or very bad news. We see His hand raised - again! But this time, not in judgment, but to recover, to bring back, the remnant of His people. The root of Jesse looks forward to the promise of a king to forever sit on David's throne. Jesus

Christ is He and on that day, He will stand as the banner so all His people will see Him and come to Him. This is the Lord's doing and it IS marvelous in our eyes!

Earlier in this book (chap 5 and verse 26) we saw YHWH lift up a banner which called the Gentiles to Himself. Here we see it again, calling people from the nation, the scattered people of Israel and those scattered from Judah - from the four corners of the earth. Herein is a clue: ethnic Israel was taken into exile in a very concentrated area. In Isaiah's time, they had not been scattered all over the globe. If we look to the apostolic teaching on who is Israel, we'll see Isaiah' reference must be speaking of the elect and redeemed from every tribe, tongue, and people.

Isaiah 11:13-14 *Ephraim's envy will cease; Judah's harassment will end. Ephraim will no longer be envious of Judah, and Judah will not harass Ephraim. But they will swoop down on the Philistine flank to the west. Together they will plunder the people of the east. They will extend their power over Edom and Moab, and the Ammonites will be their subjects.*

On that day, the striving amongst the tribes of Israel will cease. In the first part of this chapter, we read about, on that day, the wolf and the lamb, the lion and the calf, the bear and the cow will all be at peace with each other. So it will be with the tribes of man who are united together in Christ as one new man. God-haters will not be able to divide them nor stand before them, for the great day of the Lord is at hand!

Isaiah 11:15-16 *The LORD will divide the Gulf of Suez. He will wave His hand over the Euphrates with His mighty wind and will split it into seven streams, letting people walk through on foot. There will be a highway for the remnant of His people who will survive from Assyria, as there was for Israel when they came up from the land of Egypt.*

YHWH will go before His people, making the way to His kingdom clear. As Moses held up his hands to part the Red

Sea, YHWH will lift His hand over the great river Euphrates and split it into seven streams, small rivulets that men can walk through. And God will make a highway for His remnant - not all ethnic Israel. Those people He gathered from the four corners of the earth will travel on His highway to be welcomed into the eternal kingdom. *Jesus= highway*

This is the Lord's doing - and it is marvelous in our eyes!

Isaiah 12 - Song of Praise.

Chapter 12 of Isaiah is a short but deep song of praise to the Lord Christ. And it opens with a familiar phrase.

Isaiah 12:1-2 *On that day you will say: "I will praise You, LORD, although You were angry with me. Your anger has turned away, and You have had compassion on me. Indeed, God is my salvation; I will trust [Him] and not be afraid, for Yah, the LORD, is my strength and my song. He has become my salvation."*

The balance of this short chapter reveals more, but the opening phrase tells us this we will be reading about the end of days. This happens when the fullness of redemption is complete - all the elect from ethnic Israel and the world. On that day, there will no more anger evident amongst the elect, for all the elect will then be the redeemed, which means they have been translated from the domain of darkness into the glorious light of His kingdom (Col 1:13). And with His redeemed, the Lord is always compassionate - He is our salvation, our strength, and our song!

Isaiah 12:3-4 *You will joyfully draw water from the springs of salvation, and on that day you will say: "Give thanks to Yahweh; proclaim His name! Celebrate His works among the peoples. Declare that His name is exalted.*

All the redeemed of God can drink freely from the waters of salvation. This is what Isaiah will tell us in chapter 55 -

Come, everyone who is thirsty, come to the waters; and you without money, come, buy, and eat! Come, buy wine and milk without money and without cost! And this is what the Lord Himself tells us in the last chapter of His Word - Revelation 22:1-2 & 17 *Then he showed me the river of living water, sparkling like crystal, flowing from the throne of God and of the Lamb down the middle of the broad street [of the city]. ... Both the Spirit and the bride say, "Come!"* Anyone who hears should say, "Come!" And the one who is thirsty should come. Whoever desires should take the living water as a gift." The bride - God's people - say "Come!" This is the general call. The Spirit says "Come!" This is the effectual call. All who are thirsty, all who desire living water are those called by the Spirit to new life in Christ. And the redeemed will give thanks to Christ Jesus and proclaim His name to all! We will celebrate and proclaim His work - He has brought redemption to His people! Dear saints - is this not marvelous in your eyes? Exalt in the Lord Jesus and make Him known!

Isaiah 12:5-6 *Sing to Yahweh, for He has done glorious things. Let this be known throughout the earth. Cry out and sing, citizen of Zion, for the Holy One of Israel is among you in [His] greatness."*

Again, fellow saints, sing unto YHWH, for He has done glorious things! He has satisfied the Father, drank the cup of wrath that was ours, and clothed us in His righteousness. Proclaim this throughout the earth - we are citizens of Zion, free from Mount Sinai! The Holy One of Israel - the God-Man Himself - is among us in His greatness! This is the most glorious news among men; wretched men who need refuge from the judgment to come. Preach Christ to all - we the bride say "Come!" We trust the Spirit to do what only He can do - raise the dead and draw them to Christ. This is good news and it's what we should be proclaiming and singing day-by-day until He takes us home.

III. Judgment on the Nations

Isaiah 13 - Babylon is Overthrown.

Isaiah's 13th chapter is an oracle against Babylon. Curious - Assyria has been the main player in Isaiah's world so far; Babylon would rise up later in Israel's history. But the Bible often uses Babylon as the symbol for the system of the world - cultural arrogance and self-reliance, trusting in wealth and health.

Isaiah 13:1 *An oracle against Babylon that Isaiah son of Amoz saw:*

In this vision of judgment Isaiah saw, we read (verses 2 - 4) the gathering of an army. It's not until the last phrase of verse 4 we find out Who's doing this: *The LORD of Hosts is mobilizing an army for war. They are coming from a far land, from the distant horizon— the LORD and the weapons of His wrath— to destroy the whole country.* The object of YHWH's wrath is not, at this point, the nation of Israel; it is Babylon, the whore of the world's system of greed and violence. And none can stop His hand!

Isaiah 13:6 *Wail! For the day of the LORD is near. It will come like destruction from the Almighty.*

What can man do when judgment comes? Isaiah 13:7-8 *Therefore everyone's hands will become weak, and every man's heart will melt. They will be horrified; pain and agony will seize [them]; they will be in anguish like a woman in labor. They will look at each other, their faces flushed with fear.*

And again: Isaiah 13:9 *Look, the day of the LORD is coming— cruel, with rage and burning anger— to make the earth a desolation and to destroy the sinners on it.*

Ah, but aren't we told by people who know Him not that God is a gentleman Who would never do harm to anyone! Recall this from chapter 1: *If the LORD of Hosts had not left us a few survivors, we would be like Sodom, we would resemble Gomorrah.* God will save and redeem every one of His chosen ones and all not so chosen will face His wrath. This is the unchanging nature of God. Only He can please Him. Only those who are in Christ are pleasing to Him.

Verses 10-12 describes the impact of this judgment, followed by: Isaiah 13:13-14 *Therefore I will make the heavens tremble, and the earth will shake from its foundations at the wrath of the LORD of Hosts, on the day of His burning anger. Like wandering gazelles and like sheep without a shepherd, each one will turn to his own people, each one will flee to his own land.*

Verse 13 ought to cause us to think of: Hebrews 12:25-27 *Make sure that you do not reject the One who speaks. For if they did not escape when they rejected Him who warned them on earth, even less will we if we turn away from Him who warns us from heaven. His voice shook the earth at that time, but now He has promised, Yet once more I will shake not only the earth but also heaven. This expression, "Yet once more," indicates the removal of what can be shaken—that is, created things—so that what is not shaken might remain.*

And verse 14 is shown in Isaiah 53:6 *We all went astray like sheep; we all have turned to our own way* and cited in 2 Peter 2:25. Even those chosen by God to be redeemed are not inclined to seek Him or follow Him until that redemption is applied.

Verses 15-18 is a graphic description of the woe that befalls those who are sought out by the great Shepherd of our souls - they are without the compassion of the Lord, being the objects of His wrath.

Isaiah 13:19 *And Babylon, the jewel of the kingdoms, the glory of the pride of the Chaldeans, will be like Sodom and Gomorrah when God overthrew them.*

Here is the result: Babylon; the archetype of the lust of the flesh, lust of the eyes, and the pride of life; will be like Sodom and Gomorrah. The last few verses of chapter 13 reinforce this.

When judgment comes, no amount of worldly power will protect one rebel. The fool thinks his wealth (bigger barns) will satisfy his soul. Hear and heed this refrain: None but Jesus can do helpless sinners good. Keep your eyes focused on Him, fellow saints. He is the faithful one!

Isaiah 14 - The World is Judged, Zion is Established.

As we turn our attention to chapter 14 of Isaiah, it would do well to recall what we learned in chapter 1: God gave this entire book to Isaiah in a vision. As the prophet uses language to communicate God's Word to His people, let us bear in mind (remember) what He told us in chapter 1. Let's look closely at the opening of this chapter.

Isaiah 14:1-2 *For the LORD will have compassion on Jacob and will choose Israel again. He will settle them on their own land. The foreigner will join them and be united with the house of Jacob. The nations will escort Israel and bring it to its homeland. Then the house of Israel will possess them as male and female slaves in the LORD's land. They will make captives of their captors and will rule over their oppressors.*

National Israel would look at this and see the restoration of their tribes to their land, victorious over their enemies. The next section identifies Babylon as the enemy mentioned in the opening. Look at this short paragraph with gospel glasses and see the Israel of God as we are brought to our homeland. Ethnic Israel never conquered temporal nations and made slaves of them, but Christ's apostles currently sit as judges over the 12 tribes. The use of "LORD" in this passage is the personal name YHWH; YHWH's land is as Abraham saw it - a heavenly country. At the end of the age, the people of God from every nation, tribe, and tongue will escort Israel to the homeland.

There are 11 other passages in Isaiah (in chapters 31, 45, 49, 54, 60, & 61) that have similar pictures of Israel's victory, the consistent theme is God works all things to reconcile His people to Himself. This present earth cannot inherit eternity - that small parcel in the mid-east served as a picture of the heavenly country YHWH has prepared, where we will be with Him and all the saints eternally on the new earth.

Isaiah 14:3-4 *When the LORD gives you rest from your pain, torment, and the hard labor you were forced to do, you will sing this song [of contempt] about the king of Babylon.*

As was noted in the previous chapter, at the time of Isaiah Babylon was not yet a world power. Babylon was often used in the Bible to denote the system of the world - satisfaction in self, health, and wealth. Verses 4b - 21 describe the evil of that system and consequences of such rebellion, as God uses nation against nation, with the king of Babylon being a type of Satan (vs 12- 14).

YHWH responds. Isaiah 14:22-23 *"I will rise up against them"—[this is] the declaration of the LORD of Hosts—"and I will cut off from Babylon her reputation, remnant, offspring, and posterity"—[this is] the LORD's declaration. "I will make her a swampland and a region for screech owls, and I will sweep her away with a broom of destruction." [This is] the declaration of the LORD of Hosts.*

No matter what great nations of this world rise up, God is the one Who rules all things and all people. At the end of all things, He will utterly destroy Babylon - the system of the world and her people.

III. Judgment on the Nations

Isaiah 14:24-27 *The LORD of Hosts has sworn: As I have purposed, so it will be; as I have planned it, so it will happen. I will break Assyria in My land; ...This is the plan prepared for the whole earth, and this is the hand stretched out against all the nations. The LORD of Hosts Himself has planned it; therefore, who can stand in its way? It is His hand that is outstretched, so who can turn it back?*

Babylon, Assyria, and all other peoples who rage against God will be broken - and there are none who can withstand what He has planned, no one can turn it back. YHWH of Hosts has planned it and His hand is outstretched - recall His raised arm in earlier chapters? Ready to mete out judgment.

The last segment in this chapter is judgment pronounced against Philistia - their wealth has rotted and terror has overtaken them.

Isaiah 14:31-32 *Wail, you gates! Cry out, city! Tremble with fear, all Philistia! For a cloud of dust is coming from the north, and there is no one missing from [the invader's] ranks. What answer will be given to the messengers from that nation? The LORD has founded Zion, and His afflicted people find refuge in her.*

People of the earth - wail and cry out, tremble with fear! When the King returns it will be to judge the nations, gather His people, and make all things new. We see in this passage Christ coming in power "from the north" (Assyria was north of Philistia) and no one is missing from YHWH's army - all His redeemed are with Him. What is the answer? YHWH has established Zion, the place of grace where His afflicted people (poor in spirit, hated by the world) find refuge.

This is the safety, the tower of refuge and strength that God's redeemed find in the person and work of the Lord Jesus, Who is the Christ. Only trust Him, let no other trust intrude. He - alone - is able to do poor sinners good.

Isaiah 15 & 16 - Moab's Doom.

Chapters 15 & 16 will be reviewed as a unit, as it a cycle of judgment against Moab, with the attending exaltation of Christ in the midst of it.

Isaiah 15:1-4 *An oracle against Moab ... Every head is shaved; every beard is cut off. In its streets they wear sackcloth; on its rooftops and in its public squares everyone wails, falling down and weeping. ... the soldiers of Moab cry out, and they tremble.*

The pagan nations that surrounded Israel are being judged. This vision squares with what we know about the kingdom of God that is in our midst - God's anger is meted out against those who surround us; as the world rages against the Lord and His people. Even the strong and proud of the world will cry out in fear as they tremble before their Creator.

Verses 5 -9 continue: Moab's fugitives flee, weeping; the land is desolate, withered; their wealth is useless - unable to grow food! Their wailing becomes unbearable as their rivers fill with blood and YHWH brings "a lion" (the Lion of Judah?) to consume those who escape. Interestingly, the KJV and its variants have "lions" while Young's Literal and myriad others (including Strong's) have a singular lion. IF it is "lions" it must be temporal, a pride of lions literally pouncing on Moabites. IF it is "a lion" it fits into the vision of judgment/redemption, focused on Christ Jesus that characterizes this book.

In the first few verses of chapter 16 Moab sends people to mount Zion, seeking refuge and counsel. *Like a bird fleeing, forced from its nest ... Give us counsel, shelter us in the heat of the day ... hide the refugees ... be a refuge for Moab from the aggressor.* (verses 1-4). As in the days of Rahab, the pagans have heard of YHWH and they know who His people are. In their distress, they cry out for mercy from the One who is pouring our judgment on them.

Isaiah 16:5 *Then in the tent of David a throne will be established by faithful love. A judge who seeks what is right and is quick to execute justice will sit on the throne forever.*

Here is a clear reference to the promised Messiah, the shoot of Jesse, the Son of David, who will take David's throne - established by FAITHFUL LOVE! He will do what is right and will mete out justice quickly, *Because the sentence against a criminal act is not carried out quickly, the heart of people is filled with the desire to commit crime.* (Eccl 8:11). This passage has wide application to every generation.

Isaiah 16:6-7 *We have heard of Moab's pride— how very proud he is— his haughtiness, his pride, his arrogance, and his empty boasting. Therefore let Moab wail; let every one of them wail for Moab. Mourn, you who are completely devastated, for the raisin cakes of Kir-hareseth.*

Those in Zion know about the pride of Moab, their arrogant self-sufficiency. They seek after pagan delicacies (raisin cakes), yet all they will do is wail and mourn for they are completely devastated. There is no peace for the wicked! Their grapes have withered for the rulers of the other pagan nations have trampled her vines to furthest reaches of Moab's borders (vs 8).

Isaiah 16:10 *Joy and rejoicing have been removed from the orchard; no one is singing or shouting for joy in the vineyards. No one tramples grapes in the winepresses. I have put an end to the shouting.* God's judgment has put an end to Moab's boasting in her material wealth. In Rev 6 we see the rich and powerful of the world (Moab, Babylon) crying out for the mountains to fall on them and hide them from wrath of the Lamb; but there is no hiding place apart from being in Christ Jesus.

Isaiah 16:12 *When Moab appears on the high place, when he tires himself out and comes to his sanctuary to pray, it will do him no good.*

Pagan religion will offer so solace when the Son of Man returns to judge the nations. False religion will lose its allusion of comfort when the darkness it requires is stripped away by the Light that exposes every wicked way.

Isaiah 16:13-14 *This is the message that the LORD previously announced about Moab. And now the LORD says, "In three years, as a hired worker counts years, Moab's splendor will become an object of contempt, in spite of a very large population. And those who are left will be few and weak."*

YHWH had previously spoken against Moab and now (at the time of Isaiah's writing) there were only 3 years left until Assyria would wear Moab out, leaving the few survivors weak, with no vineyards, no wealth.

Hebrews 1:1-2 *Long ago God spoke to the fathers by the prophets at different times and in different ways. In these last days, He has spoken to us by [His] Son. God has appointed Him heir of all things and made the universe through Him.*

What was spoken long ago was for our benefit. But when Christ came and spoke, the time of ignorance is over.

Hebrews 1:10-13 *In the beginning, Lord, You established the earth, and the heavens are the works of Your hands; they will perish, but You remain. They will all wear out like clothing; You will roll them up like a cloak, and they will be changed like a robe. But You are the same, and Your years will never end. Now to which of the angels has He ever said: Sit at My right hand until I make Your enemies Your footstool?*

All authority in heaven and earth has been given to the One who created all things, who have His life for His sheep, and is coming again to judge the world, gather His people, and make all things new.

Today, if you hear His voice, do not harden your heart! There will come a day when it's too late and mercy will be no more.

Isaiah 17 - Judgment Against Damascus, Israel, and the World.

Chapter 17 is a quick run-through of judgments pronounced on Damascus, Israel, and "the nations." Damascus was the capital of Syria, to the north. This series of judgments proceeds from a known enemy of Israel, to Israel, then to the world. While there are local (in terms of history of geography) aspects of these judgments, the over-arching focus is eschatological.

Isaiah 17:1 -3 *"An oracle against Damascus: Look, Damascus is no longer a city. It has become a ruined heap." Her cities will be forsaken, Damascus will lie in ruins. ""The fortress disappears from Ephraim, and a kingdom from Damascus. The remnant of Aram will be like the splendor of the Israelites. [This is] the declaration of the LORD of Hosts."*

Destruction and ruin - but the remnant of Aram (a southern city) will be like the SPLENDOR of the Israelites. Why does Aram get the exception, a blessing (it appears) in the midst of this devastation? The judgment against Israel puts it in perspective.

Isaiah 17:4 *On that day the splendor of Jacob will fade, and his healthy body will become emaciated.*

We've seen this phrase before, "on that day" - it tends to point towards the Day of the Lord, when He comes to judge the nations. It shows up 3 times in this chapter. On that day, Jacob's splendor will fade, he will be emaciated - stripped of all that the world envied.

Isaiah 17:5-6 *It will be as if a reaper had gathered standing grain— his arm harvesting the heads of grain— and as if one had gleaned heads of grain in the Valley of Rephaim. Only gleanings will be left in Israel, as if an olive tree had been*

61

beaten— two or three berries at the very top of the tree, four or five on its fruitful branches. [This is] the declaration of the LORD, the God of Israel.

Jesus used the image of reaping to describe the end, as in the parable of the wheat and the weeds in Matthew 13. Beginning in verse 37 Jesus explained the field is the world, not the ekklesia of God, that the wheat was sown by the Son of Man and the weeds by Satan. The harvest is the end of the age and angels are the harvesters. As the weeds are gathered and burned up, so it will be at the end of the age, when Jesus sends His angels to gather the weeds (everything that causes sin and all who practice lawlessness); they will be thrown in the blazing furnace. If you have ears, listen to the Lord of the harvest!

Paul used the parable of the olive tree to those how most of national Israel would be broken off, as if the olive tree had been beaten. Very few olives left on the tree, onto which the Gentiles would be grafted. Of the few natural olives left on the tree, the apostle said "only a remnant (of ethnic Israel) will be saved.

This is the declaration of YHWH - the God of Israel; as she was in the mid-east and as she is becoming for eternity.

Isaiah 17:7-8 *On that day people will look to their Maker and will turn their eyes to the Holy One of Israel. They will not look to the altars they made with their hands or to the Asherahs and incense altars they made with their fingers.*

ON that day, the remnant will repent and believe on God, turning their backs on the gods made with human hands.

Isaiah 17:9-10 *On that day their strong cities will be like the abandoned woods and mountaintops that were abandoned because of the Israelites; there will be desolation. For you have forgotten the God of your salvation, and you have failed to remember the rock of your strength; therefore you will plant beautiful plants and set out cuttings from exotic vines.*

ON that day, those branches that were broken off will find their "bigger barns" worthless; for they have forgotten Who was their strength, they have forsaken the God who saved them from Egypt.

Isaiah 17:11 *On the day that you plant, you will help them to grow, and in the morning you will help your seed to sprout, [but] the harvest will vanish on the day of disease and incurable pain.*

ON that day, the works of their hands will be empty, bringing only illness and incurable pain. There is no room for repentance on that day.

Now judgment on the world. Isaiah 17:12-14 *Ah! The roar of many peoples— they roar like the roaring of the seas. The raging of the nations— they rage like the raging of mighty waters. The nations rage like the raging of many waters. He rebukes them, and they flee far away, driven before the wind like chaff on the hills and like tumbleweeds before a gale. In the evening—sudden terror! Before morning—it is gone! This is the fate of those who plunder us and the lot of those who ravage us.*

The nations that know not God roar like raging seas and mighty waters, puffed up by their sense of power and authority. YHWH rebukes them and they flee like fleas driven by gale winds, like tumbleweeds across a clear plain. They will suffer great terror and then - everything they've prized will be gone, they will be naked before their Creator. THIS is the fate of those who plunder and ravage US - the body of Christ.

This ought to cause us to think of 1 Corinthians 3:16-17: *Do you not know that you are God's temple and that God's Spirit dwells in you? If anyone destroys God's temple, God will destroy him. For God's temple is holy, and you are that temple.*

God is jealous of His own, He will mete out wrath on those who persecute His body. ON that day, you will find yourself

EITHER in Christ (SAFE from the wrath of God) or in Adam (appointed unto unending wrath). ON that day, it will be too late. IF you hear His voice, do not harden your heart - cry out for mercy while it is today.

Isaiah 18 - Cush.

Chapter 18 brings a short declaration of judgment upon Cush, ending with a vision of redemption.

Isaiah 18:1 - 2 *Ah! The land of buzzing insect wings beyond the rivers of Cush sends couriers by sea, in reed vessels on the waters. Go, swift messengers, to a nation tall and smooth-skinned, to a people feared far and near, a powerful nation with a strange language, whose land is divided by rivers.*

Cush corresponds to Ethiopia, south of Egypt; it was a nation known for its ships and the attending trade. Being blessed with many rivers, Cush was also plagued with many bugs. Verses 2b & 3 describe Cush's activity to raise up, for all the people to come to her aid - the nation of powerful, tall, smooth-skinned people with a strange language. But then, in verse 4, YHWH speaks to His prophet.

Isaiah 18:4 *For, the LORD said to me: I will quietly look out from My place, like shimmering heat in sunshine, like a rain cloud in harvest heat.*

In contrast to the frantic cries from humans, YHWH is calm, in control, seeing everything. He will cut down the fruit bearing plants before harvest time (verse 5), leaving only birds of prey and foraging beasts. This may be part of what of what formed the vision in Revelation 19:17-18 *Then I saw an angel standing on the sun, and he cried out in a loud voice, saying to all the birds flying high overhead, "Come, gather together for the great supper of God, so that you may eat the flesh of kings, the flesh of commanders, the flesh of mighty men, the flesh of horses and of their riders, and the flesh of everyone, both free and slave, small and great."*

64

That great supper is two-sided, showing in graphic terms the wrath to be poured out on those who believe not on the Lamb (John 3:18) with all of it taking place at the end of the age; just as the judgment of all flesh.

The end-of-the-age perspective is brought home with the last verse of this chapter.

Isaiah 18:7 *At that time a gift will be brought to Yahweh of Hosts from a people tall and smooth-skinned, a people feared far and near, a powerful nation with a strange language, whose land is divided by rivers—to Mount Zion, the place of the name of Yahweh of Hosts.*

"At that time" has the same impact as "on that day" - drawing our attention to the end of time. At that time, the remnant of Cush - the tall, smooth-skinned people with strange language and many rivers - will bring gifts to YHWH, on Mount Zion; the place of peace with God that none but the redeemed will ascend.

If you are having your wealth decimated, wondering why you face ruin - perhaps the Lord of the harvest is pruning you so that you will turn to Him. Harden not your heart today - for you may not have tomorrow.

Isaiah 19 - An Oracle Against Egypt.

Chapter 19 brings us to an oracle against Egypt, perhaps the most powerful nation in Isaiah's day. What we see is that God is all powerful and not the fairy-tale gentleman who never goes against the will of man.

Isaiah 19:1 *An oracle against Egypt: Look, the LORD rides on a swift cloud and is coming to Egypt. Egypt's idols will tremble before Him, and Egypt's heart will melt within it.*

Not something done in secret, the prophet declares Look! YHWH rides on a war chariot (see Ps 18:10; 68:33; 104:3;

Nah 1:3 for similar images) and Egypt's idols tremble (recall Dagon in 1 Sam 5) and her heart (the leaders) will melt, become weak in the knees. Such is the terror for those without proper refuge.

Verses 2 - 4 reveal that God will provoke Egypt against herself, brothers and friends will fight each other; the people will be driven to seek idols, ghosts, spirits of the dead, and wizards. Egypt will be delivered to a stronger, harsher master to rule over her. This is the declaration of the Lord GOD of Hosts!

Verses 5 - 15 continue the amazing list of evidence that piles up, displaying the wrath of God against Egypt. Their waters will dry up, their ship channels will stink, reed and rush will die. Fishermen will mourn; weavers will be dismayed; all her workers will be demoralized. Her leaders are fools, her counselors give stupid advice; can they know what YHWH has planned?

Isaiah 19:14-15 *The LORD has mixed within her a spirit of confusion. [The leaders] have made Egypt stagger in all she does, as a drunkard staggers in his vomit. No head or tail, palm or reed, will be able to do anything for Egypt.*

Here God takes credit for Egypt's confusion - He has done this! The reference to "head or tail, palm or reed" points to totality, nothing can protect Egypt and nothing will be spared from YHWH's judgment. Again, I am reminded of the scene at the end of Rev 6, wherein no place is found for the powerful of the world to hide from the wrath of the Lamb. Such is natural man's situation, unless the Lord has mercy on his soul.

Five times in this next section, the phrase "on that day" introduces what will happen.

Isaiah 19:16-17 *On that day Egypt will be like women. She will tremble with fear because of the threatening hand of the LORD of Hosts when He raises it against her. The land of*

Judah will terrify Egypt; whenever Judah is mentioned, Egypt will tremble because of what the LORD of Hosts has planned against it.

On THAT day, Egypt will be so weak she will tremble before Judah - this southern kingdom was never a threat to Egypt! YHWH is jealous of His own and all the kings of the earth will tremble before Him as He vindicates His people.

Isaiah 19:18 *On that day five cities in the land of Egypt will speak the language of Canaan and swear loyalty to the LORD of Hosts. One of the cities will be called the City of the Sun.*

On THAT day, a remnant in Egypt will repent and turn to YHWH; one of the cities was Heliopolis - home of Egypt's sun god.

Isaiah 19:19-22 *On that day there will be an altar to the LORD in the center of the land of Egypt and a pillar to the LORD near her border. It will be a sign and witness to the LORD of Hosts in the land of Egypt. When they cry out to the LORD because of their oppressors, He will send them a savior and leader, and he will rescue them. The LORD will make Himself known to Egypt, and Egypt will know the LORD on that day. They will offer sacrifices and offerings; they will make vows to the LORD and fulfill them. The LORD will strike Egypt, striking and healing. Then they will return to the LORD and He will hear their prayers and heal them.*

On THAT day, this remnant will worship YHWH and cry out to Him because of their oppressors. He will rescue this remnant and Egypt will know Him ON THAT DAY. YHWH will strike Egypt and heal the remnant, who will return to Him. He will hear their prayers and heal them - this is how we know they are His.

Isaiah 19:23 *On that day there will be a highway from Egypt to Assyria. Assyria will go to Egypt, Egypt to Assyria, and Egypt will worship with Assyria.*

On THAT day there will be no barriers or separation ("highway" often used to convey this idea), as the remnants from former enemies join to worship the one true God.

Isaiah 19:24-25 *On that day Israel will form a triple [alliance] with Egypt and Assyria—a blessing within the land. The LORD of Hosts will bless them, saying, "Egypt My people, Assyria My handiwork, and Israel My inheritance are blessed."*

On THAT day Israel, Egypt, and Assyria will be united, a blessing within the land. YHWH will bless them, calling them "my people, my handiwork, my inheritance." Striking words, considering what we read in Hosea, where a child bears the name of "not my people" - referring to the Hebrew nation!

Here is the bottom line: There is no advantage with God for those who trace their lineage to Abraham. YHWH has chosen and will redeem His people from every nation, tribe, and tongue; they will be His handiwork; and all who are in union with Christ share in His inheritance. This is all grace and it's all glorious, what the Lord has done for us!

Isaiah 20 - People of the World put to Shame.

Chapter 20 brings us back to a point in history, reminding us the whole Word of God is anchored in historical fact.

Isaiah 20:1-2 *In the year that the chief commander, sent by Sargon king of Assyria, came to Ashdod and attacked and captured it— during that time the LORD had spoken through Isaiah son of Amoz.*

The event Isaiah mentioned, Assyria captured Ashdod, took place between 713 -711 B.C. Isaiah is telling us that in 713 B.C. (not that he called it that) YHWH spoke through him. The balance of this short chapter is an oracle against all who put their hope in the arm of man.

Isaiah 20:2-5 *"Go, take off your sackcloth and remove the sandals from your feet," and he did so, going naked and barefoot— the LORD said, "As My servant Isaiah has gone naked and barefoot three years as a sign and omen against Egypt and Cush, so the king of Assyria will lead the captives of Egypt and the exiles of Cush, young and old alike, naked and barefoot, with bared buttocks—to Egypt's shame. Those who made Cush their hope and Egypt their boast will be dismayed and ashamed.*

Foreshadowing Jeremiah, Isaiah is told to go naked and barefoot to confront the king of Assyria, telling him that YHWH's servant, Israel, had been likewise naked and barefoot - humiliated and poor - as a sign and omen against Cush and Egypt. Chapters 18 & 19 were focused on these nations - judgment against them was pronounced. Therefore, Assyria would conquer Cush and Egypt, leading the captives and exiles naked and barefoot, to their shame.

All the wealth of all the nations cannot cover sin, cannot pay for sin. Those who do not humble themselves as the Spirit calls will be put to shame. Those who put their hopes in the riches of the nations will be dismayed and ashamed.

Scripture gives us a different picture for miserable sinners that find refuge in Christ: Romans 10:8b-11a *This is the message of faith that we proclaim: If you confess with your mouth, "Jesus is Lord," and believe in your heart that God raised Him from the dead, you will be saved. One believes with the heart, resulting in righteousness, and one confesses with the mouth, resulting in salvation. Now the Scripture says, Everyone who believes on Him will not be put to shame.*

That last phrase is a quote from Isaiah 28:16. Sinners imputed with the righteousness of Christ will not be put to shame. All who have not found refuge in Him will - just like the captives from Cush and Egypt; just like those who had put their hopes in the big barns of Cush and Egypt.

Isaiah 20:6 *And the inhabitants of this coastland will say on that day, 'Look, this is what has happened to those we relied on and fled to for help to rescue [us] from the king of Assyria! Now, how will we escape?'"*

This last verse relates the lament of those in Egypt, people of the coastland, as they realize there is always someone who can take away what you treasure. Moth and rust will take away what the king of Assyria does not. How will we escape? They are left with no hope in this chapter. Recall how the redemption of a remnant from Egypt was revealed in chapter 19. Therein is their hope, which is the Christ. Therein is mankind's only hope.

Isaiah 21 - Oracles Against Babylon and Arabia.

Chapter 21 brings us oracles against Babylon (AGAIN!) and Arabia. We saw in chapter 13 that Babylon represented the world's system of prosperity, enticing men to lust after bigger barns. Arabia makes her first appearance in Isaiah's vision.

Isaiah 21:1-2a *An oracle against the desert by the sea: Like storms that pass over the Negev, it comes from the desert, from the land of terror. A troubling vision is declared to me.*

We find out in verse 9 that it is Babylon against whom this oracle is spoken. Isaiah reveals a troubling vision that he was given, which corresponds to a storm from the land of terror. Sleep well, Babylon.

The vision has treacherous people who lay siege and destroy what's before them, perplexing and dismaying all who see them (vs 2b-3). Isaiah was filled with anguish, his heart staggered as he was terrified by the sheer horror before him (vs 4).

The next verse stands out because it's a non-sequitur. Isaiah 21:5 *Prepare a table, and spread out a carpet! Eat and drink! Rise up, you princes, and oil the shields!*

This appears to be a reference to what we find in Daniel 5:1-4, as Belshazzar held a great feast, having prepared a table for 1,000 - at which there was much drinking. They may have been getting ready for battle, as oiling shields would indicate. What awaits them?

In verses 6-8 Isaiah is told to post a lookout, who must pay close attention to the field and report when he see riders coming. The lookout stands day and night, his duties being more detailed in Ezekiel 33 & 34 where the watchman appointed by God had certain responsibilities to warn, guard, and care for the people of God. Being a watchman was post with much responsibility.

Isaiah 21:9-10 *Look, riders come— horsemen in pairs." And he answered, saying, "Babylon has fallen, has fallen. All the images of her gods have been shattered on the ground." My people who have been crushed on the threshing floor, I have declared to you what I have heard from the LORD of Hosts, the God of Israel.*

Here we see Babylon as the one spoken against. The watchman sees horsemen coming with the message, "Babylon has fallen, has fallen." Her gods have been smashed; the people of YHWH crushed on the threshing floor. Isaiah declared what he heard from YHWH, God of Israel. There is no escape from this judgment.

Next is a very short oracle against Dumah - an oasis in Arabia that was a major trade intersection.

Isaiah 21:11-12 *An oracle against Dumah: One calls to me from Seir, "Watchman, what is [left] of the night? Watchman, what is [left] of the night?" The watchman said, "Morning has come, and also night. If you want to ask, ask! Come back again."*

The watchman is asked what of the night? He responds, Morning has come as well as the night. The suffering goes on day and night.

Verse 13 begins the oracle against Arabia proper. Isaiah 21:13-15 *An oracle against Arabia: In the desert brush you will camp for the night, you caravans of Dedanites. Bring water for the thirsty. The inhabitants of the land of Tema meet the refugees with food. For they have fled from swords, from the drawn sword, from the bow that is strung, and from the stress of battle.*

Dedan and Tema were cities or regions in Arabia, representing power aligned with Babylon. Arabia will camp for a short time, with water and food for those who have fled the sword and the bow of judgment.

Isaiah 21:16-17 *For the Lord said this to me: "Within one year, as a hired worker counts years, all the glory of Kedar will be gone. The remaining Kedarite archers will be few in number." For the LORD, the God of Israel, has spoken.*

God had spoken: the glory of Kedar, another center of wealth and power in Arabia, would be gone within the year. Reference to the "hired worker" implies precise measurement of time, as those who watch the clock are famous for doing. Only a remnant will be left - for YHWH, the God of Israel, has spoken it.

The apostle to the Gentiles burned with love for his kinsmen of the flesh and he wrote that, as with the people of Arabia in Kedar, only a remnant of the people in national Israel would be saved. Our job is not to try and save everyone. Our job is to be faithful with the gospel message that is the power of life to those being saved. No matter our personal desire for any people group, a remnant will be saved from every people, tongue, and tribe.

Isaiah 22 - Oracle Against the Valley of Vision.

Isaiah 22 is an oracle against the Valley of Vision (verse 1). There is a Puritan book of prayer titled The Valley of Vision. The phrase, Valley of Vision, appears only in this passage in all of Scripture; many are convinced it is a reference to Jerusalem, a city in a valley, known to be the city wherein God met with His people.

I found it funny that the next phrase in verse 1 in the HCSB is "What's the matter with you?" as it reminds me of the often cited question from R.C. Sproul: "What's wrong with you people?" The question in our passage is followed by another: "Why have all of you gone up on the rooftops?" What follows in this chapter lends credence to the view that verse 1 relates to people going to the rooftops to get a better view of the Assyrian army's retreat from Jerusalem.

Isaiah 22:2 *The noisy city, the jubilant town, is filled with revelry. Your dead did not die by the sword; they were not killed in battle.*

Happy they are that the swords of Assyria have withdrawn, though their kinsmen who died were not killed by those swords - likely hardship and illness from a long seige.

Isaiah 22:3 *All your rulers have fled together, captured without a bow. All your fugitives were captured together; they had fled far away.*

This comment is not part of the historical record of the Assyrian siege of 701 B.C., but may be a reference to the capture of some of Hezekiah's people during a battle with Assyria.

Isaiah 22:4-5 *Therefore I said, "Look away from me! Let me weep bitterly! Do not try to comfort me about the destruction of my dear people." For the Lord GOD of Hosts had a day of tumult, trampling, and confusion in the Valley of Vision— people shouting and crying to the mountains.*

Isaiah speak in the first person, weeping over the loss of life due to the siege. He recognizes that though Assyria was the agent of wrath, it was YHWH who trampled on the Valley and caused confusion. Note the recurring picture of people

73

crying and calling out to the mountains to hide them. No place in all creation to hide from the wrath of the Lamb!

The next couple of verses note that the best warriors went out to defend the city but God removed the defenses of Judah. When that happened, the leaders of Judah went to the House of the Forrest looking for weapons. This is likely a reference a building Solomon built: 1 Kings 7:1-2 Solomon completed his entire palace complex after 13 years of construction. He built the House of the Forest of Lebanon.

"You" in these verses refers to the leadership of Judah; they looked for weapons, looked at the breaches in the city wall, collected water, calculated how many houses to tear down for materials, and made a reservoir for waters of the ancient pool. This last is a reference to a tunnel built by Hezekiah to bring water into the city. All of these actions taken by the leaders of Judah reveal men who had put their trust in their own wisdom and strength - rather than trusting in the covenant God Who had built them up into a mighty nation; the last bit of verse 11: *you did not look to the One who made it, or consider the One who created it long ago.* Self-reliance by those who know God is a wretched position - as the next passage demonstrates.

Isaiah 22:12 *On that day the Lord GOD of Hosts called for weeping, for wailing, for shaven heads, and for the wearing of sackcloth.*

Here's that phrase again, denoting the end of the age when judgment comes - on THAT day.

Isaiah 22:13-14 *But look: joy and gladness, butchering of cattle, slaughtering of sheep, eating of meat, and drinking of wine— "Let us eat and drink, for tomorrow we die!" The LORD of Hosts has directly revealed to me: "This sin of yours will never be wiped out." The Lord GOD of Hosts has spoken.*

Rather than weeping and wearing sackcloth; the people of Judah are joyful and glad, enjoying the high life - just as the people of the world before the first rain came. All in full view of the Creator, who revealed to Isaiah that the sins of Judah mentioned herein will never be wiped out. The Lord GOD of Hosts has spoken! This is one reason it is impossible for there to be a future for ethnic Judah as the people of God; their sin will ever be before them.

The last section of this chapter is an oracle against a steward of Jerusalem, a man known as Shebna, identified as a high-ranking official in Hezekiah's court (2 Kings 18:18, 26, 37; Isa 36:3, 11, 22; 37:2). He and another steward, Eliakim, are the focus. Even though Eliakim was praised by Isaiah, the lesson from this oracle is clear and applicable to us, today: Politicians CANNOT solve problems that are God's purview.

Isaiah 22:15-19 *The Lord GOD of Hosts said: "Go to Shebna, that steward who is in charge of the palace, [and say to him:] What are you doing here? Who authorized you to carve out a tomb for yourself here, carving your tomb on the height and cutting a crypt for yourself out of rock? Look, you strong man! The LORD is about to shake you violently. He will take hold of you, wind you up into a ball, and sling you into a wide land. There you will die, and there your glorious chariots will be—a disgrace to the house of your lord. I will remove you from your office; you will be ousted from your position.*

Note the tone YHWH had in giving this oracle to Isaiah: You, Shebna, think yourself a strong man. YHWH will shake you violently, wind you up into a ball and sling you far where you will die and be disgraced.

After that, Eliakim will take Shebna's place; he will have position and prestige. He will be placed in a solid place - like a peg driven into a firm place, for coats to hang.

Isaiah 22:24-25 *They will hang on him the whole burden of his father's house: the descendants and the offshoots—all the*

75

*small vessels, from bowls to every kind of jar. On that day"—
the declaration of the LORD of Hosts—"the peg that was
driven into a firm place will give way, be cut off, and fall, and
the load on it will be destroyed." Indeed, the LORD has
spoken.*

As the people of Judah are willing to put ALL their problems
on Eliakim's shoulders (more trusting in man than in God),
the peg will give way, be cut off, and all that was hanging on
it destroyed. When the people got to the place where they
took no responsibility for themselves, expected their
government to handle everything, God removed the
government He had established - cut him off - and destroyed
those who had forgotten Him in favor of the government.

Indeed - YHWH has spoken.

Brothers and sisters - as we seek an honest and truthful
outcome to our national elections, let us not put our hope in
this party or that one; let us not get emotionally invested in
the kingdom of this world. But let be responsible pilgrims
with our eyes fixed on the Lord of Glory.

Isaiah 23 - Oracle Against Tyre.

Chapter 23 of Isaiah is an oracle against Tyre, a trade center
on the coast of the Mediterranean Sea through which much
of the trade from Europe found entry into what we now call
the Middle East. As this chapter opens, we see how people
of the world treasure the things of this world.

*Isaiah 23:1-3 An oracle against Tyre: Wail, ships of Tarshish,
for your haven has been destroyed. Word has reached them
from the land of Cyprus. Mourn, inhabitants of the coastland,
you merchants of Sidon; your agents have crossed the sea on
many waters.*

I want you to note how the verse numbers were assigned here.
Look at where "3" is - smack in the middle of a phrase. These

numbers make it easy for us to be at the same place, but they often distract us from reading as intended.

More importantly, take note of how the people wail and mourn because mechanisms of transferring wealth have been destroyed. Ships from Tarshish - a trade center in Spain - unable to dock in Tyre. Side note - Jonah was trying to run from God by booking a trip on ship from Joppa (south of Tyre) to Tarshish - a long route. Jonah didn't get to Tarshish and, in our passage - ships from Tarshish cannot get to Tyre. This bad news reached Cyprus - an island 75 miles off Tyre's coast and the last port before Tyre, described as "the merchant among the nations" (verse 3). When Tyre's harbors were destroyed, people of the world mourned and wept.

Isaiah 23:4 *"Be ashamed Sidon, the stronghold of the sea ..."* Sidon - another port (north of Tyre) who is brought to shame when her trade is decimated. Verses 5 - 8 describe the anguish in Egypt when they hear the news of Tyre's demise, the wailing of Tarshish - asking with sarcasm, Is this your jubilant city, which has been around since ancient times? And this: Isaiah 23:8 *Who planned this against Tyre, the bestower of crowns, whose traders are princes, whose merchants are the honored ones of the earth?*

Verse 8 reveals carnal man's view of disaster. Who did this, regarding the unthinkable? Who destroyed Tyre? She was the one who gave crowns, is higher than others, bestowing prestige on traders and merchants. When man denies God, shaking his fist at the One he refuses to submit to, he cannot fathom why bad things happen.

Isaiah 23:9 & 11 *The LORD of Hosts planned it, to desecrate all [its] glorious beauty, to disgrace all the honored ones of the earth. ... He stretched out His hand over the sea; He made kingdoms tremble. The LORD has commanded that the Canaanite fortresses be destroyed.*

I remember when Hurricane Katrina hit New Orleans and thousands of people fled to Houston. I heard several well-known Baptist preachers assert that God had nothing to do with that, betraying their own temporal view of good and a cotton-candy view of God. In addition to our current passage, there are myriad passages that refute this view. Psalm 135:6-7, for example: *Yahweh does whatever He pleases in heaven and on earth, in the seas and all the depths. He causes the clouds to rise from the ends of the earth. He makes lightning for the rain and brings the wind from His storehouses.* If your view of God is that He only does what carnal man thinks is good, you have a false view of God. Like the people in our text.

Isaiah 23:12 *He said, "You will not rejoice anymore, ravished young woman, daughter of Sidon. Get up and cross over to Cyprus— even there you will have no rest!"*

Creator God - the God of the Bible - is not worried that man might think He is unloving. If God didn't judge sin, He would not be God. He loves truth so He must hate sin. He taunts the people who are suffering - and goes on (vs 13) to chide the Chaldeans and Assyrians and people of Tarshish for trusting in their "horses and chariots."

Isaiah 23:15-16 *On that day Tyre will be forgotten for 70 years—the life span of one king. At the end of 70 years, what the song [says] about the prostitute will happen to Tyre: Pick up [your] lyre, stroll through the city, prostitute forgotten [by men]. Play skillfully, sing many a song, and you will be thought of again.*

Here's an instance where the phrase "on that day" does NOT refer to the Day of Judgment. In this case, it refers to a limitation of Tyre's demise, after a perfect, complete time of 70 years. The prostitute's song would be a reminder that the core of Tyre is hedonism.

Having sent the 70 out to proclaim the kingdom, Jesus pronounces woes upon cities familiar to the Jewish people, in the region of Galilee - from where Jesus came. As John recorded, *He came to His own and His own people did not receive Him* (John 1:10). Those who have the oracles of God and reject His Son face a more harsh judgment than those who know Him only by general revelation. Luke 10:13-14 *"Woe to you, Chorazin! Woe to you, Bethsaida! For if the miracles that were done in you had been done in Tyre and Sidon, they would have repented long ago, sitting in sackcloth and ashes! But it will be more tolerable for Tyre and Sidon at the judgment than for you."* Tyre and Sidon were pagan cities used by God and they knew Him not. People in Israel had many advantages yet did not receive their Messiah. It will be very bad for them. Countless people in our country have had every advantage with Bible teaching available everywhere and everyhow. Those who hear of the kingdom and reject the Messiah are in league with national Israel and will suffer more than ignorant people who know little.

Isaiah 23:17 *And at the end of the 70 years, the LORD will restore Tyre and she will go back into business, prostituting herself with all the kingdoms of the world on the face of the earth.*

It was YHWH that humbled Tyre; it was YHWH that restored Tyre. The city would be back in business, serving the traders and merchants in a way normally associating with Babylon.

Isaiah 23:18 *But her profits and wages will be dedicated to the LORD. They will not be stored or saved, for her profit will go to those who live in the LORD's presence, to provide them with ample food and sacred clothing.*

Here's the end of it. God restores Tyre; Tyre doesn't change her M.O., but He does change who benefits. Rather than saving and storing her profits and wages, Tyre will give to the Levite priests who serve YHWH, providing them food and fine linen for their priestly garments.

Saints - at the end of this age, God will not change the way this world and its corrupt systems work. He will feed us with good food every month and will clothe us with His righteousness. Even while some of us are disappointed with the recent events in the USA, this nation is not our home and her wages are not our wealth. Our God will provide what we need and He tells us not to worry about these things (Matt 5:25-34), and He is our righteousness, having made peace with God for us. Sleep well - Jesus is King!

IV. Judgment and Promise, Part 1

Isaiah 24 - The Day of Judgment.

Isaiah's 24th chapter is accurately titled "The Earth Judged" in the HCSB. ESV has "Judgment on the Whole Earth" while the KJV has "The doleful judgments of God upon the land." I would say that seeing this chapter as "judgments upon the land" conveys too small a picture. This judgment is described in terms that force us to consider what the Bible says elsewhere of the end of this age.

The structure is poetic, with repeats of certain phrase and pairing of others. Isaiah 24:1a *Look, the LORD is stripping the earth bare and making it desolate.* Verses 1b & 2 describe the effects of stripping the earth and making it desolate - the earth's surface will be twisted, its inhabitants scattered, without regard to status or condition of the people. Verse 3 repeats part of verse 1: *The earth will be stripped completely bare and will be totally plundered for the LORD has spoken this message.*

How do we know these things will happen? YHWH has spoken it! I read a book once wherein the author asserted some of the good stuff from age - even that done by unbelievers - would be deemed by God to be so good that they would survive judgment and be extant on the new earth. There are so many passages that flatly deny that idea, including verse 3 of this passage: "The earth will be stripped completely bare and will be totally plundered." Not partially or mostly stripped bare; completely. Nothing man can do is truly good: *If you make a stone altar for Me, you must not build it out of cut stones. If you use your chisel on it, you will defile it.* (Ex 20:25)

Verses 4-12 describe the effects of the judgment of God mentioned in verses 1 & 3. Isaiah used couplets to emphasize the totality of the devastation. Isaiah 24:4 *The earth mourns and withers; the world wastes away and withers; the exalted people of the earth waste away.* Note how the earth mourns and withers, wastes and withers and the rulers of earth waste away. The repetition of terms conveys the idea of completion.

Verse 5 tells us those who dwell on the earth have polluted it, they have transgressed His teaching and decrees, and violated "the everlasting covenant." The language here likely refers to Genesis 6, where man is wicked in every thought, full of violence, having corrupted their way on the earth; and Genesis 9, where God gave law to Noah and all the earth and set His bow in the sky as a sign of "the everlasting covenant."

As an aside, read Gen 9:1-7 and then read Acts 15:23-29 and think of other passages in the New Covenant Scriptures that touch on what YHWH told Noah. The continuity of God's law does not depend on His covenant with national Israel.

In Isaiah 24:6-12 we see "only a few survive" the judgement of God upon the earth, after a curse consumed it and burned up most of the inhabitants. The vineyards have withered, the tambourines are quiet, earth's rejoicing has gone into exile - only desolation remains as the city's gate has collapsed in ruin.

Verse 13 brings a change in perspective, *For this is how it will be on earth among the nations: like a harvested olive tree, like a gleaning after a grape harvest.* When an olive tree or vineyard is harvested, only a few olives or grapes remain. This remnant sings and praises the majesty of God (vs 14), *From the ends of the earth we hear songs: The Splendor of the Righteous One* (vs 16a). What a contrast from those who pollute and corrupt the earth - despising their Creator.

Verse 16b brings Isaiah's voice to our attention: *But I said, "I waste away! I waste away! Woe is me." The treacherous act treacherously; the treacherous deal very treacherously.* This ought to draw our attention to something written much later, as an angel spoke: Revelation 22:10-11 *He also said to me, "Don't seal the prophetic words of this book, because the time is near. Let the unrighteous go on in unrighteousness; let the filthy go on being made filthy; let the righteous go on in righteousness; and let the holy go on being made holy."* At the end, there is no room for repentance, no second opportunity for salvation. Only judgment for those who are not in Christ while those in Christ can only sing His praises.

Verses 17 & 18 bring poetic terms of trouble that await those who deal treacherously - "Panic, trip, and trap" await them; windows in heaven are opened up and the foundations of the earth are shaken - just as noted in Hebrews 12:25-27, which I have cited several times already.

Scripture cannot be broken. When the foundations of the earth are shaken, the end is nigh. The security for the saints is found not in this world but in Christ and the kingdom that CANNOT be shaken, which shall remain forever.

Verses 19 & 20 continue to describe God's judgment on earth: Isaiah 24:19-20 *The earth is completely devastated; the earth is split open; the earth is violently shaken. The earth staggers like a drunkard and sways like a hut. Earth's rebellion weighs it down, and it falls, never to rise again.* The totality of God's judgment, the completeness of man's depravity are on display.

Isaiah 24:21-23a *On that day the LORD will punish the host of heaven above and kings of the earth below. They will be gathered together like prisoners in a pit. They will be confined to a dungeon; after many days they will be punished. The moon will be put to shame and the sun disgraced.*

Peter had this to say: 2 Peter 3:10-13 *But the Day of the Lord will come like a thief; on that [day] the heavens will pass away with a loud noise, the elements will burn and be dissolved, and the earth and the works on it will be disclosed. Since all these things are to be destroyed in this way, [it is clear] what sort of people you should be in holy conduct and godliness as you wait for and earnestly desire the coming of the day of God. The heavens will be on fire and be dissolved because of it, and the elements will melt with the heat. But based on His promise, we wait for the new heavens and a new earth, where righteousness will dwell.*

The angels that rebelled and all the people of the world will be thrown into hell and all the saints eagerly await the NEW heaven and the NEW earth, where RIGHTEOUSNESS dwells. Do you yearn for that?

Isaiah 24:23b - *the LORD of Hosts will reign as king on Mount Zion in Jerusalem, and He will [display His] glory in the presence of His elders.* This is displayed in another book based on a vision from God:

Revelation 5:8-14 *When He took the scroll, the four living creatures and the 24 elders fell down before the Lamb. Each one had a harp and gold bowls filled with incense, which are the prayers of the saints. And they sang a new song: You are worthy to take the scroll and to open its seals, because You were slaughtered, and You redeemed [people] for God by Your blood from every tribe and language and people and nation. You made them a kingdom and priests to our God, and they will reign on the earth. Then I looked and heard the voice of many angels around the throne, and also of the living creatures and of the elders. Their number was countless thousands, plus thousands of thousands. They said with a loud voice: The Lamb who was slaughtered is worthy to receive power and riches and wisdom and strength and honor and glory and blessing! I heard every creature in heaven, on earth, under the earth, on the sea, and everything in them say: Blessing and honor and glory and dominion to the One seated on the throne, and to the Lamb, forever and ever! The four living creatures said, "Amen," and the elders fell down and worshiped.*

When the end us upon us, YHWH reigns as King of kings, displaying His glory in the presence of His elders. And all will sing praises to the One who is worthy to open the seals;

the One who ransomed His people from every tribe and tongue, people and nation. Countless redeemed people will never tire of praising the Lamb Who is worthy to receive power and riches and wisdom and strength and honor and glory and blessing!

If you cannot say "Amen!" to that, perhaps you are of those who corrupt the earth. While it is yet today, before He returns ON THAT DAY, cry out for mercy and harden not your heart. For time is running out and there is a day appointed wherein Christ will judge the works of man. He stands as a refuge for all who trust in Him.

Isaiah 25 - Salvation and Judgment.

Chapter 25 of Isaiah is a proclamation of God's people about His victory and their redemption; His victory over the world.

Isaiah 25:1 *Yahweh, You are my God; I will exalt You. I will praise Your name, for You have accomplished wonders, plans [formed] long ago, with perfect faithfulness.* Here the remnant exalt YHWH, calling them "my God" whose name they will praise for the wonders of the plans He set out long ago. Who other than God can make a plan with absolute assurance it will be accomplished?

Isaiah 25:2 *For You have turned the city into a pile of rocks, a fortified city, into ruins; the fortress of barbarians is no longer a city; it will never be rebuilt.* This fortified city is symbolic of the world, as with the city of chaos in 24:10. It's defeat is YHWH's victory over the world - when He returns a new earth will be raised up and the city of this world will never be rebuilt.

Isaiah 25:3 *Therefore, a strong people will honor You. The cities of violent nations will fear You.* Those who honor God have His strength; those who depend on their own strength are violent men who will greatly fear Him when they discover they have no refuge.

Isaiah 25:4-5 *For You have been a stronghold for the poor, a stronghold for the needy person in his distress, a refuge from the rain, a shade from the heat. When the breath of the violent is like rain [against] a wall, like heat in a dry land, You subdue the uproar of barbarians. As the shade of a cloud [cools] the heat of the day, [so] He silences the song of the violent.*

His people testify of His provision for the poor and needy (blessed are the poor in spirit!), His refuge from the rain and a shade from the heat. Do you recall Jonah, the reluctant prophet? Disappointed in God's mercy on repentant Ninevites, Jonah pouted and sat down to see what would happen. Jonah 4:6 *Then the LORD God appointed a plant, and it grew up to provide shade over Jonah's head to ease his discomfort. Jonah was greatly pleased with the plant.* YHWH provided shade for Jonah just as He had for the remnant in Isaiah's vision. He subdued the barbarians and shuts the mouths of the violent.

Isaiah 25:6-8 *The LORD of Hosts will prepare a feast for all the peoples on this mountain— a feast of aged wine, choice meat, finely aged wine. On this mountain [He] will destroy the [burial] shroud, the shroud over all the peoples, the sheet covering all the nations; He will destroy death forever. The Lord GOD will wipe away the tears from every face and remove His people's disgrace from the whole earth, for the LORD has spoken.*

Does this not bring to your mind the wedding feast of the Lamb? The peace with God found on Mt Zion? The promise of the new earth where He will wipe every tear and clothe us with His righteousness completely? So much of John's Apocalypse is taken from Old Testament passages, we should not be surprised to find his source material here.

Isaiah 25:9-10a *On that day it will be said, "Look, this is our God; we have waited for Him, and He has saved us. This is the LORD; we have waited for Him. Let us rejoice and be glad in His salvation." For the LORD's power will rest on this mountain.* Verse 10 is another place where ya got to wonder what they were thinking, including the second sentence here rather than in verse 11. On THAT day, when Christ Jesus comes to judge the nations He will also bring salvation to those who eagerly await Him (Heb 9:28). This salvation is not justification, but the final salvation that free us from the presence of sin.

Isaiah 25:10b-12 *For the LORD's power will rest on this mountain. But Moab will be trampled in his place as straw is trampled in a dung pile. He will spread out his arms in the middle of it, as a swimmer spreads out [his arms] to swim. His pride will be brought low, along with the trickery of his hands. The high-walled fortress will be brought down, thrown to the ground, to the dust.*

Then end of this chapter is the sad record of the judgment on Moab - symbolic of the pride of life that dominates the city of this age. Swimming in dung - how's that for a word picture? No pride left, no tricks, no wealth - all undone when the Creator and Judge of all things returns.

Are you the joyful remnant praising God for His victory? Or are you still full of pride and self-sufficiency? Time is running out and none of us knows when He will return. Today, if you hear His voice, do not harden your heart.

Isaiah 26 - God's People Sing His Praises.

Chapter 25 of Isaiah revealed the salvation of the remnant, with the redeemed unable to keep quiet as they boasted in the salvation of YHWH. Chapter 26 continues with that theme, as Judah is lifted in rejoicing.

Isaiah 26:1-4 *On that day this song will be sung in the land of Judah: We have a strong city. Salvation is established as walls and ramparts. Open the gates so a righteous nation can come in— one that remains faithful. You will keep the mind [that is] dependent [on You] in perfect peace, for it is trusting in You. Trust in the LORD forever, because in Yah, the LORD, is an everlasting rock!*

On THAT day, when Christ returns to judge the nations, He also gathers His people. And on THAT day, the saints will sing and boast about the salvation and security they have in Christ; they will rejoice with all His people who are gathered in. YHWH will keep in perfect peace the soul that trusts in Him; He is trustworthy because Jesus is the everlasting Rock which gushes out refreshing water, provides a sure foundation in any storm, and will not be moved when all hell breaks loose.

Isaiah 26:5-6 *For He has humbled those who live in lofty places— an inaccessible city. He brings it down; He brings it down to the ground; He throws it to the dust. Feet trample it, the feet of the humble, the steps of the poor.*

We see, again, what happens to those filled with the pride of life - God humbles them, no matter how secure they think themselves. He knocks down all the idols of man and leaves the debris to be trampled on by the very people that were despised and mistreated by the proud, boastful men of the world. The meek SHALL inherit the earth - the new earth!

Isaiah 26:7 *The path of the righteous is level; You clear a straight path for the righteous.*

The praise of His people continues, as they declare He makes a straight, level path for His people. A sermon I heard many years contained this pearl, which stuck with me: "The path of least resistance makes both MEN and rivers crooked. The Lord God makes man's path straight." People who "let go and let God" are drifting in the sea of humanity. Once raised we must be deliberate and determined, by the grace of God, to walk as children of the light.

Verses 8 - 10 continue with the praise of God and the vindication of His judgment, as some people learn righteousness while the wicked do not - they do not see the majesty of the Lord.

Isaiah 26:11 *LORD, Your hand is lifted up [to take action], but they do not see it. They will see [Your] zeal for [Your] people, and they will be put to shame. The fire for Your adversaries will consume them!*

If you recall from the early chapters, YHWH's hand being raised is a symbol of impending judgment. Wicked people will not see His zeal to defend His name and His people until it is too late and His fire consumes them.

Isaiah 26:12-13 *LORD, You will establish peace for us, for You have also done all our work for us. Yahweh our God, lords other than You have ruled over us, but we remember Your name alone.*

Read that again, slowly. YHWH establishes peace for His people, He has done ALL the work. They were ruled by lesser gods that were not gods and He put His name in their minds. Where, oh man, have ye room to boast of ANYTHING other the grace of God? If you have been feeling satisfied in anything you've done, repent.

Verse 14 reveals the doom of the wicked - they die and have no peace nor place with God. But -

Isaiah 26:15-16 *You have added to the nation, LORD. You have added to the nation; You are honored. You have expanded all the borders of the land. LORD, they went to You in their distress; they poured out whispered [prayers because] Your discipline [fell] on them.*

YHWH has added to the nation - bringing Gentiles to Mt. Zion where His righteousness reigns. The poor in spirit, people in distress, cried out to God in prayer and His chastisement fell on them, the chastisement that brings peace - Isaiah 53:5 (KJV) *But he was wounded for our transgressions, he was bruised for our iniquities: the chastisement of our peace was upon him; and with his stripes we are healed.* If His chastisement does not bring you peace, you will never have peace with God.

The next two verse describe how the chastisement of peace is akin to the travails of a pregnant woman giving birth. And the birth was without life, but a breeze - as someone passing gas (as one commentary put it); no victory or lineage in which to boast. But there is cause for boasting -

Isaiah 26:19 *Your dead will live; their bodies will rise. Awake and sing, you who dwell in the dust! For you will be covered with the morning dew, and the earth will bring out the departed spirits.*

Contrary to the death of the wicked, those who die in Christ will live - their bodies will be raised on the last day! Awake and sing, you who dwell in the dust - if Christ be your king, for on THAT day all who have died in YHWH will come up out of the earth to meet Him!

Isaiah 26:20-21 *Go, my people, enter your rooms and close your doors behind you. Hide for a little while until the wrath has passed. For look, the LORD is coming from His place to punish the inhabitants of the earth for their iniquity. The earth will reveal the blood shed on it and will no longer conceal her slain.*

While judgment is meted out on the nations in Israel's day, she was told to hide - the battle belongs to the Lord. As in the day of the angel of death, when the children of Moses hid in their homes with the blood of the lamb on their doorframe, so all His redeemed will hide in Him, covered by the blood of the victorious Lamb Who exposes the sin of the world and renders eternal judgment. As the nations are judged, we have refuge in Christ, who will then gather us to Himself as He makes a new heaven (the universe) and new earth.

Is Christ your peace? The chastisement, the punishment, laid upon Him - did He bring you peace? Trust not a man who says, "Peace, peace!" where there is no peace. Trust in the Man who brings peace and gives is to His people.

Isaiah 27 - The Vineyard of YHWH.

Some Bibles title Isaiah 27 as "Leviathan Slain," as this is what the opening verse declares: Isaiah 27:1 *On that day the LORD with His harsh, great, and strong sword, will bring judgment on Leviathan, the fleeing serpent—Leviathan, the twisting serpent. He will slay the monster that is in the sea.*

We have seen that the phrase "On that day" often means Judgment Day, but not exclusively. Leviathan is mentioned by Job and God (Job 3:8; 41:1) and in Psalms 74:14 and 104:26; where it is portrayed as a terrifyingly strong sea monster that God alone can handle; and that will be destroyed and fed to creatures of the desert when He restores His people (Ps 74). Leviathan was known in Canaanite mythology, representing evil. It is thought that Leviathan is mentioned in Scripture to convey the idea that when YHWH comes the second time He will destroy not only the historical and temporal forms of evil but the cosmic or spiritual forms as well. Just as Satan is portrayed as a serpent, evil is portrayed as Leviathan.

The balance of this chapter is about YHWH's vineyard - a wealth of metaphorical wisdom! Isaiah 27:2-3 *On that day sing about a desirable vineyard: I, Yahweh, watch over it; I water it regularly. I guard it night and day so that no one disturbs it.*

It's implied that YHWH planted this vineyard, He is the One Who tends it. It is a most desirable vineyard that is guarded so no one who unbid may come in and disturb it. Verses 4 & 5 describe how wild vines are trampled down and burned and good ones rely on God and have peace with Him. Anyone else think of John 15?

Isaiah 27:6 *In days to come, Jacob will take root. Israel will blossom and bloom and fill the whole world with fruit.* Similar to "On that day" we see that Jacob will take root and Israel will bloom and the whole world will be filled with their fruit. We know that YHWH has always had people from every nation, tongue, and tribe marked out to be included in His kingdom - to yield fruit keeping with repentance. We know from the parable of the soils (Mark 4) that only in good soil will seed grow healthy roots and only healthy roots produce fruit and all that do not yield good fruit are trampled down and burned.

Verses 7 & 8 describe how God disciplines His people, they will not be annihilated as will His enemies. His people will be scattered like the seed freely cast along the way, so that people in every nation, tongue, and tribe will hear the gospel and be brought into His sheepfold (mixed metaphors!).

Isaiah 27:9 *Therefore Jacob's iniquity will be purged in this way, and the result of the removal of his sin will be this: when he makes all the altar stones like crushed bits of chalk, no Asherah poles or incense altars will remain standing.* This is the result of God's people being purified, purged of sin: false gods will be removed and their altars torn down. As when Jacob flew Laban and Rachel secretly brought pagan idols with them, so it is with many of God's people - we unknowingly carry the baggage of false gods and false worship with us - and have need to examine ourselves and our walk, asking for eyes to as God does and repent of all false ways. Asherah was a Canaanite goddess of fertility, mother of Baal; the wooden pole was like an altar or shrine to her. If we fail to rid ourselves of false ways, and we are His sheep, He will purge us and, while it will not seem pleasant, it is for our good and His glory.

Verses 10 & 11 describe the desolation of temporal wealth and power: the fortified city will be deserted, the trees will dry up (not yielding good fruit) and be burned as firewood.

They are people without understanding and Creator God will not be compassionate or gracious to them.

Isaiah 27:12-13 *On that day the LORD will thresh grain from the Euphrates River as far as the Wadi of Egypt, and you Israelites will be gathered one by one. On that day a great trumpet will be blown, and those lost in the land of Assyria will come, as well as those dispersed in the land of Egypt; and they will worship the LORD at Jerusalem on the holy mountain.*

On THAT day, YHWH will thresh His grain, from the north boundary to the southern boundary. John the Baptizer gave a preview of THAT day, telling the self-righteous Jews that Jesus was the Christ and had His winnowing fork in His hand, ready to clear His threshing floor and gather His wheat; leaving the chaff to be burned with fire that never goes out (Matt 3:12). Jesus told a parable of wheat and chaff confirming this:

Matthew 13:37-43 *He replied: "The One who sows the good seed is the Son of Man; the field is the world; and the good seed—these are the sons of the kingdom. The weeds are the sons of the evil one, and the enemy who sowed them is the Devil. The harvest is the end of the age, and the harvesters are angels. Therefore, just as the weeds are gathered and burned in the fire, so it will be at the end of the age. The Son of Man will send out His angels, and they will gather from His kingdom everything that causes sin and those guilty of lawlessness. They will throw them into the blazing furnace where there will be weeping and gnashing of teeth. Then the righteous will shine like the sun in their Father's kingdom. Anyone who has ears should listen!"*

God's judgment is true and none of His wheat will be burned up, but there will be fiery wrath poured out on many who claim they know Him and do not. On THAT day, a great trumpet will be blown - just as on the 7th day, the walls of Jericho fell as the last trumpet sounded (Joshua 6:15-20), so it will be on THAT day, when the all lost from all the lands will come and worship YHWH on the Mount Zion. Here's a little homework: Search out every instance of the word "lost" in the New Testament and see if anyone described as such (except Judas) is not found and brought home. Jesus came to seek and save that which was LOST. Those who are not found were not lost; they are not His sheep, but are goats of the world. But all the lost sheep of Israel, the Israel of God, on that day that the last trumpet sounds, will be found and brought into the sheepfold of God but that great shepherd and savior of His people, Jesus - Who is the Christ!

V. Woes on Unbelieving Israel

Isaiah 28 - Woe and Bliss.

Isaiah 28 is another contrast between the woe that comes to people of the world and the true bliss of knowing God.

Isaiah 28:1 *Woe to the majestic crown of Ephraim's drunkards, and to the fading flower of its beautiful splendor, which is on the summit above the rich valley. [Woe] to those overcome with wine.*

Another oracle begins, this time against Samaria. We see repeated references to obsession with intoxicating drink - described here as symbols of wealth and positions of influence (the crown may refer to the capital city, which sat on a hill overlooking the region); all of which will fade.

Isaiah 28:2-4 *Look, the Lord has a strong and mighty one— like a devastating hail storm, like a storm with strong flooding waters. He will bring it across the land with [His] hand. The majestic crown of Ephraim's drunkards will be trampled underfoot. The fading flower of his beautiful splendor, which is on the summit above the rich valley, will be like a ripe fig before the summer harvest. Whoever sees it will swallow it while it is still in his hand.*

We see that God has a strong and mighty one to fulfill His will - one like a hail storm, a strong storm with floods; think Gen chapter 7. The symbols of wealth and power will be trampled down and shown as a sign of shame for those who trusted in uncertain things of this world. Unlike the fig tree in Matt 21:18-22, the fig tree in this passage had ripe fruit, ready for the picking - but not by those who found their security in their large barns.

Isaiah 28:5-6 *On that day the LORD of Hosts will become a crown of beauty and a diadem of splendor to the remnant of His people, a spirit of justice to the one who sits in judgment, and strength to those who turn back the battle at the gate.*

On THAT day, YHWH of Hosts will become the crown of beauty and splendor to His people, a remnant of the world. This passage recalls the devastation in verses 2-4, using similar terms to describe the glory of being united with YHWH. He bring justice and strength to His people.

Verses 7-12 reveal the futility of trusting one's wisdom and abusing drink meant for reasonable pleasure. When people partake of too much beer and wine (or pizza and donuts) there are consequences. Drunkards have a very hard time dealing with life, they stumble confused as to what's going on. Their vision is muddled, their judgment is muddled, their tables are covered in vomit! Nobody will listen to them.

Isaiah 28:13 *Then the word of the LORD came to them: "Law after law, law after law, line after line, line after line, a little here, a little there," so they go stumbling backward, to be broken, trapped, and captured.*

YHWH speaks and throws their own words into their teeth, quoting the drunkard from verse 10. These aimless people stumble backward, to be broken, trapped, and captured. Woe to these who tempt God by abusing gifts given to man. Woe to those who trust in wealth rather than the Creator and Lord of all.

Isaiah 28:14-15 *Therefore hear the word of the LORD, you mockers who rule this people in Jerusalem. For you said, "We have cut a deal with Death, and we have made an agreement with Sheol; when the overwhelming scourge passes through, it will not touch us, because we have made falsehood our refuge and have hidden behind treachery."*

Here YHWH addresses the leaders in Judah, rulers over the people in Jerusalem, who had made a deal with a nation identified as Death to provide protection from Assyria from overwhelming them. They bragged that lies were their refuge and treachery their strong wall. This will not end well for them.

Isaiah 28:16-17a *Therefore the Lord GOD said: "Look, I have laid a stone in Zion, a tested stone, a precious cornerstone, a sure foundation; the one who believes will be unshakable. And I will make justice the measuring line and righteousness the mason's level. Hail will sweep away the false refuge, and water will flood your hiding place.*

Here we find architectural references to Christ, which are repeated in the gospels and epistles. Contrary to the papists who believe Peter is the cornerstone of "the church" God almighty has established His Son as the cornerstone, the sure foundation. As Jesus would later say, the one who builds on the Rock will withstand the fiercest storm, but the one who builds on sand will be devastated when the flood comes. YHWH's justice, not man's perverted "justice" will be the plumb line and His righteousness, not man's filthy rags, will the level.

Isaiah 28:17b-18 *"And I will make justice the measuring line and righteousness the mason's level." Hail will sweep away the false refuge, and water will flood your hiding place. Your deal with Death will be dissolved, and your agreement with Sheol will not last. When the overwhelming scourge passes through, you will be trampled.*

Those who continue to trust in man will swept away in the judgment, as in the day of Noah. Juda's treacherous deal with Death and Sheol will not protect them; for when the Lord Jesus returns on that great and terrible day, the time of patience and place for repentance will have ended; and not a mortal soul will be able to find any refuge from the storm if they had not already found it in Christ. As we read in the previous chapter, Isaiah 27:11b *Therefore their Maker will not have compassion on them, and their Creator will not be gracious to them.* This will be the end of time, and all who continued in their rebellion will face the Judge who has no compassion or grace for them. Indeed, in verse 19 we see that *only terror will cause you to understand the message.* He will have compassion and grace only for those clothed in His righteousness, and we all will be in awe as we consider how little we understood and how much He has done for us.

Isaiah 28:21-22 *For the LORD will rise up as [He did] at Mount Perazim. He will rise in wrath, as at the Valley of Gibeon, to do His work, His strange work, and to perform His task, His disturbing task. So now, do not mock, or your shackles will become stronger. Indeed, I have heard from the Lord GOD of Hosts a decree of destruction for the whole land.*

These references to well-known places in Israel bring home the message to those who dwell in the land, seeking comfort in large barns. Yet almighty God has spoken: what He will do will seem strange and disturbing to those who rest on Moses and Abraham. He will burden them with unbreakable shackles and destroy the whole land. He will take the kingdom from them and give it to a nation of kings and priests that will bear fruit (Matt 21:43 & 1 Peter 2:4-6).

The last part of this chapter breaks into a new line of thought. Isaiah 28:23 *Listen and hear my voice. Pay attention and hear what I say.* With this call to listen up, God begins giving instruction on farming!

Isaiah 28:24-26 *Does the plowman plow every day to plant seed? Does he [continuously] break up and cultivate the soil? When he has leveled its surface, does he not then scatter black cumin and sow cumin? He plants wheat in rows and barley in plots, with spelt as their border. His God teaches him order; He instructs him.*

As He teaches the animals where to forage for food, as He tells the clouds where to go pour out their rain, so He teaches brute man how to tend the land so he can feed his family.

Isaiah 28:28-29 *Bread grain is crushed, but is not threshed endlessly. Though the wheel of [the farmer's] cart rumbles, his horses do not crush it. This also comes from the LORD of Hosts. He gives wonderful advice; He gives great wisdom.*

Simple truth about temporal things, properly used, is wisdom from God - wonderful news! Proper use of good things He has given us is wise; thanksgiving for His mercies in giving us bread and meat is the proper response. What a contrast to the attitude of Israel in Isaiah's day; for they had forgotten YHWH and had slid into the thankless, conceited position of thinking they were entitled to comfortable living, safe from the terrors of Assyria and the other pagans.

In the USA at this hour, we have our own pagans at the gate - claiming they own the nation and want to trample justice and exalt all sorts of sin and horror. Let us who know God - or rather are known by Him - stand for His Truth but never lose sight of which kingdom we belong to. As the ancient preacher taught, Ecclesiastes 9 *Go, eat your bread with pleasure, and drink your wine with a cheerful heart, ... Enjoy life with the wife you love all the days of your fleeting life, ... Whatever your hands find to do, do with [all] your strength, because there is no work, planning, knowledge, or wisdom in Sheol where you are going.*

Trust God, meditate on His Word. If you are His, He will be your wisdom and give you light to take the next step. If you are not His, cry out for mercy while you yet have breath.

Isaiah 29 - Who is Ariel?

Chapter 29 is titled "Woe to Jerusalem" in the HCSB. The ESV, ASB, and KJV each have similar titles. And yet, Jerusalem is not mentioned in this chapter.

Isaiah 29:1a *Woe to Ariel, Ariel, the city where David camped!*

Woe to Ariel, not Jerusalem, Ariel - the city where David camped. Ariel shows up in several places (2 Sam 23 & 1 Chron 11) as a man from Moab and in Ezra 8 as an Israelite. Three times in this chapter it refers to a city - which every serious commentator believes is Jerusalem; the context reveals this. The Hebrew word is obscure, but thought to mean the hearth place of an altar - alluding to judgment manifested as fire.

Isaiah 29:1b-4 *Continue year after year; let the festivals recur. I will oppress Ariel, and there will be mourning and crying, and she will be to Me like an Ariel. I will camp in a circle around you; I will besiege you with earth ramps, and I will set up my siege towers against you. You will be brought down; you will speak from the ground, and your words will come from low in the dust. Your voice will be like that of a spirit from the ground; your speech will whisper from the dust.*

God taunts Jerusalem, which was the pride of Israel. While they continue their normal routine, He is preparing to punish them. As in the days of Noah, when people were eating and drinking and getting married when the rains came down, so here will the people of Israel will be taken as they ignore the warnings - just as in the days of Noah. Read the military language of God's attack on Jerusalem; He will destroy their walls and the city, people will mourn and cry as they are brought low and grovel in the dust.

Isaiah 29:5-8 *Your many foes will be like fine dust, and many of the ruthless, like blowing chaff. Then suddenly, in an instant, you will be visited by the LORD of Hosts with thunder, earthquake, and loud noise, storm, tempest, and a flame of consuming fire. All the many nations going out to battle against Ariel— all the attackers, the siege works against her, and those who oppress her— will then be like a dream, a vision in the night. It will be like a hungry one who dreams he is eating, then wakes and is still hungry; and like a thirsty one who dreams he is drinking, then wakes and is still thirsty, longing for water. So it will be for all the many nations who go to battle against Mount Zion.*

In the midst of Israel's doom, God turns His wrath on their enemies as YHWH meets with Israel in full strength to consume all who wage war against Ariel. These enemies will seem like a dream that cannot satisfy - a vapor with no substance. So it will be for all who wage war against Mt. Zion - the scene changes from earthly Jerusalem to the true kingdom of Mt Zion as a reminder of who God defends.

Isaiah 29:9-12 *Stop and be astonished; blind yourselves and be blind! They are drunk, but not with wine; they stagger, but not with beer. For the LORD has poured out on you an overwhelming urge to sleep; He has shut your eyes—the prophets, and covered your heads—the seers. For you the entire vision will be like the words of a sealed document. If it is given to one who can read and he is asked to read it, he will say, "I can't read it, because it is sealed." And if the document is given to one who cannot read and he is asked to read it, he will say, "I can't read."*

This scene ought to seem familiar, for we've read similar things in Isaiah. Recall the commissioning of Isaiah as a prophet in chapter 6, as he was sent to a people who would hear but not understand, would see but not perceive. Their eyes would be heavy with sleep - so they would not see and hear and be saved. And anther prophet was told to keep the book sealed: Daniel 12:4 *But you, Daniel, keep these words secret and seal the book until the time of the end. Many will roam about, and knowledge will increase.* Until THAT day arrives, the mystery of the gospel will be hidden from those not chosen. Many will claim to be wise but have not the wisdom that reveals Jesus as the Christ.

This is what God reveals next: Isaiah 29:13-14 *The Lord said: Because these people approach Me with their mouths to honor Me with lip-service— yet their hearts are far from Me, and their worship [consists of] man-made rules learned [by rote]— therefore I will again confound these people with wonder after wonder. The wisdom of their wise men will vanish, and the understanding of the perceptive will be hidden.*

Rote religion cannot please God nor save sinners. Traditions of man neither please God not benefit sinners. Such self-righteous nonsense characterizes those who build large barns on foundation of sand. And the One who created all and will judge all confounds these people, as in the days of the Tower of Babel. Even as late as when the promised Messiah walked the earth, the Jewish people were self-satisfied in their "law-keeping" and their fleshly lineage. The wonders that would confound them were the same as in Isaiah's time: Gentiles would be brought into the kingdom! Their wise men were found to be fools - with a few notable exceptions such as Simeon and Caiaphas.

Isaiah 29:15-16 *Woe to those who go to great lengths to hide their plans from the LORD. [They do] their works in darkness, and say, "Who sees us? Who knows us?" You have turned things around, as if the potter were the same as the clay. How can what is made say about its maker, "He didn't make me"? How can what is formed say about the one who formed it, "He doesn't understand [what he's doing]"?*

Harken unto the warning from God: nothing is done in darkness that He does not see! To think that the creature can keep secrets from the Creator is akin to thinking the clay has power over the potter! Paul alluded to this in his rebuke to self-righteous Jews of his day. Romans 9:20-21 *But who are you, a mere man, to talk back to God? Will what is formed say to the one who formed it, "Why did you make me like this?" Or has the potter no right over the clay, to make from the same lump one piece of pottery for honor and another for dishonor?* The mystery is not why are *some* people doomed to wrath; the mystery is why not *all*?

Isaiah 29:18-21 *On that day the deaf will hear the words of a document, and out of a deep darkness the eyes of the blind will see. The humble will have joy after joy in the LORD, and the poor people will rejoice in the Holy One of Israel. For the ruthless one will vanish, the scorner will disappear, and all those who lie in wait with evil intent will be killed—those who, with [their] speech, accuse a person of wrongdoing, who set a trap at the gate for the mediator, and without cause deprive the righteous of justice.*

Note the contrast: blind will see, humble (poor in spirit) will have unending joy, the wicked will be gone, justice will prevail - all in the presence of the Holy One of Israel! What a contrast to what we've just read where He kept some in darkness, without understanding, in fear of the doom that awaits them.

Isaiah 29:22-24 *Therefore, the LORD who redeemed Abraham says this about the house of Jacob: Jacob will no longer be ashamed and his face will no longer be pale. For when he sees his children, the work of My hands within his [nation], they will honor My name, they will honor the Holy One of Jacob and stand in awe of the God of Israel. Those who are confused will gain understanding, and those who grumble will accept instruction.*

On THAT day, the promise to Abraham will be fulfilled as the New Covenant is completed, when the people of Israel (House of Jacob) are not ashamed - none of this remnant will think himself righteous, knowing he is not; all will fully trust in YHWH. When Jacob sees his children - his redeemed kinsmen of the flesh - all the ransomed sons of Israel will honor Him, knowing it was the Christ who redeemed them; as they stand in awe (true reverence and adoration) of the God of Israel. This is the Israel of God, the redeemed from every nation, tribe, and tongue - all children of Abraham according to the promise. Both Jew and Gentile will no longer be confused about Who the Messiah is nor about the nature of His kingdom. The confused and grumbling will be no more confused and no more grumbling, for their eyes see and their ears hear and their minds understand the glories of the grace of God in the person of Christ!

Here is the sum of the matter: Natural man, Jew and Gentile, is blind to truth, confounded about the gospel, unable to reconcile himself to God. According to His plan, Jesus (the Good Shepherd) is seeking out all those the Father has given Him, to bring them into His sheepfold. He gives grace to these, gives understanding, and loves them to the uttermost. If you are His, stand in awe of Who He is and what He has done!

Isaiah 30 - This is the Way, Walk in it.

Isaiah 30 is a lengthy rebuke of Israel's reliance on the strength of man, the doom of those who present themselves as worthy of such trust, and a reminder of the bliss that awaits those reconciled to God.

Isaiah 30:1-2 *Woe to the rebellious children! [This is] the LORD's declaration. They carry out a plan, but not Mine; they make an alliance, but against My will, piling sin on top of sin. They set out to go down to Egypt without asking My advice, in order to seek shelter under Pharaoh's protection and take refuge in Egypt's shadow.*

Note the judgment of God: His people, ethnic Israel, proved themselves to be rebels by pursuing a plan of their own. Not being merely ignorant of YHWH's ways but being deliberately against what they know of His ways. They pile up sin upon sin by seeking refuge in the strength of man! These are the same people who declared that some may trust in chariots but THEY would trust in the name of their God. And here they are. Saints - how is it with your soul? Are you THIS DAY trusting in Him or have you slouched into a false security of seeking refuge in wealth, comfort, political success, or those who preach "peace, peace!" where there is none?

Note how it will end for ethnic Israel: Isaiah 30:3 *But Pharaoh's protection will become your shame, and refuge in Egypt's shadow your disgrace.* This was written for our benefit - we can expect no better result if we have misplaced trust.

Verses 4 - 8 bring us more details of the consequences of this misplaced trust, describing the land as "in distress" and Egypt's help as "completely worthless." Our prophet is given instructions:

Isaiah 30:8-9 *Go now, write it on a tablet in their presence and inscribe it on a scroll; it will be for the future, forever and ever. They are a rebellious people, deceptive children, children who do not want to obey the LORD's instruction.*

We will read later of another message that is to be written on a tablet so all can read it - bringing the good news of the gospel. This message, written on a tablet, is bad news - God's judgment comes upon those who rebel against God and do not obey YHWH's instructions.

Isaiah 30:10-11 *They say to the seers, "Do not see," and to the prophets, "Do not prophesy the truth to us. Tell us flattering things. Prophesy illusions. Get out of the way! Leave the pathway. Rid us of the Holy One of Israel."*

This reminded me of the encounter between the kings of the two kingdoms in 1 Kings 22. Ahab, king of Israel (northern kingdom) wanted a military alliance with Jehoshaphat, king of Judah (southern kingdom). Jehoshaphat is agreeable, but wants Ahab to get confirmation from God (verse 7). *The king of Israel said to Jehoshaphat, "There is still one man who can ask Yahweh, but I hate him because he never prophesies good about me, but only disaster. He is Micaiah son of Imlah.* (1 Kings 22:8) All the other "prophets" had told Ahab he would succeed in this campaign. And this was the result: *But the king said to him, "How many times must I make you swear not to tell me anything but the truth in the name of Yahweh?" So Micaiah said: I saw all Israel scattered on the hills like sheep without a shepherd. And the LORD said, "They have no master; let everyone return home in peace." So the king of Israel said to Jehoshaphat, "Didn't I tell you he never prophesies good about me, but only disaster?"* (1 Kings 22:16-18)

The Jews had developed their own brand of the prosperity gospel - thinking God only wanted them to prosper as a nation, conquering all the pagan nations; thinking poverty and illness was a sure sign of sin. We see this highly developed as early as Job's day. It didn't line up with God's plan then and it doesn't now.

Isaiah 30:12-14 *Therefore the Holy One of Israel says: "Because you have rejected this message and have trusted in oppression and deceit, and have depended on them, this iniquity of yours will be like a spreading breach, a bulge in a high wall whose collapse will come in an instant—suddenly! Its collapse will be like the shattering of a potter's jar, crushed to pieces, so that not even a fragment of pottery will be found among its shattered remains— no fragment large enough to take fire from a hearth or scoop water from a cistern."*

We man trusts in man, he has trusted in oppression and deceit; and this will ALWAYS bring judgment and dismay. The description of this judgment is in detail that would imprint itself in the minds of the Hebrews - wall breached and collapsing, reduced to small pieces like a shattered ceramic pot that are good for nothing. If we trust in man for satisfaction in this life or protection from His wrath, we will be dismayed.

Isaiah 30:15-17 *For the Lord GOD, the Holy One of Israel, has said: "You will be delivered by returning and resting; your strength will lie in quiet confidence. But you are not willing." You say, "No! We will escape on horses"— therefore you will escape!— and, "We will ride on fast horses"— but those who pursue you will be faster. One thousand [will flee] at the threat of one, at the threat of five you will flee, until you alone remain like a [solitary] pole on a mountaintop or a banner on a hill.*

Here God lays out His plan - return to Him and rest! But they were not willing - natural man is ALWAYS unwilling, trusting in horses and barns. Any excuse to run away from God will do - but all excuses will end badly. But YHWH is unchanging and patient with His chosen ones, no matter how circumstances look to us.

Isaiah 30:18-22 *Therefore the LORD is waiting to show you mercy, and is rising up to show you compassion, for the LORD is a just God. All who wait patiently for Him are happy. For you people will live on Zion in Jerusalem and will never cry again. He will show favor to you at the sound of your cry; when He hears, He will answer you. The Lord will give you meager bread and water during oppression, but your Teacher will not hide Himself any longer. Your eyes will see your Teacher, and whenever you turn to the right or to the left, your ears will hear this command behind you: "This is the way. Walk in it." Then you will defile your silver-plated idols and your gold-plated images. You will throw them away like menstrual cloths, and call them filth.*

YHWH is just and He will satisfy those who hunger for Him; they will live with Him on Mt. Zion where there will be no more tears - sound familiar? He will ensure we have enough to live on while we are our earthly pilgrimage, and He will be with us - gave His Spirit to comfort and guide us - during this time. He will instruct us in His way: "This is the way. Walk in it." A better way than man (even Mandalorian!) can show us. And there will be evidence of this change in heart: we will be cast away false idols - consider them filthy rags (another familiar phrase). Saints: do you cling to idols? Think they yet have value? Consider your ways and make sure you are not mistaken about whose way you follow.

Verses 23 - 26 continue with the description of the care YHWH has for His people, Isaiah 30:26 *The moonlight will be as bright as the sunlight, and the sunlight will be seven times brighter—like the light of seven days—on the day that the LORD bandages His people's injuries and heals the wounds He inflicted.* This ought to draw our minds to John's Apocalypse: Revelation 22:5 *Night will no longer exist, and people will not need lamplight or sunlight, because the Lord God will give them light. And they will reign forever and ever.* Oh the glory and the true AWE of being in Christ and knowing Him as He knows us! No more tears, no more sin, no darkness!

The balance of this chapter is an oracle against Assyria, the main pain for national Israel. God's judgment on His enemies ought to comfort us just as it did national Israel - for it demonstrates His justice. Our sins weren't "winked at" - Jesus suffered the Father's wrath for our sin. This is part of the covenant God made with Noah and all creation: Genesis 9:6 *Whoever sheds man's blood, his blood will be shed by man, for God made man in His image.* This is why the Son of God put on man-flesh. To know we are reconciled to God, our sin-debt PAID, ought to cause us to rejoice with unspeakable joy.

So He tells Israel to, *Look, Yahweh comes from far away, His anger burning and heavy with smoke. His lips are full of fury, and His tongue is like a consuming fire.* (Isaiah 30:27) This wrath is against Assyria for their vengeance against ethnic Israel. Isaiah 30:28 *His breath is like an overflowing torrent that rises to the neck. [He comes] to sift the nations in a sieve of destruction and to put a bridle on the jaws of the peoples to lead [them] astray.* Note that God not only sifts the nations to destroy them, He leads His enemies astray - into that destruction.

Isaiah 30:29 *Your singing will be like that on the night of a holy festival, and [your] heart will rejoice like one who walks [to the music] of a flute, going up to the mountain of the LORD, to the Rock of Israel.* In the midst of the doom falling on Assyria, we see this snippet of grace poured out His people. Does your heart rejoice in the knowledge that you are seated with Christ in the heavenlies, destined to be with Him on the New Earth (Mt Zion!) for eternity? Pray for the Spirit of God to stir you - and me! - up to be honestly excited and joyful at being His possession.

Verse 30 shows God's arm raised to strike, and He will make known the splendor of His voice. Isaiah 30:31 *Assyria will be shattered by the voice of the LORD. He will strike with a rod.* Isaiah 30:33b *The breath of the LORD, like a torrent of brimstone, kindles it.* No matter how strong man considers himself, the breath of YHWH will shatter him. There is NO refuge from this judgment apart from union with Christ. If you are His, rejoice!

Isaiah 31 - Repent and Trust in YHWH.

The 31st chapter of Isaiah appears to be a short rehash of chapter 30 - an oracle against Egypt and against ethnic Israel for trusting in Egypt.

Isaiah 31:1 *Woe to those who go down to Egypt for help and who depend on horses! They trust in the abundance of chariots and in the large number of horsemen. They do not look to the Holy One of Israel and they do not seek the LORD's help.*

I've noted several times in this walk through Isaiah that Israel once declared that OTHERS might boast in horses and chariots, but THEY would boast in the name of their God. Oh how often they forgot this! Fearful of the Assyrians, Israel sought help from Egypt - wealthy in horses and chariots; the machinery of war! By doing so, they turned their back on YHWH - the One who brought them out of Egypt with a strong arm. He freed them from Egypt so long ago - now they seek refuge from the Pharaoh of that land.

Isaiah 31:2-3 *But He also is wise and brings disaster. He does not go back on what He says; He will rise up against the house of wicked men and against the allies of evildoers. Egyptians are men, not God; their horses are flesh, not spirit. When the LORD raises His hand [to strike], the helper will stumble and the one who is helped will fall; both will perish together.*

The Holy One of Israel is the only wise god, the only true God; the only One who does not need a "plan B." Evil doers will not last long, though it may seem they do. Egypt's help is merely flesh (which profits nothing, Jesus observed, in John 6) and they will be cast down and perish with YHWH raises His hand to strike them. We have seen this raised hand of God several times as well - He saves with His strong outstretched arm and He destroys His enemies with His strong outstretched arm.

Isaiah 31:4-5 *For this is what the LORD said to me: As a lion or young lion growls over its prey when a band of shepherds is called out against it, and is not terrified by their shouting or subdued by their noise, so the LORD of Hosts will come down to fight on Mount Zion and on its hill. Like hovering birds, so the LORD of Hosts will protect Jerusalem— by protecting [it], He will rescue [it], by sparing [it], He will deliver [it].*

Isaiah pronounces what God has told him, and it's about how almighty and trustworthy He is! Those who reside on Mt Zion will be under His protection, rescued and delivered from their own evil sins. No fear of Assyria or any other army or beast because the battle belongs to YHWH and He will vanquish all His enemies - just as He rescues and preserves all His sheep.

Isaiah 31:6-9 *Return to the One the Israelites have greatly rebelled against. For on that day, every one of you will reject the silver and gold idols that your own hands have sinfully made. Then Assyria will fall, but not by human sword; a sword will devour him, but not one made by man. He will flee from the sword; his young men will be put to forced labor. His rock will pass away because of fear, and his officers will be afraid because of the signal flag. [This is] the LORD's declaration—whose fire is in Zion and whose furnace is in Jerusalem.*

Those who repent and turn to God will reject the idols once held dear. Recall this from chapter 30: Isaiah 30:21-22 *whenever you turn to the right or to the left, your ears will hear this command behind you: "This is the way. Walk in it." Then you will defile your silver-plated idols and your gold-plated images. You will throw them away like menstrual cloths, and call them filth.* God grants repentance to His people; but He doesn't repent for us. If repentance is not part of your life, cry out to God for this!

Assyria will not be put down by men - Egyptian or any other. A sword not from a human will devour them one by one. The sword of Truth, wielded by the victorious Christ will do this. Those who flee will be imprisoned, their source of pride - their rock - will pass away, and no one will look to the battle flag of Assyria any longer. YHWH has decreed this - His fire in on Mt Zion, burning from the furnace in Jerusalem. Righteousness from God wherein He sits as He rules, Jerusalem will be that city on Mt Zion!

Again and again we see the same cycle - trust in men and strongholds of this world are attractive to us, we are but frail men and women. But the only refuge the provide safety from the storm of God's wrath is to have the righteousness of Christ imputed to your account!

Isaiah 32 - The Kingdom Revealed.

Chapter 32 is mostly good news, as the prophet hails the kingdom that will never end. But there is the warning against drifting away, with the wrath that awaits those who do not trust in YHWH.

Isaiah 32:1-2 *Indeed, a king will reign righteously, and rulers will rule justly. Each will be like a shelter from the wind, a refuge from the rain, like streams of water in a dry land and the shade of a massive rock in an arid land.*

These two verses announce the structure of God's kingdom: a righteous king and just rulers. Saints rule with Christ now (2 Tim 2:12; Rev 20:4 - 6) and Jesus is the righteous King (1 Cor 15:20-28; Eph 1:20-22). Such rule is not a terror to men, but serve as a shelter and refuge from wickedness, providing refreshment and shade in desert climes.

Isaiah 32:3-5 *Then the eyes of those who see will not be closed, and the ears of those who hear will listen. The reckless mind will gain knowledge, and the stammering tongue will speak clearly and fluently. A fool will no longer be called a noble, nor a scoundrel said to be important.*

When the kingdom of God is consummated, all will see clearly, understand what they hear, and speak truth and they grow in grace and knowledge. No longer will the culture elevate fools and scoundrels. Compare verse 3 with the commissioning of the prophet in chapter 6: *Go! Say to these people: Keep listening, but do not understand; keep looking, but do not perceive. Dull the minds of these people; deafen their ears and blind their eyes; otherwise they might see with their eyes and hear with their ears, understand with their minds, turn back, and be healed.* Quite the contrast! All His chosen ones will see and perceive, will hear and understand; and be healed.

Verses 6 & 7 describe the fools, which are exalted by worldly cultures. They speak foolishness, plot wickedness: godless people who abuse the poor and seek to destroy everything. Isaiah 32:8 *But a noble person plans noble things; he stands up for noble causes.* Israel's history is pock-marked by her abuse of widows and orphans, cheating people with false scales, and seeking the fleeting glory of a temporal kingdom. The noble person seeks to honor God by taking care of the poor and weak, dealing honestly with people, and trusting God to deal with wickedness.

Verses 9 - 14 are the warnings of what will happen to those who mindlessly (those without understanding) depend on their bigger barns. The prophet addresses this warning to the women, perhaps as a contrast to the woman described in Proverbs 31. Isaiah 32:9 *Stand up, you complacent women; listen to me. Pay attention to what I say, you overconfident daughters.* Complacent and overconfident - characteristics of those who pay no heed to the warnings of the age-to-come. This passage reveals how their land will fail and be full of thorns, the palace deserted and the city forsaken; and this rebuke: Isaiah 32:11 *Shudder, you complacent ones; tremble, you overconfident ones! Strip yourselves bare and put [sackcloth] around your waists.* People ought to tremble at the thought of what is to come, at how fragile their lives are. Time is running out.

The cities will continue to fall, the vineyards become barren, *until the Spirit from heaven is poured out on us. Then the desert will become an orchard, and the orchard will seem like a forest. Then justice will inhabit the wilderness, and righteousness will dwell in the orchard. The result of righteousness will be peace; the effect of righteousness will be quiet confidence forever. Then my people will dwell in a peaceful place, in safe and secure dwellings.* (Isaiah 32:15-18)

On the new earth, the Spirit will rule in every heart, the provision of YHWH will be untarnished by sin, and justice and righteousness (recall the righteous king and just rulers from the opening of this chapter?) will be the rule, providing peaceful, safe dwellings. Again quite the contrast to Israel's condition - and ours! Does your soul ache to have this peace and safety? It will be ours if we are His.

This chapter comes to an end with a short contrast to drive the message home. Contrary to those who trust in YHWH, those who care not for His rule will be in despair. Isaiah 32:19 *But hail will level the forest, and the city will sink into the depths.* Hail symbolizes the reign of God over weather, as He knocks the wind out of the prideful.

Isaiah 32:20 *Those who sow seed are happy beside abundant waters; they let ox and donkey range freely.* But those who are content with food and shelter, not seeking the vainglory of earthly wealth, will be satisfied with land that provides produce and provision for the animals. I hear the Lord's counsel as He taught on the mount:

Matthew 6:25-34 *This is why I tell you: Don't worry about your life, what you will eat or what you will drink; or about your body, what you will wear. Isn't life more than food and the body more than clothing? Look at the birds of the sky: They don't sow or reap or gather into barns, yet your heavenly Father feeds them. Aren't you worth more than they? Can any of you add a single cubit to his height by worrying? And why do you worry about clothes? Learn how the wildflowers of the field grow: they don't labor or spin thread. Yet I tell you that not even Solomon in all his splendor was adorned like one of these! If that's how God clothes the grass of the field, which is here today and thrown into the furnace tomorrow, won't He do much more for you—you of little faith? So don't worry, saying, 'What will we eat?' or 'What will we drink?' or 'What will we wear?' For the idolaters eagerly seek all these things, and your heavenly Father knows that you need them. But seek first the kingdom of God and His righteousness, and all these things will be provided for you. Therefore don't worry about tomorrow, because tomorrow will worry about itself. Each day has enough trouble of its own.*

Israel's history provided the backdrop to Jesus' words, as He had provided food and clothing during their 40 years of wandering. His counsel stands in our day, as we see the wealth of this world taken away from the workers and stored up by the "landowners." This is YHWH's reminder that with food and clothing, we are to be content, for our God has gone to prepare a place for us and will return to take us to be with

Him forever. So while we live here as pilgrims, let us sojourn with our eyes fixed on Him. He is our rock and strong tower. And He gives peace to His own - peace the world cannot comprehend. What cause do we have to worry?

Isaiah 33 - Victory in Jesus!

Isaiah chapter 33 continues the contrast of the man's wickedness and God's self-existent power and righteousness.

The opening reveals the doom of those who rebel against God and abuse people for selfish gain. Isaiah 33:1 *Woe, you destroyer never destroyed, you traitor never betrayed! When you have finished destroying, you will be destroyed. When you have finished betraying, they will betray you.*

Note: those powerful men who appeared to have a firm grip on their destiny, destroyers never destroyed - such Babylon under Nebuchadnezzar - will be destroyed when, according to YHWH's plan, they themselves will be destroyed. Those whose lives are marked by betraying others will be betrayed by them. This is God's plan.

Isaiah 33:2 *LORD, be gracious to us! We wait for You. Be our strength every morning and our salvation in time of trouble.*

The contrast with those who belong to YHWH wait for Him; these cry out to Him for grace, for strength, and for salvation - for refuge from destroyers.

Isaiah 33:3-4 *The peoples flee at the thunderous noise; the nations scatter when You rise in Your majesty. Your spoil will be gathered as locusts are gathered; people will swarm over it like an infestation of locusts.*

When God makes Himself known to the world, as when the Lord Jesus returns, people who know Him not will flee, seeking safety on earth. Nations that rage against Him will be scattered like dust in the wind when the majesty of God is revealed. The spoils of His war will be picked over like bugs swarming a garbage heap.

Isaiah 33:5 *The LORD is exalted, for He dwells on high; He has filled Zion with justice and righteousness.*

In all of this, YHWH is exalted, reigning from on high, having filled Mt Zion with justice and righteousness - the two characteristics of the saints ruling with Him and His rule over all things, as we read in the beginning of chapter 32.

Isaiah 33:6 *There will be times of security for you— a storehouse of salvation, wisdom, and knowledge. The fear of the LORD is Zion's treasure.*

Those who are known by YHWH are secure - the storehouse of salvation, wisdom, and knowledge of Him! Do you see, dear saints - we are heirs of all that the Father has given His Son because we are united to Him by grace working through faith! Nothing this weary world has can satisfy the soul of the one who has been brought to life by the Spirit of the living God.

Verses 7 - 9 reveal the dismal state of those rebel against their Creator. Bitter weeping, cities broken down, promises broken, land become worthless, and human life without meaning.

Isaiah 33:10-13 *"Now I will rise up," says the LORD. "Now I will lift Myself up. Now I will be exalted. You will conceive chaff; you will give birth to stubble. Your breath is fire that will consume you. The peoples will be burned to ashes, like thorns cut down and burned in a fire. You who are far off, hear what I have done; you who are near, know My strength."*

When YHWH rises up, He will be exalted. Chaff consumed, leaving stubble. His voice is a fire that will destroy the destroyers, burning them to ashes. Those who are far off - a phrase used by Paul and Luke to denote Gentiles - will hear

116

of His mighty deeds and those are near will know His strength. Children - do you hear Him, do you see Him? He is mighty to save and will have mercy on all He calls to Himself.

Isaiah 33:14-16 *The sinners in Zion are afraid; trembling seizes the ungodly: "Who among us can dwell with a consuming fire? Who among us can dwell with ever-burning flames?" The one who lives righteously and speaks rightly, who refuses gain from extortion, whose hand never takes a bribe, who stops his ears from listening to murderous plots and shuts his eyes to avoid endorsing evil—he will dwell on the heights; his refuge will be the rocky fortresses, his food provided, his water assured.*

Pretenders in the midst of the saints will greatly fear Him; they will tremble in terror as they recognize the nature of His judgment that is being poured out. Those who live in righteousness will dwell on high with his God, Who will be his strong tower of refuge - providing food and water.

Isaiah 33:17-20 *Your eyes will see the King in His beauty; you will see a vast land. Your mind will meditate on the [past] terror: "Where is the accountant? Where is the tribute collector? Where is the one who spied out our defenses?" You will no longer see the barbarians, a people whose speech is difficult to comprehend— who stammer in a language that is not understood. Look at Zion, the city of our festival times. Your eyes will see Jerusalem, a peaceful pasture, a tent that does not wander; its tent pegs will not be pulled up nor will any of its cords be loosened.*

When His people see Him, in His glory and beauty unsurpassed by anything, they will how vast His dwelling is. They will remember the terror that filled their life on this earth, where all those who were to protect them took advantage of them instead. In contrast, the New Jerusalem will be a peaceful pasture with unmovable boundaries, stable in all circumstances.

Isaiah 33:21-22 *For the majestic One, our LORD, will be there, a place of rivers and broad streams where ships that are rowed will not go, and majestic vessels will not pass. For the LORD is our Judge, the LORD is our lawgiver, the LORD is our King. He will save us.*

All these things mentioned above are so because YHWH the majestic One dwells there with His own, where rivers need not carry the ships of man - He provides food and water for His own (verse 16). For YHWH is our lawgiver, Judge, King, and Savior! No matter how bad 2020 was, no matter how good you think 2021 might be, nothing can compare with the security and provision that Creator God provides for His own.

Isaiah 33:23-24 *Your ropes are slack; they cannot hold the base of the mast or spread out the flag. Then abundant spoil will be divided, the lame will plunder it, and none there will say, "I am sick." The people who dwell there will be forgiven [their] iniquity.*

Those who stand on their own merit will find their symbols of substance failing, as their ships fall limp and useless. Its cargo will be taken from her, divided among the weak - leaving gleanings for those who are refuse in the eyes of the world's powerful. These are provided for by God, just as He ordained the corners of Israel's fields to be left for the poor. All who are called and seek Him will dwell with Him in forgiveness.

To be forgiven by your lawgiver and Judge is a precious thing. This is the Lord's doing and it is marvelous in our eyes!

VII. Judgment and Promise, Part 2

Isaiah 34 - Judgment Against the Nations.

Isaiah 34 is titled by many Bibles as "The Judgment Against the Nations" while the KJV has it as "The judgment with which God avenges His church." What is clear is that this chapter DOES reveal God's judgment against the nations; and it is clear in many places in earlier chapters that this judgment is because the nations were used by God to punish Israel for rebellion. Wicked men do what wicked men do - and there are consequences for that. God uses wicked men for His purposes but their wickedness does not proceed from Him, but from within the men. Read Acts 2:22 & 23 for a clear example of this.

Isaiah 34:1-2 *You nations, come here and listen; you peoples, pay attention! Let the earth hear, and all that fills it, the world and all that comes from it. The LORD is angry with all the nations— furious with all their armies. He will set them apart for destruction, giving them over to slaughter.*

This is notice, not to the pagan nations around Israel, but to the entire world. YHWH is angry with ALL the nations and their military and He calls them to sit up and listen! To what are they to listen? God has sanctified them - SET THEM APART - for destruction. God is not passive towards His enemies, He does not, as some teach, merely "pass over them" and allow them drift to destruction. He sets them apart, devotes them to (Josh 10:28-43), gives or delivers them over to (Romans 1:26) their destruction.

Isaiah 34:3-4 *Their slain will be thrown out, and the stench of their corpses will rise; the mountains will flow with their blood. All the heavenly bodies will dissolve. The skies will roll up like a scroll, and their stars will all wither as leaves wither on the vine, and foliage on the fig tree.*

These two verses ought to pull you to John's Apocalypse, where we see blood flowing far and high (Rev 14:19 & 20) and we also see the sky rolled up like a scroll (Rev 6:12-14). We also find Peter alluded to this in 2 Peter 3:10 *But the Day of the Lord will come like a thief; on that [day] the heavens will pass away with a loud noise, the elements will burn and be dissolved, and the earth and the works on it will be disclosed.* Scripture interprets Scripture - the apostolic references show us Isaiah's vision here is in regards to the day of the Lord's return. The vineyard and fig tree being withered away are other word pictures of temporal wealth being reduced to nothing.

Isaiah 34:5-7 *When My sword has drunk its fill in the heavens, it will then come down on Edom and on the people I have set apart for destruction. The LORD's sword is covered with blood. It drips with fat, with the blood of lambs and goats, with the fat of the kidneys of rams. For the LORD has a sacrifice in Bozrah, a great slaughter in the land of Edom. The wild oxen will be struck down with them, and young bulls with the mighty bulls. Their land will be soaked with blood, and their soil will be saturated with fat.*

The imagery we're used to seeing in John's Apocalypse keeps showing up here! Read Rev 19:11-16 to see the Lord Jesus presented as the victorious King, whose robe is stained with blood and wields a sword to defeat the nations. See also Deut 32:41-43; Jere 46:10; and Ezek 21:3-5 for direct correlations to Isaiah's words. Again, symbols of temporal wealth (livestock and land) are described as slaughtered and made worthless. Mother Nature is not in control of the weather or circumstance or chance. There is one God by Whom all things were made and in Whom all things are held together. He directs the clouds where to go drop the rain He metes out destruction on those chosen to be vessels of wrath.

Isaiah 34:8-10 *For the LORD has a day of vengeance, a time of paying back [Edom] for its hostility against Zion. [Edom's] streams will be turned into pitch, her soil into sulfur; her land will become burning pitch. It will never go out—day or night. Its smoke will go up forever. It will be desolate, from generation to generation; no one will pass through it forever and ever.*

Here we see why Edom - an ancient nation south of Moab - is a vessel of wrath; she has been hostile to Zion, the people of YHWH. Vengeance is mine, says the Lord! And He will have it! Sodom and Gomorrah are brought before us to show what end Edom will face: burning pitch, sulfur, and smoke from a never-ending fire. Edom will pass into shadow, never again to be a nation but only a memory. A signpost of warning for those who disregard God or stand, shaking their fists at Him.

Verses 11 - 15 describe the desolation of Edom with various word pictures, including the presence of unclean birds (owls), hyenas and wild goats, thorns and chaos. YHWH will stretch out a plumb line to make sure the plan is complete, the destruction comprehensive - and precisely as His wisdom has determined it should be. Edom will have no more kings - a line of rulers more ancient than Israel's. Edom's princes will come to nothing. This is a contrast to the righteous king and just rulers of God's kingdom that we read of in chapter 32.

Isaiah 34:16-17 *Search and read the scroll of the LORD: Not one of them will be missing, none will be lacking its mate, because He has ordered it by my mouth, and He will gather them by His Spirit. He has ordained a lot for them; His hand allotted their portion with a measuring line. They will possess it forever; they will dwell in it from generation to generation.*

This "scroll of YHWH" is likely the Scriptures Israel had in her possession, she had the recurring habit of putting them aside and following after the pagan nations. Isaiah tells them to find and read YHWH's Words, wherein they will find His hand of providence providing all they had need of as well as keeping the wolves they desired from consuming them entirely. Verse 15 ended with a picture of wild, unclean birds making nests in Edom; verse 16 tells us God will insure none of the birds will miss their mates. This is because God had ordained it, has gathered these birds by His Spirit, and allotted their portion by His plumb line. NOTHING is left to "chance."

If you are unhappy with your circumstances, be careful you do not grumble against God, as though you deserve something better. This is my daily challenge right now, as I have been looking for work for 6 months and tend to get discouraged. But God is my strength and my portion - we who are in Christ have no reason and no right to grumble against that which God has allotted to us. Praise Him in "good times" and in "bad times." He is always working for good for those who love God, those who are called according to His purpose. For those He has known from eternity past He has called and is causing us to be conformed to His Son. And the end of all this is our glorification and eternal life with Christ Jesus on the new earth. What reason DO we have to grumble? To the contrary, we have no reason to grumble - but countless reasons of far more weight to rejoice!

Isaiah 35 - The Ransomed Return to Zion.

Chapter 35 of Isaiah brings good news to those who know and love the Messiah. Most Bibles title it something along the lines of "The Ransomed Return to Zion." This is good news!

Isaiah 35:1-2 *The wilderness and the dry land will be glad; the desert will rejoice and blossom like a rose. It will blossom abundantly and will also rejoice with joy and singing. The glory of Lebanon will be given to it, the splendor of Carmel and Sharon. They will see the glory of the LORD, the splendor of our God.*

What a contrast to the gloom and doom of the land in the nations of chapter 34! The desert will blossom abundantly like a rose and rejoice with joy and singing - as when the trees clap their hands! This wilderness is not left to scavengers but is redeemed by God for the redeemed of God. And all with see the splendor and glory of YHWH as He reveals Zion.

Isaiah 35:3-4 *Strengthen the weak hands, steady the shaking knees! Say to the cowardly: "Be strong; do not fear! Here is your God; vengeance is coming. God's retribution is coming; He will save you."*

We see a New Covenant allusion to this: Hebrews 12:7, 12 - 13 *Endure [suffering] as discipline: God is dealing with you as sons. For what son is there that a father does not discipline? Therefore strengthen your tired hands and weakened knees, and make straight paths for your feet, so that what is lame may not be dislocated but healed instead.* God's vengeance is coming upon those who hate Him, retribution for the evil they've done. This same God, vengeful towards some, is merciful towards others. He WILL save His own - the Great Shepherd will find EVERY lost sheep and bring EACH one home to the sheepfold of God.

Isaiah 35:5-7 *Then the eyes of the blind will be opened, and the ears of the deaf unstopped. Then the lame will leap like a deer, and the tongue of the mute will sing for joy, for water will gush in the wilderness, and streams in the desert; the parched ground will become a pool of water, and the thirsty land springs of water. In the haunt of jackals, in their lairs, there will be grass, reeds, and papyrus.*

Jesus referred to the first part of this passage when John's disciples came to Him with the question, *"Are you the One who is to come or should we look for another?"* Matthew 11:4-6 *Jesus replied to them, "Go and report to John what you hear and see: the blind see, the lame walk, those with skin diseases are healed, the deaf hear, the dead are raised, and the poor are told the good news. And if anyone is not offended because of Me, he is blessed."* This is how we know this passage in Isaiah describes the kingdom of God given through Jesus - He said it is proof that He is the One is to come. Again we see parched land revived, scavengers no longer at home because of this. If this is not cause to join the land and rejoice with great joy I fail to find any reason to do so.

Isaiah 35:8 *A road will be there and a way; it will be called the Holy Way. The unclean will not travel on it, but it will be for the one who walks the path. Even the fool will not go astray.*

In chapter 11 we read of a highway that brings God's remnant to Zion; here that road is a Holy Way that no rebels can travel. This road is set apart for those clothed in the righteousness of Christ, who walk His path; even fools that once denied Him will be kept on the narrow path since they now belong to Him.

Isaiah 35:9-10 *There will be no lion there, and no vicious beast will go up on it; they will not be found there. But the redeemed will walk [on it], and the redeemed of the LORD will return and come to Zion with singing, crowned with unending joy. Joy and gladness will overtake [them], and sorrow and sighing will flee.*

Zion is in view here - no vicious animals or people will be there. Here we see them outside instead of tame, not in conflict what Isaiah wrote in Isaiah 11:6-7 *The wolf will live with the lamb, and the leopard will lie down with the goat. The calf, the young lion, and the fatling will be together, and a child will lead them. The cow and the bear will graze, their young ones will lie down together, and the lion will eat straw like the ox.* Two references to Zion with word pictures using animals to describe the peace the redeemed will have. Neither reference should be seen as a focus on the animals, but on the peace of God He gives His people. We will walk on His revived land (new earth), wherein peace rules. We will sing His praise without end, full of joy and gladness. Not only will there be no vicious beasts, there will no sorrow.

Revelation 21:1-4 *Then I saw a new heaven and a new earth, for the first heaven and the first earth had passed away, and the sea no longer existed. I also saw the Holy City, new Jerusalem, coming down out of heaven from God, prepared like a bride adorned for her husband. Then I heard a loud voice from the throne: Look! God's dwelling is with humanity, and He will live with them. They will be His people, and God Himself will be with them and be their God. He will wipe away every tear from their eyes. Death will no longer exist; grief, crying, and pain will exist no longer, because the previous things have passed away.*

God's plan of redemption, unfolded from Genesis through Revelation - it's all about the One who was to come, the promised Messiah. He gives joy unbounded to those He brings into His sheepfold. Do you know Him? There is no politician, no business, no husband or wife, no child or parent that provide this peace and joy. Christ ALONE gave His life to save His OWN; to bring the ransomed to Zion.

Isaiah 36 - Anchored in History.

While much of Isaiah is designed to bring the eternal kingdom of God into view, chapter 36 serves to remind us that His redemptive plan is revealed in time, that ours is a faith that is anchored in the events that happened in time. For national Israel, this was a time to be reminded of their enemies' plans to draw them away from reliance upon God.

Isaiah 36:1 *In the fourteenth year of King Hezekiah, Sennacherib king of Assyria attacked all the fortified cities of Judah and captured them.*

The 14th year of Hezekiah's reign was 701 B.C. Twenty one years prior, Assyria had conquered the northern kingdom and had pressured Judah to pay an annual ransom - protection money like the US mafia is infamous for. Now, Judah has fallen; perhaps the annual tribute failed to satisfy Sennacherib, who became king of Assyria in 703.

Isaiah 36:2-3 *Then the king of Assyria sent the Rabshakeh, along with a massive army, from Lachish to King Hezekiah at Jerusalem. The Assyrian stood near the conduit of the upper pool, by the road to the Fuller's Field. Eliakim son of Hilkiah, who was in charge of the palace, Shebna the court secretary, and Joah son of Asaph, the court historian, came out to him.*

Lachish was an important city in Judah, a garrison some 30 miles west of Jerusalem. This aid to the king was sent with a massive army and he stood at the same place Isaiah had stood when he confronted Ahaz (see chapter 7 and verse 3). 3 important officials from Judah were sent to meet him, including Shebna - who was responsible for the king's household (chapter 22:15). This display was to show Assyria Judah was taking this invasion seriously.

Isaiah 36:4-7 *The Rabshakeh said to them, "Tell Hezekiah: The great king, the king of Assyria, says this: What are you relying on? I say that your strategy and military preparedness are mere words. What are you now relying on that you have rebelled against me? Look, you are trusting in Egypt, that splintered reed of a staff that will enter and pierce the hand of anyone who leans on it. This is how Pharaoh king of Egypt is to all who trust in him. Suppose you say to me, 'We trust in the LORD our God.' Isn't He the One whose high places and altars Hezekiah has removed, saying to Judah and Jerusalem, 'You are to worship at this altar'?*

Sennacherib's aid is not polite, replaying a sarcastic message from his king, who saw Israel's God as merely another god among countless others. By relying on Egypt to protect them (recall how Egypt was shown by YHWH as totally inadequate in chapter 30:3-7), Israel was demonstrating their lack of faith in YHWH. Sennacherib picked up on this and threw into their teeth. He also reminded them that Hezekiah had torn down some of the (pagan) places of worship that Israel had a habit of clinging to - this to try and drive a wedge between the king of Judah and his people.

The Assyrian continued: Isaiah 36:8-10 *Now make a deal with my master, the king of Assyria. I'll give you 2,000 horses if you're able to supply riders for them! How then can you drive back a single officer among the weakest of my master's officers and trust in Egypt for chariots and horsemen? Have I attacked this land to destroy it without the LORD's [approval]? The LORD said to me, 'Attack this land and destroy it.'"*

Since Israel has shown she doesn't trust in YHWH, she is taunted by Assyria to submit to that nation, as Sennacherib's aid implies Israel doesn't have riders, much less horses, with which to wage war. The least of his officers would be able to withstand all the machinery of war Israel could bring. The might and success of Assyria convinced her king that Israel's God had sanctioned his conquest of both kingdoms.

There were men of Judah within the hearing of this discussion, leading to this. Isaiah 36:11-12 *Then Eliakim, Shebna, and Joah said to the Rabshakeh, "Please speak to your servants in Aramaic, since we understand [it]. Don't speak to us in Hebrew within earshot of the people who are on the wall." But the Rabshakeh replied, "Has my master sent me to speak these words to your master and to you, and not to the men who are sitting on the wall, [who are destined] with you to eat their own excrement and drink their own urine?"*

The three representatives of Hezekiah feared for their personal safety and their reputation back home, asking the Assyrian to speak in a language the Jewish people did not know. But the Assyrian would have none of it, replying with what must have been the most rude, crude way imaginable to communicate how powerless Israel was.

He then addresses the men of Judah directly. Isaiah 36:13-20 *Then the Rabshakeh stood and called out loudly in Hebrew: Listen to the words of the great king, the king of Assyria! This is what the king says: "Don't let Hezekiah deceive you, for he cannot deliver you. Don't let Hezekiah persuade you to trust in the LORD, saying, 'The LORD will certainly deliver us! This city will not be handed over to the king of Assyria.'" Don't listen to Hezekiah, for this is what the king of Assyria says: "Make peace with me and surrender to me. Then every one of you may eat from his own vine and his own fig tree and drink water from his own cistern until I come and take you away to a land like your own land—a land of grain and new wine, a land of bread and vineyards. [Beware] that Hezekiah does not mislead you by saying, 'The LORD will deliver us.' Has any one of the gods of the nations delivered his land from the power of the king of Assyria? Where are the gods of Hamath and Arpad? Where are the gods of Sepharvaim? Have they delivered Samaria from my power? Who among all the gods of these lands [ever] delivered his land from my power? So will the LORD deliver Jerusalem."*

The men of Judah were told, repeatedly, that their own king, Hezekiah, was unable to save or protect them. Hezekiah's reliance upon YHWH is mocked and presented as ineffective, whereas the king of Assyria is presented as almighty and compassionate. The false ever tries to sell itself as the real thing, always failing to deliver what is promised. No other god was able to stand before Assyria - Arpad and Hamath were well known conquests in Syria. Why would the men of Judah persist in thinking YHWH would deliver them in the face of such great opposition?

Isaiah 36:21-22 *But they kept silent; they didn't say anything, for the king's command was, "Don't answer him." Then Eliakim son of Hilkiah, who was in charge of the palace, Shebna the court secretary, and Joah son of Asaph, the court historian, came to Hezekiah with their clothes torn and reported to him the words of the Rabshakeh.*

The emissaries of Hezekiah had no authority to negotiate with Assyria. Their job was to listen and report back to the king of Judah. They did this in the common way that conveyed distress and mourning. Their report to Hezekiah was like that of the ten spies sent across the Jordan - we cannot stand before these people!

Such was the dire state of Judah in 701 B.C. Who can relate to political defeat and the turmoil that brings? Who doesn't have a little bit of uncertainty in what the new regime will bring? In the next chapter of Isaiah we see Hezekiah's response. What is your response - and mine - in our day? Do we fear the Assyrians who have conquered our land, mocked our God, and ridiculed us for trusting in Him? Brothers and sisters, let not your heart be troubled! Believe in God and the One He sent! This place and time is not our home. The Lord Jesus has gone to prepare a place for us and He has promised to come back and receive us to Himself so that where He is we will be also! (John 14:1-3). Trust in Him and live like you do! He is faithful! He has promised it and He will do it!

Isaiah 37 - YHWH Answers Sennacherib.

Chapter 37 of Isaiah remains rooted in the history of national Israel; a continuation of the scenario from chapter 36. Hezekiah seeks counsel from God's prophet, Isaiah. Recall that Hezekiah's advisors had returned from meeting Sennacherib's top man - it was bad news from man from man. Isaiah 37:1 *When King Hezekiah heard [their report], he tore his clothes, put on sackcloth, and went to the LORD's temple.*

The king of Judah was shaken, as a man, by what Assyria intended. His first response was to weep and mourn in a display of humility and to seek wisdom from YHWH. After this, Isaiah 37:2-4 *Then he sent Eliakim, who was in charge of the palace, Shebna the court secretary, and the leading priests, who were wearing sackcloth, to the prophet Isaiah son of Amoz. They said to him, "This is what Hezekiah says: 'Today is a day of distress, rebuke, and disgrace, for children have come to the point of birth, and there is no strength to deliver [them]. Perhaps Yahweh your God will hear all the words of the Rabshakeh, whom his master the king of Assyria*

129

sent to mock the living God, and will rebuke [him for] the words that Yahweh your God has heard. Therefore offer a prayer for the surviving remnant.'

Hezekiah knew Isaiah was God's prophet; he wanted to hear from him. His message, carried by the three, revealed the dismay and disgrace of what was happening to Israel with a plea for Isaiah to petition YHWH to preserve the remnant of Israel.

Isaiah 37:5-7 *So the servants of King Hezekiah went to Isaiah, who said to them, "Tell your master this, 'The LORD says: Don't be afraid because of the words you have heard, which the king of Assyria's attendants have blasphemed Me with. I am about to put a spirit in him and he will hear a rumor and return to his own land, where I will cause him to fall by the sword.'*

Here's another example of verse number insertions that ought to make you scratch your head - verse 6 begins in the middle of a sentence. Do not allow verse and chapter divisions to disrupt your reading and understanding of Scripture.

Isaiah's response to Hezekiah's henchmen is what the saints today need to hear: DO NOT FEAR WHAT MAN MAY DO! He tells us to fear not - only believe! YHWH was not ignorant of what Assyria was up to - He knew the king's aid was a blasphemer and He had planned to ruin that man's best life. God would a spirit in Rabshakeh that would cause him to fear and then God would cause Rabshakeh to be killed. Yes, God did that.

In verses 8 - 13, Sennacherib had moved on to the next city on his march to Jerusalem when Rabshakeh caught up with him. The king of Assyria had heard from the prince of Egypt that Judah might be ready to fight them in this town - Libnah. Sennacherib sent a message to Hezekiah, the same as Rabshakeh had given earlier, testifying of Assyria's might and Judah's hopelessness. The same taunting style, meant to cause Judah to doubt YHWH and fear Sennacherib.

Isaiah 37:14-20 *Hezekiah took the letter from the messengers, read it, then went up to the LORD's temple and spread it out before the LORD. Then Hezekiah prayed to the LORD: LORD of Hosts, God of Israel, who is enthroned above the cherubim, You are God—You alone—of all the kingdoms of the earth. You made the heavens and the earth. Listen closely, LORD, and hear; open Your eyes, LORD, and see. Hear all the words that Sennacherib has sent to mock the living God. LORD, it is true that the kings of Assyria have devastated all these countries and their lands. They have thrown their gods into the fire, for they were not gods but made by human hands—wood and stone. So they have destroyed them. Now, LORD our God, save us from his power so that all the kingdoms of the earth may know that You are the LORD—You alone.*

Again, Hezekiah went alone to seek wisdom from YHWH. This time we see what was on the king's mind. He admits the Assyrians' are fearful men and have defeated nations that followed gods that were not God. He adores and worships the one true God who created all things and rules all things. And he cries out for YHWH - the God of Judah! - to save them from Assyria so that everyone on earth would know the YWHW is God and there is none other. Proper prayer seeks to bring glory to God. Hezekiah did not have his reputation on his tongue but the honor and glory of God who had promised to all to keep a man on the throne of David forever.

God sends Isaiah to answer the prayers of the king of Judah. Isaiah 37:21-22a *Then Isaiah son of Amoz sent [a message] to Hezekiah: "The LORD, the God of Israel, says: 'Because you prayed to Me about Sennacherib king of Assyria, this is the word the LORD has spoken against him."*

Beginning in verse 22b, YHWH has a lengthy message for Assyria, beginning with His declared affection for the afflicted "daughters" Zion and Jerusalem, which scorn Sennacherib and mock him behind his back - knowing YHWH will avenge them because the king of Assyria had mocked and waged war against the Holy One of Israel; God Himself! All the plans of destruction carried by Assyria were proudly announced by them as their own accomplishments. Isaiah 37:26 God asks, *"Have you not heard? I designed it long ago; I planned it in days gone by. I have now brought it to pass."* All the destruction at the hands of the Assyrians were His doing! Isaiah 37:28-29 *But I know your sitting down, your going out and your coming in, and your raging against Me. Because your raging against Me and your arrogance have reached My ears, I will put My hook in your nose and My bit in your mouth; I will make you go back the way you came.* Creator God will show the Assyrians whose in charge - He will put His hook in their nose and His bit in their mouth to make them go back to where they started. It's as if He had said, in another place, Proverbs 21:1 *A king's heart is like streams of water in the LORD's hand: He directs it wherever He chooses.* Indeed - and Sennacherib's heart was subject to YHWH's hand, He directed it as He chose.

To Hezekiah, God spoke: Isaiah 37:30-32 *'This will be the sign for you: This year you will eat what grows on its own, and in the second year what grows from that. But in the third year sow and reap, plant vineyards and eat their fruit. The surviving remnant of the house of Judah will again take root downward and bear fruit upward. For a remnant will go out from Jerusalem and survivors, from Mount Zion. The zeal of the LORD of Hosts will accomplish this.'*

No matter what Assyria threatened them with, they were to count on God's provision; this is a reminder of the Sabbath year God gave them in Lev 25:1-7. The remnant would take root and bear fruit; the remnant from both "daughters" - Jerusalem and Zion. And the zeal of YHWH would accomplish this. Has God rejected His people? God forbid! Though the number of Israel's sons be like the sand of sea, only the remnant will be saved, for YHWH will execute His sentence completely and decisively on the earth (Paul, in Romans 11 and 9, where He quotes Isaiah).

YHWH has a final word for Sennacherib - he will not enter Jerusalem nor even shoot an arrow into it. He will go back to where he started. Isaiah 37:34b-35 *[This is] the LORD's declaration. I will defend this city and rescue it because of Me and because of My servant David.* Here is God's own declaration of why the remnant will be saved: for His name and His servant David's sake. The Messiah was the promised son of David that made David valuable. All is from God, through God, and for God.

Here's how it played out, YHWH's decree: Isaiah 37:36-37 *Then the angel of the LORD went out and struck down 185,000 in the camp of the Assyrians. When the people got up the [next] morning—there were all the dead bodies! So Sennacherib king of Assyria broke camp and left. He returned [home] and lived in Nineveh.*

BOOM! Proud, arrogant, tyrannical king of Assyria - defeated by an angel of YWHW. Do you fear the wrath of those tyrants who seized power in the US on January 20th, 2021? Do you not know that, as with Sennacherib, all their goings up and down are known by Him, are directed by Him? Do you not think His counsel for us would be exactly the same today as it was for Hezekiah so many years ago? Trust in God for your daily bread, do not fear man - only believe on Him!

Some 20 years later, here's how Sennacherib ended. Isaiah 37:38 *One day, while he was worshiping in the temple of his god Nisroch, his sons Adrammelech and Sharezer struck him down with the sword and escaped to the land of Ararat. Then his son Esar-haddon became king in his place.*

Appels fall close to apple trees. Men who do evil tend to die at the hands of evil men; even kin. This is the way of the world. It is not the way of God's people. Vengeance is YWHW's, not yours or mine. As one author put it, to be disappointed in one's self reveals misplaced trust. Trust the King - not your ability to follow Him! No matter how you or

I try to make things work out "good" - we should NEVER trust that we can make things right. Trust the King - alone! Let no other trust intrude.

Isaiah 38 - Hezekiah falls ill and is given recovery.

In this chapter, we see Hezekiah as a type of Christ in that he is stricken with a mortal illness (is close to death) and God grants him recovery to health (a type of resurrection). This aligns with the type Scripture confirms elsewhere, when Isaac was offered up for sacrifice and restored to life with Abram.

Isaiah 38:1 *In those days Hezekiah became terminally ill. The prophet Isaiah son of Amoz came and said to him, "This is what the LORD says: 'Put your affairs in order, for you are about to die; you will not recover.'"*

God sets the times and boundaries of men's lives - see Acts 17. Seldom do any of us get the advance notice that Hezekiah did, as Isaiah brought the Word of YHWH to him: *'Put your affairs in order, for you are about to die; you will not recover.'* How many of us will die without notice and leave our affairs in disorder?

Isaiah 38:2-3 *Then Hezekiah turned his face to the wall and prayed to the LORD. He said, "Please, LORD, remember how I have walked before You faithfully and wholeheartedly, and have done what pleases You." And Hezekiah wept bitterly.*

When Abraham was told of the looming demise of Sodom, he pleaded with God to save the city for the sake of his nephew, Lot. While some see that the conversation in Genesis 19 is Abraham bargaining with God, YHWH is, in fact, helping Abraham see the depths of man's depravity. In our passage, Hezekiah is confronted with his own mortality - not far different from Abraham facing that of Lot - and he pleads with God to remember his, Hezekiah's, faithfulness.

134

We see from this side of history that we should go to God pleading His faithfulness, as Moses did when he asked God to not wipe out the Hebrew nation for the sake of His name - otherwise the pagans would think the Hebrews' God was unable to keep His promises. Hezekiah wept, perhaps because he did not yet have an heir, and that was personal and national embarrassment.

Isaiah 38:4-6 *Then the word of the LORD came to Isaiah: "Go and tell Hezekiah that this is what the LORD God of your ancestor David says: I have heard your prayer; I have seen your tears. Look, I am going to add 15 years to your life. And I will deliver you and this city from the power of the king of Assyria; I will defend this city."*

Verses 21 & 22 fit here, chronologically. We have no hint as to why they are at the end of this chapter. Isaiah 38:21-22 *Now Isaiah had said, "Let them take a lump of pressed figs and apply it to his infected skin, so that he may recover." And Hezekiah had asked, "What is the sign that I will go up to the LORD's temple?"*

Isaiah 38:7-8 *"This is the sign to you from the LORD that He will do what He has promised: I am going to make the sun's shadow that goes down on Ahaz's stairway go back by 10 steps." So the sun's shadow went back the 10 steps it had descended.*

YHWH had a promise that must be kept - a seed would come through the royal line of Israel (a son of David) that would save Israel. He tells Isaiah to tend to the sores and He provides and answer to the larger question. God hears the prayers of His people and He granted Hezekiah 15 additional years. Hezekiah would have a son, Manasseh, 3 years after this "resurrection", 12 years before his death (2 Kings 21:11). The issue was not Hezekiah's life; human life is never the reason for God's actions. He had sworn by Himself (Heb 6:13) and His promises WILL NOT FAIL. To that end, Hezekiah was given a longer life.

The sign given Hezekiah to prove it was YHWH making the promise to him went against the natural order, as when fire came down to consume Elijah's altar. The account in 2 Kings 20 reveals more detail, with Hezekiah being given the choice of whether the sun's shadow would advance or retreat. Hezekiah asked that the shadow retreat, since this is - from man's perspective - less natural, more difficult. For the One who created all things, moving the shadow up or back is nothing - the nations are as dust in His scales.

But that this One condescended to answer him prompted Hezekiah to break forth in song. Isaiah 38:9 *A poem by Hezekiah king of Judah after he had been sick and had recovered from his illness:*

The first part of his poem is focused on his looking death and the realization of the finality therein. Isaiah 38:12 *My dwelling is plucked up and removed from me like a shepherd's tent. I have rolled up my life like a weaver; He cuts me off from the loom. You make an end of me from day until night.*

The last part of the poem is his praise to God for giving him life. Isaiah 38:15 *What can I say? He has spoken to me, and He Himself has done it.* Isaiah 38:16-17 *Lord, because of these [promises] people live, and in all of them is the life of my spirit as well; You have restored me to health and let me live. Indeed, it was for [my own] welfare that I had such great bitterness; but Your love [has delivered] me from the Pit of destruction, for You have thrown all my sins behind Your back.*

He is amazed that the One who spoke creation into existence has spoken to him! He realizes that people live because of promises God has made; perhaps reflecting on the Covenant with Noah, wherein YHWH promised seed time and harvest until the end of the age. Hezekiah confesses his bitterness was because he was vain and selfish; but he sees that it was God's loving kindness that rescued him and threw all his sins behind His back. Hezekiah sees the bigger picture - not merely more years added to his walk on this earth; FORGIVENESS of sins that will never be laid to his account! Are we amazed He has spoken to us, or do we take His Word for granted?

Isaiah 38:18-20 *For Sheol cannot thank You; Death cannot praise You. Those who go down to the Pit cannot hope for Your faithfulness. The living, only the living can thank You, as I do today; a father will make Your faithfulness known to children. The LORD will save me; we will play stringed instruments all the days of our lives at the house of the LORD.*

Those who are in the grave awaiting the second death, those who go down to the pit, cannot praise God. Only the living - those whose sins have been thrown behind God's back - can praise Him. Having been saved, the redeemed will desire to praise Him in many ways all the rest of his days. This is the happy state of all who have forgiveness, who are reconciled to YHWH. Endless praise because of His faithfulness and for redeeming helpless sinners.

Is your heart filled with praise for this God? Do you realize what's been done to redeem sinners? Salvation is of the LORD - Jonah knew this, Hezekiah declared this. Do you know this - or do you believe your salvation depends, even in part, on you? None but Jesus can do helpless sinners good. Trust Him wholly, let no other trust intrude. Make His faithfulness known to your children. They need to see their earthly fathers for what we are - no help in saving them beyond proclaiming Christ to them. Your faithfulness and mine isn't what anyone needs. God's faithfulness is what insures every lost sheep will be brought into the sheepfold of Christ.

Isaiah 39 - Hezekiah's Folly

"Hezekiah's Folly" is how the HCSB titles this chapter. The ESV has it "Envoys From Babylon" and the KJV has "Merodach-baladan sends visitors to Hezekiah to examine his treasures." A read through this short chapter convinced me the HCSB had the best focus on the theme of this chapter.

From Noah Webster's 1828 dictionary:

FOL'LY, noun [See Fool.]
1. Weakness of intellect; imbecility of mind. want of understanding.
A fool layeth open his folly Proverbs 13:16.

Folly is the hallmark of a fool; one who commits folly is foolish. May God keep us from folly!

Isaiah 39:1 *At that time Merodach-baladan son of Baladan, king of Babylon, sent letters and a gift to Hezekiah since he heard that he had been sick and had recovered.*

At that time - this was around 703 B.C., after Sennacherib had removed Merodach-baladan from being king of Babylon. Merodach-baladan was a constant pain for Sennacherib, plotting with Assyria to overthrow him. The gifts and letters to Hezekiah were, no doubt, part of his plan or revenge against Sennacherib. Timing was perfect - Hezekiah was feeling good, having received healing and more years from God.

Isaiah 39:2 *Hezekiah was pleased with them, and showed them his treasure house—the silver, the gold, the spices, and the precious oil—and all his armory, and everything that was found in his treasuries. There was nothing in his palace and in all his realm that Hezekiah did not show them.*

Here then, is the folly of a foolish man. Apparently puffed up because he sees himself as having favor with God, Hezekiah reveals everything to a man long-bent on destroying Israel. This action is not lost on our prophet.

Isaiah 39:3-4 *Then the prophet Isaiah came to King Hezekiah and asked him, "Where did these men come from and what did they say to you?" Hezekiah replied, "They came to me from a distant country, from Babylon." Isaiah asked, "What have they seen in your palace?" Hezekiah answered, "They have seen everything in my palace. There isn't anything in my treasuries that I didn't show them."*

Something didn't set right with Isaiah, seeing Babylonians walking around the king's palace. Not fearful of the man, Isaiah asks him bluntly what he has done; the foolish king answers honestly. He has "lifted his skirt" to show his enemy everything.

Is this how people of God are supposed to act? We have the benefit of having more of God's Word in writing and His Spirit indwelling us. We read in Matthew 10:16: *Look, I'm sending you out like sheep among wolves. Therefore be as shrewd as serpents and as harmless as doves.* God's people are sent by God into the world of wolves, knowing we are but sheep - needing our great Shepherd. While He will defend us He also equips us to walk in wisdom towards the world. Be wise as serpents - do not allow the world to take advantage of you. Here's one place in the Old Testament where we DO see a morality lesson - Don't be like Hezekiah!

Isaiah 39:5-7 *Then Isaiah said to Hezekiah, "Hear the word of the LORD of Hosts: 'The time will certainly come when everything in your palace and all that your fathers have stored up until this day will be carried off to Babylon; nothing will be left,' says the LORD. 'Some of your descendants who come from you will be taken away, and they will become eunuchs in the palace of the king of Babylon.'"*

Here's how we know Hezekiah was foolish: YHWH pronounces judgment on him for his actions. Everything that Hezekiah proudly revealed to the Babylonian would be carried off to Babylon - nothing would be left. Some of Hezekiah's children would be taken to Babylon, in exile for a time; some serving as eunuchs in the Babylonian palace. This came true nearly 100 years later, as Nebuchadnezzar conquered Jerusalem and took gold and people back to Babylon. Daniel 1:6 *Among them, from the descendants of Judah, were Daniel, Hananiah, Mishael, and Azariah.*

Isaiah 39:8 *Then Hezekiah said to Isaiah, "The word of the LORD that you have spoken is good," for he thought: There will be peace and security during my lifetime.*

More foolishness from this foolish king. He is fat, dumb, and happy because he will be spared the consequences of his folly. The fool that Hezekiah had become does not care what will happen after he is dead, he does not care his offspring will suffer greatly for his actions. But in 605 B.C. all Israel would wail and moan as the great and terrible king Nebuchadnezzar devastated their land and left only those who were of no use to him - and no use to their own.

If you have been translated from darkness into the glorious light of the kingdom of God and His Christ, then you - and I - MUST diligently seek to walk in wisdom toward the world, knowing it as at war with the Lord Jesus and His body; knowing we are called to be a light in this dark place, proclaiming His gospel and equipping His people so we won't be tossed about by the wiles of sinister men. Like Hezekiah was. Don't be like Hezekiah. Follow the teaching of the Word, the guidance of His Spirit. Our children and grandchildren are watching, the other saints in our local fellowship need us to walk with them. For His glory and the good of all who know Him, or rather are known by Him.

Selah.

VIII. Comfort for Spiritual Israel

Isaiah 40 - The Lord of Glory.

Chapter 40 of Isaiah brings another shift in focus by the Prophet. Chapter 38 & 39 were primarily about specifics things that took place around 700 B.C. This was, in part, a reminder that though God is outside His creation, His plan of redemption is worked out in time with real people going through myriad trials. While the revelation of His plan of redemption is complete, all people will continue to experience various trials until Christ returns.

The HCSB and ESV title this chapter "God's People Comforted" and "Comfort for God's People", while the KJV has "The promulgation of the gospel." While comforting God's people is one theme in this chapter, the major theme that I identified when I read it was the glory of God. KJV's outline is a nice one:

Vs 1-2: The promulgation of the gospel

Vs 3-8: The preaching of John the Baptist

Vs 9-11: The preaching of the Apostles

Vs 12-17: The prophet, by the Omnipotence of God

Vs 18-31: and because He is incomparable, comforts His people

The chapter does start out with words of comfort. Isaiah 40:1-2 *"Comfort, comfort My people," says your God. "Speak tenderly to Jerusalem, and announce to her that her time of forced labor is over, her iniquity has been pardoned, and she has received from the LORD's hand double for all her sins."*

Isaiah is likely being commanded by YHWH to speak these words, telling Jerusalem her time of slavery is over, her iniquity pardoned, and her sin paid for double. This sounds like New Covenant language, where the remnant of Israel finds reconciliation with God.

Isaiah 40:3-5 *A voice of one crying out: Prepare the way of the LORD in the wilderness; make a straight highway for our God in the desert. Every valley will be lifted up, and every mountain and hill will be leveled; the uneven ground will become smooth and the rough places, a plain. And the glory of the LORD will appear, and all humanity together will see [it], for the mouth of the LORD has spoken.*

We recognize John's words, as he quoted to this passage in his early preaching (Luke 3: 4-6). We've seen highways and straight, level paths mentioned in Isaiah before, in context to leading the way to Zion. This is the message of Isaiah as it was of John - Christ has gone before us, making the way to peace with God possible. And if you don't hear Handel's music from The Messiah as you read verse 5, go listen to it right now. The KJV is what he used: "*And the glory of the LORD shall be revealed, and all flesh shall see it together: for the mouth of the LORD hath spoken it.*" As with everything else that has come to pass, even this - when Christ returns with the blast of the trumpet and shout of the archangel, the glory of YHWH will be revealed to all mankind; for the mouth of YHWH has spoken it! What a glorious day for all who know Him, or rather are known by Him!

Isaiah 40:6-8 *A voice was saying, "Cry out!" Another said, "What should I cry out?" "All humanity is grass, and all its goodness is like the flower of the field. The grass withers, the flowers fade when the breath of the LORD blows on them; indeed, the people are grass. The grass withers, the flowers fade, but the word of our God remains forever."*

Voices call out, reminding man that his life is as grass - frail and short. All creation will come to an end when YHWH blows on them, for nothing and nobody can withstand Him.

142

Yet His Word remains. What is of God cannot be overturned or ended.

Isaiah 40:9-11 *Zion, herald of good news, go up on a high mountain. Jerusalem, herald of good news, raise your voice loudly. Raise it, do not be afraid! Say to the cities of Judah, "Here is your God!" See, the Lord GOD comes with strength, and His power establishes His rule. His reward is with Him, and His gifts accompany Him. He protects His flock like a shepherd; He gathers the lambs in His arms and carries [them] in the fold of His [garment]. He gently leads those that are nursing.*

Zion and Jerusalem are heralds of good news to Judah, just as we each are messengers of reconciliation are heralds of good news to lost sheep everywhere. We tell them, "Here is your God! He rules with power and gathers His own, carrying them back to His the safety of His sheepfold." Oh, we have read so much about the wrath of God poured out on His enemies. Savor this passage revealing Him as a gentle shepherd who knows how to care for His flock and is tenderhearted towards them in caring for them. Do you sense His arms around you or does this sound foreign to you? Saints of God - raise your voices LOUDLY! Jesus came to save sinners!

Isaiah 40:12-17 *Who has measured the waters in the hollow of his hand or marked off the heavens with the span [of his hand]? Who has gathered the dust of the earth in a measure or weighed the mountains in a balance and the hills in the scales? Who has directed the Spirit of the LORD, or who gave Him His counsel? Who did He consult with? Who gave Him understanding and taught Him the paths of justice? Who taught Him knowledge and showed Him the way of understanding? Look, the nations are like a drop in a bucket; they are considered as a speck of dust in the scales; He lifts up the islands like fine dust. Lebanon is not enough for fuel, or its animals enough for a burnt offering. All the nations are as nothing before Him; they are considered by Him as nothingness and emptiness.*

This paragraph resounds with the last several chapters of Job, wherein that righteous man was reminded of how glorious and almighty YHWH is. How can any human read these Scriptures and not be taken aback at how the Creator describes Himself? No creature can counsel Him or give Him knowledge. No matter how big a farm you may own, look at His handiwork and see how small and insignificant the NATIONS are! This is why it was foolish for Israel to seek a partnership with Egypt to help them fight Babylon. This is also why it is foolish for Christians to get fraught with anxiety over the sad state of our national governments.

When the Lord Jesus returns, Revelation 6:15-17 *Then the kings of the earth, the nobles, the military commanders, the rich, the powerful, and every slave and free person hid in the caves and among the rocks of the mountains. And they said to the mountains and to the rocks, "Fall on us and hide us from the face of the One seated on the throne and from the wrath of the Lamb, because the great day of Their wrath has come! And who is able to stand?"*

The nations are as dust on God's scales, they are considered as nothing and empty. For apart from Christ, man can do nothing good nor is he capable of being good. Only those who are known by the Good Shepherd have cause to rejoice always and give thanks in all circumstances (1 Thess 5:14 &18).

Isaiah 40:18-20 *Who will you compare God with? What likeness will you compare Him to? To an idol?—[something that] a smelter casts, and a metalworker plates with gold and makes silver welds [for it]? To one who shapes a pedestal, choosing wood that does not rot? He looks for a skilled craftsman to set up an idol that will not fall over.*

Here the nations are reminded that their gods are not gods at all, but stupid idols crafted by their own hands. Nothing made by man can compare with the One Who created all things! The best of what man can craft is like Dagon, which was knocked over for being in the same tent as the Ark of God's covenant with Israel (1 Sam 5). Why work to make a stupid thing when the one true God has revealed Himself in creation and spoken to us in His Word and by His Son?

Isaiah 40:21-24 *Do you not know? Have you not heard? Has it not been declared to you from the beginning? Have you not considered the foundations of the earth? God is enthroned above the circle of the earth; its inhabitants are like grasshoppers. He stretches out the heavens like thin cloth and spreads them out like a tent to live in. He reduces princes to nothing and makes judges of the earth irrational. They are barely planted, barely sown, their stem hardly takes root in the ground when He blows on them and they wither, and a whirlwind carries them away like stubble.*

Does Romans 10 come to mind when you read this? Romans 10:14a *But how can they call on Him they have not believed in? And how can they believe without hearing about Him?* Have you not heard, do you not know, has it not been proclaimed to you, even from the created order? Don't be misled by those who point to verse 22 and claim the Bible supports a flat earth; that is a "literal" hermeneutic that strains itself to the breaking point. Rather see this as evidence that the Spirit revealed to the prophet that earth is curved - looks like a circle if you see it in 2 dimensions. The point is that God cannot be contained in His creation - He handles the heavens (our galaxy) as a thin cloth.

This next word picture is most interesting to me right now. God reduces the princes (rich, powerful men) to nothing and MAKES JUDGES of the earth IRRATIONAL! Now the rich people in the USA are getting richer - their big barns will not protect them when the Lord returns. Our judges ARE irrational - and this the Lord's doing, is it marvelous in your eyes? They think they are high and mighty - He says they are plants with no root that will wither and be blown away like stubble when the winds blow. Have faith in God, be ye not worried that your country is coming apart at the seams! We in the USA have grown to think wealth, health, and comfort are our rights! This unique experiment in human history has been a tremendous blessing to uncounted people. But it is not the norm and we should not murmur when it withers and is blown away like stubble.

Isaiah 40:25-26 *"Who will you compare Me to, or who is My equal?" asks the Holy One. Look up and see: who created these? He brings out the starry host by number; He calls all of them by name. Because of His great power and strength, not one of them is missing.*

This is one my favorite passages. How many of you parents have had trouble grabbing the name of the child you wanted at a particular time? We had two children live and our son heard his mother run through the names of his sister and the family dog trying to get his name to come out of her mouth. The boxer George Foreman had 6 sons and named each of them George because he knew he would have this trouble. Compare our feeble minds to that of God! not only did He create all things, He hung each star where He wanted it and calls each one by name - and they are NOT all named George! And none of the countless stars are missing because by Him all things hold together (Col 1:17). That is POWER beyond what our puny minds can comprehend! Ponder this. Every star, put in the sky and kept in place by the very One Who gave His life so we would have life.

The transcendent God is immanent! He is beyond our ability to comprehend yet He has come close to us, became like us, to reveal Himself to those He would save. The bridge in a hymn brought back to life by Matthew Smith (What Wondrous Love is This!) shows our need of Him and the way He transcends the gap between Him and us to save us:

> And what wondrous love is this
> Though I raised my clenched fist

He opened up my hand to received His gift

And what wondrous love is here
The God Immortal has drawn near
And shed His blood to close the rift

While we were His enemies, Christ died for us. We do not reach out for Him - He reached down to where we were in spiritual death, pried open our clenched fist to receive His gift. And ponder this for a long time: God immortal has drawn near and shed His blood to close the rift! Does your soul rejoice, has Christ drawn close to you and drawn to Himself? Praise Him all ye saints!

Isaiah 40:27-31 *Jacob, why do you say, and Israel, why do you assert: "My way is hidden from the LORD, and my claim is ignored by my God"? Do you not know? Have you not heard? Yahweh is the everlasting God, the Creator of the whole earth. He never grows faint or weary; there is no limit to His understanding. He gives strength to the weary and strengthens the powerless. Youths may faint and grow weary, and young men stumble and fall, but those who trust in the LORD will renew their strength; they will soar on wings like eagles; they will run and not grow weary; they will walk and not faint.*

It is a common complaint - nobody understand me, nobody even knows I exist! Others claim they can have their hidden sins - nobody sees them, nobody is hurt. How foolish we are! Jacob and Israel are often used as a reference for the remnant, not the ethnic nation. The remnant, from every nation, has heard, knows, YHWH is the everlasting God! Recall those stupid gods we read about earlier? YHWH is not like that. He created all things and He does not get tired; His wisdom is limitless! The highest IQ known to man is empty and nothing compared to the wisdom of God.

And this holy God; One Who is not like us - He is set apart from us - He is our tender shepherd (verse 11). He gives strength to the weary and powerless - come unto me, Jesus

147

said, ALL who are weak and weary and I will give you rest! The young and powerful men of the world will stumble and fall - they will fade like grass and be blown away by the breath of God! But all who trust in Him will be renewed in strength, soaring like eagles, running and not growing weary, walking and not faint. Have you seen a man in his 70s and 80s who still on fire for the Lord, preaching and teaching the gospel with a fire in his belly that won't stop? This is the Lord's doing - He promised right here He would do it! - and it IS marvelous in our eyes!

Dear brothers and sisters - do not go quietly into the night. Cry out for mercy, for renewed strength to teach your grandkids about Jesus, to tell your neighbors about the glories of Christ. He who began a good work in you WILL BE faithful to bring it to completion.

Isaiah 41 - The Holy One of Israel Reigns!

Chapter 40 began a renewed focus on the glory of God as He reveals Himself to His people. Chapter 41 continues, with a triumphant proclamation of YHWH's power and glory in the judgment of the nations.

Isaiah 41:1 *Be silent before Me, islands! And let peoples renew their strength. Let them approach, then let them testify; let us come together for the trial.*

We see in the first verse the setting for this passage: it's a courtroom, where someone will be on trial and someone else will be the Judge. The One before Whom all people are to be silent is the Judge.

Isaiah 41:2-4 *Who has stirred him up from the east? He calls righteousness to his feet. The LORD hands nations over to him, and he subdues kings. He makes [them] like dust [with] his sword, like wind-driven stubble [with] his bow. He pursues them, going on safely, hardly touching the path with his feet. Who has performed and done [this], calling the*
148

generations from the beginning? I, Yahweh, am the first, and with the last—I am He.

Another person has entered the scene - has been stirred up from the east, who calls righteousness to his feet. YHWH hands nations over to him and He subdues kings, makes then like dust, drives them as stubble. He is hardly touched by the creation, calling generations into being. This is YHWH, the Alpha and Omega - God the Son!

Isaiah 41:5-7 *The islands see and are afraid, the whole earth trembles. They approach and arrive. Each one helps the other, and says to another, "Take courage!" The craftsman encourages the metalworker; the one who flattens with the hammer [supports] the one who strikes the anvil, saying of the soldering, "It is good." He fastens it with nails so that it will not fall over.*

The earth and all her peoples tremble at the sight of the Son. They try to encourage (give courage to) one another as they build their idols. Man loves to admire the work of his hands. God warned the infant Hebrew nation not to put their tools on the rocks of the altar they were building because they would pollute the altar (Exodus 20:25). There is only One who does not pollute what He touches; mankind is by nature full of sin and unable to do anything good. Making dumb gods is the height of man's rebellion as he shamelessly declares his allegiance to the work of his hands.

Isaiah 41:8-10 *But you, Israel, My servant, Jacob, whom I have chosen, descendant of Abraham, My friend—I brought you from the ends of the earth and called you from its farthest corners. I said to you: You are My servant; I have chosen you and not rejected you. Do not fear, for I am with you; do not be afraid, for I am your God. I will strengthen you; I will help you; I will hold on to you with My righteous right hand.*

In stark contrast to the people of the world, Israel - the servant of Jacob, the chosen One, descended from Abraham, the friend of God - has been brought from the ends of the earth.

I ask you, dear reader: who does the Bible describe in these terms, who is this Israel? Jacob was later named Israel, foreshadowing the true Israel of God, the Lord Jesus Christ! His servants are the saints. 1 Corinthians 4:1-2 *A person should consider us in this way: as servants of Christ and managers of God's mysteries. In this regard, it is expected of managers that each one [of them] be found faithful.* These are the true descendants of Abraham. Galatians 3:29 *And if you belong to Christ, then you are Abraham's seed, heirs according to the promise.* The saints are His friends. John 15:15 *I do not call you slaves anymore, because a slave doesn't know what his master is doing. I have called you friends, because I have made known to you everything I have heard from My Father.* And these are called from the four corners of the earth. Revelation 5:9 *And they sang a new song: You are worthy to take the scroll and to open its seals, because You were slaughtered, and You redeemed [people] for God by Your blood from every tribe and language and people and nation.*

Dear brothers and sisters - all we have that is worthwhile is because we have been redeemed by and united to Christ! God set His affection on people and done EVERYTHING necessary to bring them to Himself.

Isaiah 41:11-14 *Be sure that all who are enraged against you will be ashamed and disgraced; those who contend with you will become as nothing and will perish. You will look for those who contend with you, but you will not find them. Those who war against you will become absolutely nothing. For I, Yahweh your God, hold your right hand and say to you: Do not fear, I will help you. Do not fear, you worm Jacob, you men of Israel: I will help you— [this is] the LORD's declaration. Your Redeemer is the Holy One of Israel.*

God continues to encourage (give courage to) His people, assuring us that all who rage against us will come to nothing and perish. YHWH holds His people, He brings help to His own - though we are but worms. No mortal can withstand Him! This is the Lord's doing and it is marvelous in our eyes!

Isaiah 41:15-16 *See, I will make you into a sharp threshing board, new, with many teeth. You will thresh mountains and pulverize [them] and make hills into chaff. You will winnow them and a wind will carry them away, a gale will scatter them. But you will rejoice in the LORD; you will boast in the Holy One of Israel.*

A threshing board was a heavy wooden sledge with stones or iron teeth on the bottom side. It was dragged across sheaves of wheat to separate grain from chaff, winnowing the wheat. John declared that Jesus had His winnowing fork in His hand as he told the self-righteous Jews that they could not rest on their fleshly connection to Abraham. Those who are shown to be grain and not chaff will rejoice in YHWH and boast in the Holy One of Israel - the redeemer and advocate of all who believe.

Verses 17-20 continue the revelation of God's tender care for His own, is word pictures drawn from national Israel's history. All of this to be done *so that all may see and know, consider and understand, that the hand of the LORD has done this, the Holy One of Israel has created it."* (41:20)

The scene changes in verse 21, as court (alluded to in verse 1) is now in session. Isaiah 41:21 *"Submit your case,"* says the LORD. *"Present your arguments,"* says Jacob's King.

These people summoned are asked to testify in verses 22 & 23; judgment is rendered Isaiah 41:24 *Look, you are nothing and your work is worthless. Anyone who chooses you is detestable.*

Apart from Jesus, we can do nothing. These people who have not been redeemed are nothing, their work is worthless, their associates are detestable.

Another stark contrast as God declares, Isaiah 41:25 *I have raised up one from the north, and he has come, one from the east who invokes My name. He will march over rulers as if they were mud, like a potter who treads the clay.* This One who is raised up and invokes YHWH's name will march over kings as though they are mud, as a potter with his clay. Anybody else think of the potter mentioned in Romans 9? This idea of God who makes vessels from dirt or clay is replete in Scripture, always showing Him as the One who forms what He wants. His associates are vessels for honor, made as such by His hands. Jesus will rule the nations with a rod of iron as He judges the world.

Isaiah 41:26-29 *Who told about this from the beginning, so that we might know, and from times past, so that we might say: He is right? No one announced it, no one told it, no one heard your words. I was the first to say to Zion: Look! Here they are! And I gave a herald of good news to Jerusalem. When I look, there is no one; there is no counselor among them; when I ask them, they have nothing to say. Look, all of them are a delusion; their works are nonexistent; their images are wind and emptiness.*

Our chapter comes to an end with another passage reminiscent of the last few chapters of Job, as the people of the world are asked if they knew about these things from the beginning. But no one told of it, none had heard it. YHWH was the One to give good news to Jerusalem from Zion. But He looked and found no wise men among them; these people can say nothing in their defense when He queries them. They are in a delusion; their works are nothing; the idols are like the wind and empty.

Futility is the hallmark of natural man. Again - if you are not in Christ you are empty and driven before the wind; deluded and worthless. Behold the Lord Jesus - He is the good news, God become man to save sinners! Look unto Him and be saved - there is no other!

Isaiah 42 - A Tale of Two Servants.

This chapter continues with the theme of the preceding one - showing the provision of redemption in the Promised One, how He is to be praised by His people; and showing the depravity of man and his desperate need of redemption.

Isaiah 42:1-4 *This is My Servant; I strengthen Him, [this is] My Chosen One; I delight in Him. I have put My Spirit on Him; He will bring justice to the nations. He will not cry out or shout or make His voice heard in the streets. He will not break a bruised reed, and He will not put out a smoldering wick; He will faithfully bring justice. He will not grow weak or be discouraged until He has established justice on earth. The islands will wait for His instruction.*

We need to see a few things here: This Servant is the Chosen One of God, the One in Who God delights. Six times we read of what this Servant WILL DO, not try to do, not fail to do. He will bring justice to the nations; not open His mouth in His own defense; not break a bruised reed; will establish justice on the earth. Also, the Spirit of God has put on Him - just as the dove settled on Christ when He was baptized.

Some theologians say God speaks of national Israel here, but every sentence in this paragraph reveals that which is assigned to the Christ and which no mortal man or group of men can do. The next paragraph continues this description; again, a quote from God the Father.

Isaiah 42:5-9 *This is what God, Yahweh, says— who created the heavens and stretched them out, who spread out the earth and what comes from it, who gives breath to the people on it and life to those who walk on it— "I, Yahweh, have called You for a righteous [purpose], and I will hold You by Your hand. I will keep You and appoint You [to be] a covenant for the people [and] a light to the nations, in order to open blind eyes, to bring out prisoners from the dungeon, [and] those sitting in darkness from the prison house. I am Yahweh, that is My name; I will not give My glory to another or My praise to idols. The past events have indeed happened. Now I declare new events; I announce them to you before they occur."*

As if the people had forgotten who He is, YWHW reminds them He is the Creator, the One who gives life and breath to those who dwell on earth. About this Servant from the first 4 verses, YHWH says He was called for a righteous purpose and will be kept - the serpent will not gain victory! This Servant will be a covenant for the people, a light to the nations; He will give sight to the blind and free the prisoners. This is the work of the Messiah Who brings true Jubilee, not the Hebrew nation! These are things said about Him in the gospel accounts! John describes Jesus as the light that came into the world; Jesus told John the Baptist's disciples, when asked whether He was the Christ, to tell John that the blind were given sight along with other healings. Jesus cut the New Covenant with His blood - He is the covenant of redemption for His people. Those who were blind to the light of truth were given sight to see Him!

And the Father will not give His glory to another - He shares it with and gains it from the faithful Servant! No idols or deaf and mute gods can share in this. God declares what WILL happen - as He did in verses 1 - 4; He announces what will be, whereas man cannot even boast that he will have life when the sun comes up.

All of this talk from God about Himself and what His Servant WILL DO give the people of Israel every reason to praise Him.

Isaiah 42:10-13 *Sing a new song to the LORD; [sing] His praise from the ends of the earth, you who go down to the sea with all that fills it, you islands with your inhabitants. Let the desert and its cities shout, the settlements where Kedar dwells [cry aloud]. Let the inhabitants of Sela sing for joy; let them cry out from the mountaintops. Let them give glory to the LORD and declare His praise in the islands. The*

LORD advances like a warrior; He stirs up His zeal like a soldier. He shouts, He roars aloud, He prevails over His enemies.

People are said to "sing a new song" in Isaiah, Psalms, and Revelation. Nearly all these are songs about YHWH as the victorious warrior. Most of this paragraph calls out to everyone, from deserts to islands to mountains - let everyone sing for joy and give Him glory and praise! BECAUSE YHWH is a warrior Who roars loudly and, with zeal, He prevails over His enemies. Note this: even in this song, God is praised for being victorious over His enemies, not Israel's enemies. All of history is about God just as all of Scripture is about His faithful Servant.

Isaiah 42:14-17 *I have kept silent from ages past; I have been quiet and restrained Myself. [But now,] I will groan like a woman in labor, gasping breathlessly. I will lay waste mountains and hills and dry up all their vegetation. I will turn rivers into islands and dry up marshes. I will lead the blind by a way they did not know; I will guide them on paths they have not known. I will turn darkness to light in front of them and rough places into level ground. This is what I will do for them, and I will not forsake them. They will be turned back [and] utterly ashamed— those who trust in idols and say to metal-plated images: You are our gods!*

God answers them. He has been quiet in the past, only revealing Himself to a few. He restrained Himself so national Israel would not be consumed before the fullness of time. BUT NOW, He says, there will be noise of labor and He will judge the earth - laying waste the mountains and countryside. And He will lead the blind, turn their darkness to light; make their path straight and level. This echoes what the Servant WILL DO in the first part of this chapter, tying together God the Father with His faithful Servant. There is a remnant not forsaken as He judges the world. But those who trust in the work of their hands will turn back from Him in shame. *And because they did not think it worthwhile to acknowledge God,*

God delivered them over to a worthless mind to do what is morally wrong. They are filled with all unrighteousness, evil, greed, and wickedness. They are full of envy, murder, quarrels, deceit, and malice. They are gossips, slanderers, God-haters, arrogant, proud, boastful, inventors of evil, disobedient to parents, undiscerning, untrustworthy, unloving, and unmerciful. Although they know full well God's just sentence—that those who practice such things deserve to die—they not only do them, but even applaud others who practice them. (Romans 1:28-32)

God then turns His attention directly on the nation of Israel, addressing the unfaithful servant.

Isaiah 42:18-20 *Listen, you deaf! Look, you blind, so that you may see. Who is blind but My servant, or deaf like My messenger I am sending? Who is blind like [My] dedicated one, or blind like the servant of the LORD? Though seeing many things, you do not obey. Though [his] ears are open, he does not listen.*

These are the people Isaiah was sent to prophecy to; recall from chapter 6: *Go! Say to these people: Keep listening, but do not understand; keep looking, but do not perceive. Dull the minds of these people; deafen their ears and blind their eyes; otherwise they might see with their eyes and hear with their ears, understand with their minds, turn back, and be healed.* Though He had called them out of the dust of humanity to be His covenant people, they were blind, deaf, disobedient; unable to see or hear the truth told to them.

Isaiah 42:21 *The LORD was pleased, because of His righteousness, to magnify [His] instruction and make it glorious.*

We might wonder why God's prophets were told to do things that were rejected by people; we might wonder why we should proclaim the gospel when so many will not hear it. Here we see why: God is pleased to make His instructions known - write it large so all can see! - because His

156

instructions are glorious and He is righteous. This ought to be reason enough for us; I pray it is for me.

Isaiah 42:22-25 But this is a people plundered and looted, all of them trapped in holes or imprisoned in dungeons. They have become plunder with no one to rescue [them] and loot, with no one saying, "Give [it] back!" Who among you will pay attention to this? Let him listen and obey in the future. Who gave Jacob to the robber, and Israel to the plunderers? Was it not the LORD? Have we not sinned against Him? They were not willing to walk in His ways, and they would not listen to His instruction. So He poured out on Jacob His furious anger and the power of war. It surrounded him with fire, but he did not know [it]; it burned him, but he paid no attention.

But this people - those led into the promised land by Joshua and Caleb - were plundered and looted with no one to rescue them. Was there any among them that would learn a lesson, to do better next time? Because ethnic Israel was unfaithful as God's servant, they would not listen to His glorious teaching; He gave them over to be plundered. By way of Assyria and Babylon, YWHW poured out His fury and power on Jacob/Israel - but he paid no attention. There was no repentance among most of Israel, merely a longing to have comfort and safety again.

Brothers and sisters - this world is not our home and while we are to be thankful for comfort and safety, these cannot be our first priority. We must seek diligently to listen to God, study His Word, walk as obedient children in this wicked world - for His glory! For if we are His, we display His righteousness to the world as we do so.

Isaiah 43 - A Tale of Two Jacobs

This chapter is a good place to remind ourselves that Isaiah is communicating a vision given to him by God (see the first verse in this book). Visions from God are not normal prophecy, filled with images related in word more than with plain speech. In this chapter, we read of Jacob in the first section and the last section, with the promise of restoration of Israel in the middle. I believe these two Jacobs are different, as the context in each segment reveals.

The KJV labels the first segment "The Lord Comforts the Church with His Promises." I think they nailed it.

Isaiah 43:1-2 *Now this is what the LORD says— the One who created you, Jacob, and the One who formed you, Israel— "Do not fear, for I have redeemed you; I have called you by your name; you are Mine. I will be with you when you pass through the waters, and [when you pass] through the rivers, they will not overwhelm you. You will not be scorched when you walk through the fire, and the flame will not burn you.*

God calls Jacob and Israel by name, indicating familiarity. This could refer to either Jacob and Israel of the flesh, or the children of promise represented by these names. The second verse would also be either, using figurative language of protection for children of the flesh or literal protection for children of promise. We who are children of the promise will be protected from the fire that will burn everything that is not in union with Christ.

Isaiah 43:3-7 *For I Yahweh your God, the Holy One of Israel, and your Savior, give Egypt as a ransom for you, Cush and Seba in your place. Because you are precious in My sight and honored, and I love you, I will give people in exchange for you and nations instead of your life. Do not fear, for I am with you; I will bring your descendants from the east, and gather you from the west. I will say to the north: Give [them] up! and to the south: Do not hold [them] back! Bring My sons from far away, and My daughters from the ends of the earth— everyone called by My name and created for My glory. I have formed him; indeed, I have made him.*

YHWH is the only God, the Holy One of Israel - physical and spiritual - and the Savior of His people; providing temporal salvation from certain trails for fleshly people and eternal life for His spiritual people. YHWH gives Egypt, Cush, and Seba as ransoms for His people - this transaction is not recorded for the temporal nation of Israel, but all the nations of the earth will be judged as true Israel has been ransomed and redeemed from wrath. He tells us "do not fear for I am with you" just as in Matt 5:36 Jesus told His followers "*Do not fear, only believe.*" YHWH will bring His people from the four corners of the world; the restoration of national Israel after the Babylonian exile was not this expansive, but the gathering of the lost sheep is! All these sons and daughters have been called by His name - something we read about in Acts 15:14-18 *Simeon has reported how God first intervened to take from the Gentiles a people for His name. And the words of the prophets agree with this, as it is written: After these things I will return and rebuild David's fallen tent. I will rebuild its ruins and set it up again, so the rest of humanity may seek the Lord— even all the Gentiles who are called by My name, declares the Lord who does these things, known from long ago.*

Here Peter reveals that the rebuilding of David's tent (referring to Jerusalem) is taking place as people from every nation, tribe, and tongue - all four corners of the planet - are called by His name and brought into the His glorious kingdom of light.

This is why I agree with the KJV section title - Spiritual Jacob is in sight in this section. The next two verses support this view.

Isaiah 43:8-9 *Bring out a people who are blind, yet have eyes, and are deaf, yet have ears. All the nations are gathered together, and the peoples are assembled. Who among them can declare this, and tell us the former things? Let them present their witnesses to vindicate [themselves], so that people may hear and say, "It is true."*

Blind that see, deaf that hear - these are those Jesus brings into the sheepfold of God. We can declare the salvation of the Lord and the wickedness of who we used to be; we will be witnesses to the manifold mercy of God in Christ and other saints will hear and say, "It is true!" Again - the blind seeing is a mark of the Messiah having come into the world, as Jesus testified to the disciples of John the Baptist.

Isaiah 43:10-13 *"You are My witnesses"— [this is] the LORD's declaration— "and My servant whom I have chosen, so that you may know and believe Me and understand that I am He. No god was formed before Me, and there will be none after Me. I, I am Yahweh, and there is no other Savior but Me. I alone declared, saved, and proclaimed— and not some foreign god among you. So you are My witnesses"— [this is] the LORD's declaration— "and I am God. Also, from today on I am He [alone], and none can deliver from My hand. I act, and who can reverse it?"*

The redeemed are His witnesses, we are called to be so unto the ends of the earth, until the last sheep is brought home. He has chosen us so we would know Him and believe on Him. Then God tells us things about Him that unbelievers cannot understand: *"I, I am Yahweh, and there is no other Savior but Me. I alone declared, saved, and proclaimed— and not some foreign god among you. So you are My witnesses."* Verse 10 begins by declaring we are His witnesses and He wraps it up, after declaring Who He is, declaring we are His witnesses. To those who think the God of the Bible is like their gods, He will have none of it! There is none like Him! To those think Christianity is a "private religion" - Christ would have you know that He is God and ALL of His ransomed people ARE His witnesses!

The last verse in this segment is not well interpreted in the HCSB. I think the KJV is the most clear: *Yea, before the day was I am he; and there is none that can deliver out of my hand: I will work, and who shall let it?* It's not that God STARTED being God "today" - before day was created, God is. Fear not, only believe, for none can deliver anything or anyone from His hand and when He acts, no one can reverse it (I don't get the KJV - "who shall let it?" Here's what one KJV advocate says about it: This is one of the classic "archaisms" of the King James Version, where the English word "let" does not mean "allow" (as we now use the word) but almost the exact opposite. This particular English word was originally written and pronounced "lat" and was from the same Teutonic root as the word "late." Thus, to our Old English ancestors, it meant essentially "make late," or "hinder.").

The middle section describes how YHWH will deliver rebellious Israel. Isaiah 43:14-15 *This is what the LORD, your Redeemer, the Holy One of Israel says: Because of you, I will send to Babylon and bring all of them as fugitives, even the Chaldeans in the ships in which they rejoice. I am Yahweh, your Holy One, the Creator of Israel, your King.*

Isaiah tells Israel how things will move forward. This deliverance contains some temporal aspects - as the judgment on Babylon and Chaldea, even though Babylon is frequently used to portray the system of world. YHWH describes Himself as the Creator and King of Israel, leading me to think He is addressing national Israel in these verses. He created that nation as a people unto Himself and set Himself up as their King - until they clamored for a human king like the pagan nations around them.

Isaiah 43:16-21 *This is what the LORD says— who makes a way in the sea, and a path through surging waters, who brings out the chariot and horse, the army and the mighty one together (they lie down, they do not rise again; they are extinguished, quenched like a wick)—"Do not remember the past events, pay no attention to things of old. Look, I am about to do something new; even now it is coming. Do you not see it? Indeed, I will make a way in the wilderness, rivers in the desert. The animals of the field will honor Me, jackals and ostriches, because I provide water in the wilderness, and*

161

rivers in the desert, to give drink to My chosen people. The
people I formed for Myself will declare My praise.

And here we see YHWH changing the scope of His
deliverance, making a way in the sea that will destroy all who
oppose Him, reminding all of the destruction of the Egyptian
army. He tells Israel not to remember the past events, the old
way, for He is about to do something new. And here we have
it - the peace with nature He describes is a picture of the new
earth; not something that can happen on this earth which is
racked with sin. God provides living water for His chosen
people these will declare His praise! All who are given life in
Christ are made new creations - this is the something new He
mentioned. Another clue that this deliverance is spiritual.

In the last segment of this chapter, our attention is drawn to
the second Jacob, Israel of the flesh. Isaiah 43:22-24 *But*
Jacob, you have not called on Me, because, Israel, you have
become weary of Me. You have not brought Me your sheep
for burnt offerings or honored Me with your sacrifices. I have
not burdened you with offerings or wearied you with incense.
You have not bought Me aromatic cane with silver, or
satisfied Me with the fat of your sacrifices. But you have
burdened Me with your sins; you have wearied Me with your
iniquities.

Here we read the same complaints against the nation that
prophet after prophet lamented over. Isaiah warned them
about the abject failure of rote religion earlier in this book
(chapter 29), but the nation was fleshly and this is the way of
all flesh. They did not bring as offerings their best, but they
brought what they wouldn't miss. None of this religious
practice was acceptable to God they were BURDENSOME
and WEARISOME to Him. Dear reader - do you ever
consider or wonder if your worship is pleasing to God or not?
It is a fearful thing to bring to him worship that burdensome
and wearisome.

Isaiah 43:25-28 *It is I who sweep away your transgressions for My own sake and remember your sins no more. Take Me to court; let us argue our case together. State your [case], so that you may be vindicated. Your first father sinned, and your mediators have rebelled against Me. So I defiled the officers of the sanctuary, and set Jacob apart for destruction and Israel for abuse.*

Here we see that forgiveness of sin is for the glory of God, not primarily for our benefit. We do not comprehend His holiness if we think our redemption is first for ourselves. To sweep away transgressions by pouring out His wrath on His Son is demonstrating the enormity of our sin as rebellion against God. His name and His glory must be maintained and that is a higher priority than our salvation.

We return the court room, where Jacob is told to take God to court! He is state his case so he might be vindicated. His trouble is compound - his first father (likely the first Jacob, later named Israel) sinned (it was his nature) and all the priests that served over the years rebelled against God - who can stand? Jacob's case fails, God put down (defiled) the priests and set the two kingdoms apart for destruction.

No escape from the justice of God's court room. God is able to raise up from rocks sons who will worship Him. Let no one put confidence in the flesh - your parents nor your family history can anything to help you. National Israel did not learn this lesson that the kingdom of God was taken from them and given to a nation bearing fruit. Those who believe in Christ are children of Abraham according to promise. Are you in that nation?

Isaiah 44 - Gospel preview.

The 44th chapter of Isaiah is easily divided into three section. The difficulty comes in rightly seeing what the true meaning of each of these three sections is. I see clues in the first section, where God uses terms of tenderness that a parent has towards a child. Ethnic Israel knew God as King (yes, they failed there) but did not in any of their history see Him as Father. This leads me to think the main message of the first part is comfort to the elect. John Gill agrees, seeing the elect of ethnic Israel being the people.

Isaiah 44:1-2 *And now listen, Jacob My servant, Israel whom I have chosen. This is the word of the LORD your Maker who formed you from the womb; He will help you: Do not fear; Jacob is My servant; I have chosen Jeshurun.*

This "forming you from the womb" is tenderness that is attached to His eternally elect, as David knew this (Psalms 51) and Jesus used similar language when He desires to gather the children of Israel as a hen does her chicks. The name Jeshurun is a term of endearment (seen in Deut 32 and 33). This may be God speaking to elect ethnic Jews, but his promise in the following verses applies to all who know Him as Lord.

Isaiah 44:3-5 *For I will pour water on the thirsty land and streams on the dry ground; I will pour out My Spirit on your descendants and My blessing on your offspring. They will sprout among the grass like poplars by flowing streams. This one will say, 'I am the LORD's'; another will call [himself] by the name of Jacob; still another will write on his hand, 'The LORD's,' and name [himself] by the name of Israel."*

National Israel didn't experience this type of earthly renewal; agricultural metaphors were common to describe the blessings of YHWH on His people because they could understand them. The redeemed of God WILL sprout and grow strong - recall what took root in the good soil (Mark 4). The flowing stream points to the river of life in Rev 22. And with one saying "I am the Lord's" and another calling himself Jacob, and another write on himself that he is the Lord's and is Israel - all these echo realities found only in the New Covenant! Jeremiah says in that covenant that everyone will know the Lord and will not have to tell his neighbor "know the Lord!" All who are in Christ are Israel for He is the Israel of God, and we are all children of Abraham according to the promise.

This next section starts out with a wonderful declaration of who God is, which is well received by all who are reconciled to Him.

Isaiah 44:6-8 *This is what the LORD, the King of Israel and its Redeemer, the LORD of Hosts, says: I am the first and I am the last. There is no God but Me. Who, like Me, can announce [the future]? Let him say so and make a case before Me, since I have established an ancient people. Let these gods declare the coming things, and what will take place. Do not be startled or afraid. Have I not told you and declared it long ago? You are my witnesses! Is there any God but Me? There is no [other] Rock; I do not know any.*

Hear what YHWH has to say! He is the King, redeemer, Lord of the hosts of heaven; He is the first and last. There is no God but Him - we will have commentary on those other gods shortly. As He demanded of Job, He demands of His people here; who among you is like Me? God is the one who called national Israel out of the dust bin of humanity and kept them until the fullness of time. He declared it long ago and has done it; the children of ethnic Israel are witnesses! These other gods cannot declare a thing. So do not be afraid, only believe (Matt 5:36).

Isaiah 44:9-11 *All who make idols are nothing, and what they treasure does not profit. Their witnesses do not see or know [anything], so they will be put to shame. Who makes a god or casts a metal image for no profit? Look, all its worshipers will be put to shame, and the craftsmen are humans. They all will assemble and stand; they all will be startled and put to shame.*

In the segment, man's religion is examined. Those who make idols are nothing, treasuring rust, with witnesses who are as blind and dumb as their gods. Shame is their lot!

Isaiah 44:12-20 *The ironworker labors over the coals, shapes the idol with hammers, and works it with his strong arm. Also he grows hungry and his strength fails; he doesn't drink water and is faint. The woodworker stretches out a measuring line, he outlines it with a stylus; he shapes it with chisels and outlines it with a compass. He makes it according to a human likeness, like a beautiful person, to dwell in a temple. He cuts down cedars for his use, or he takes a cypress or an oak. He lets it grow strong among the trees of the forest. He plants a laurel, and the rain makes it grow. It serves as fuel for man. He takes some of it and warms himself; also he kindles a fire and bakes bread; he even makes it into a god and worships it; he makes an idol from it and bows down to it. He burns half of it in a fire, and he roasts meat on that half. He eats the roast and is satisfied. He warms himself and says, "Ah! I am warm, I see the blaze." He makes a god or his idol with the rest of it. He bows down to it and worships; He prays to it, "Save me, for you are my god." Such people do not comprehend and cannot understand, for He has shut their eyes so they cannot see, and their minds so they cannot understand. No one reflects, no one has the perception or insight to say, "I burned half of it in the fire, I also baked bread on its coals, I roasted meat and ate. I will make something detestable with the rest of it, and I will bow down to a block of wood." He feeds on ashes. [His] deceived mind has led him astray, and he cannot deliver himself, or say, "Isn't there a lie in my right hand?"*

This long paragraph is God's commentary on the futility of vain worship of the work of man. How weary the man is who spends his time and energy on worthless things. Note how the carpenter grows wood that he uses, in part, for good things and, the other part, to make a god for himself. What does YHWH say about them? They do not comprehend and cannot understand. Why is this? Because God has shut their eyes and minds so they cannot see or understand. This should remind us of the people Isaiah was sent to prophecy to - those would have eyes but be unable to see; have ears but be unable to hear; and dull minds that cannot understand. Natural man in inclined to self-worship. Those who hide from general revelation are shut up so they will not be able see and understand the gospel. Jesus did this by speaking in parables, so those who were not supposed to understand would not.

Idolatry comes in many forms and is NOT restricted to worshiping stone and wood idols. I've mentioned large barns several times in this walk through Isaiah; wealth is an idol for many and they know it not, just as that farmer did not. Dear brothers and sisters, let us be brutally honest with ourselves and ask God to reveal any and all idols we may have - and grant repentance while it is yet today.

Isaiah 44:21-23 *Remember these things, Jacob, and Israel, for you are My servant; I formed you, you are My servant; Israel, you will never be forgotten by Me. I have swept away your transgressions like a cloud, and your sins like a mist. Return to Me, for I have redeemed you. Rejoice, heavens, for the LORD has acted; shout, depths of the earth. Break out into singing, mountains, forest, and every tree in it. For the LORD has redeemed Jacob, and glorifies Himself through Israel.*

Here, God returns to tender language to remind His elect to avoid idolatry because they belong to Him. What is said here cannot be said to apply to the whole of national Israel - their transgressions (this word applies specifically to breaking the law) are swept away like a cloud; forgiven. These people have been redeemed - not just from exile in Babylon but from sin and hell. This is cause for all - heavens, mountains, forests, and depths of the earth - to rejoice in God for He has redeemed His people and glorified Himself in them.

Isaiah 44:24-28 *This is what the LORD, your Redeemer who formed you from the womb, says: I am Yahweh, who made everything; who stretched out the heavens by Myself; who alone spread out the earth; who destroys the omens of the false prophets and makes fools of diviners; who confounds the wise and makes their knowledge foolishness; who confirms the message of His servant and fulfills the counsel of His messengers; who says to Jerusalem, "She will be inhabited," and to the cities of Judah, "They will be rebuilt," and I will restore her ruins; who says to the depths of the sea, "Be dry," and I will dry up your rivers; who says to Cyrus, "My shepherd, he will fulfill all My pleasure" and says to Jerusalem, "She will be rebuilt," and of the temple, "Its foundation will be laid."*

Our chapter ends with a reminder of why YHWH is worthy of worship. He returns to the tender parental language of the first part of the chapter. He is truly the Lord of all, Creator of all, Judge of all. He confounds and destroys the false prophets; He confirms what He has told His people, reminding them Jerusalem will be rebuilt and re-inhabited. God will do these things, even using a pagan king to do His pleasure in the temporal rebuilding of Jerusalem. John Gill advises that this reference to Cyrus *makes way for a particular prophecy concerning him in the next chapter.*

Remind yourselves of Who God is, in Christ is our assurance of the salvation that He has purchased for us. Walk humbly with the saints, knowing each of us has been gifted to serve one another. None of us lives to himself and serves God; we are to live unto the Lord Christ Jesus and that is the only way we can be fruitful.

Isaiah 45 - God raises up a king.

Chapter 44 of Isaiah should include the first 8 verses of chapter 45, as the end of 44 reveals God's choice of Cyrus to make the restoration of Jerusalem happen and the first part of 45 explains how He will do this.

Chapter 44 ends (vs 28) with God declaring He would use Cyrus for His good pleasure, not Cyrus', to rebuild Jerusalem and the temple therein. Our current chapter begins:

Isaiah 45:1 *The LORD says this to Cyrus, His anointed, whose right hand I have grasped to subdue nations before him, to disarm kings, to open the doors before him and the gates will not be shut:*

The One True God is Creator of all and Lord/King/Judge over all. As He kept Abimelech (king of Philistia) from sinning by taking Sarah as his wife, so He calls Cyrus (king of Persia) His right hand for the task at hand. Cyrus will subdue nations, disarm kings, open doors and keep gates open - all for the purpose of rebuilding Jerusalem and its temple. Is there any doubt Proverb 21:1 is true: *A king's heart is like streams of water in the LORD's hand: He directs it wherever He chooses.* Let those who hold high office in our day be not deceived - God is not mocked, He is not asleep; His winnowing fork is in His hand.

Isaiah 45:2-4 *I will go before you and level the uneven places; I will shatter the bronze doors and cut the iron bars in two. I will give you the treasures of darkness and riches from secret places, so that you may know that I, Yahweh, the God of Israel call you by your name. I call you by your name, because of Jacob My servant and Israel My chosen one. I give a name to you, though you do not know Me.*

Here it begins, God explaining to one who knows Him not how things will be laid out. All of these actions are similar to how God describes His provision for Israel - think back to the description of how they would take Canaan. YHWH tells Cyrus that He will make his way smooth, breaking down the barriers, giving him treasure from places Cyrus would never know; He does all this so Cyrus would know Who called him by name to be used in this glorious way. He chose Israel not because they were great; He chose them because He is great.

So with Cyrus - a man we might not know if he hadn't been chosen by YHWH, the God of Israel.

Isaiah 45:5-8 *I am Yahweh, and there is no other; there is no God but Me. I will strengthen you, though you do not know Me, so that all may know from the rising of the sun to its setting that there is no one but Me. I am Yahweh, and there is no other. I form light and create darkness, I make success and create disaster; I, Yahweh, do all these things. "Heavens, sprinkle from above, and let the skies shower righteousness. Let the earth open up so that salvation will sprout and righteousness will spring up with it. I, Yahweh, have created it."*

YHWH drives home the point about Who He is; Cyrus doesn't know Him so God is making it clear. Reminds me of Paul on Mars Hill in Act 17, telling the Oprah Winfrey crowd of his day about the "unknown god" who really is the Lord of all things, seeing as how He created all things and does not need anything that human hands can give. Here YHWH explains that He is creator, Who creates light and darkness, makes success and disaster, causes the sun to rise and set, tells the rain where to fall, and creates righteousness; THERE IS NO ONE BUT YHWH!

Ponder this. We all have the tendency to think too highly of ourselves and not highly enough of God. We tend to humanize God in our mind so we can live with ourselves. If you claim Christ, make it your goal to see Him as He is, worthy of worship and beyond all you can imagine. Thanos is a gnat! Loki was a puny god. All of these tales tend to "help" us reduce God into one of these lesser things. He will have none of it and neither should we! These fantasy gods ought to remind us of the eternal truth that the One true God is the only God. The most fantastic god of man's imagination is less than a gnat. The nations are dust on His scales (Isaiah 40:15)!

Isaiah 45:9-10 *Woe to the one who argues with his Maker— one clay pot among many. Does clay say to the one forming it, 'What are you making?' Or does your work [say], 'He has no hands'? How absurd is the one who says to [his] father, 'What are you fathering?' or to [his] mother, 'What are you giving birth to?'*

We have a change in scenery, leaving Cyrus behind and picking up a warning to ALL who do not humble themselves before their maker. Woe! is pronounced on those who argue with Him. When you or I complain that life is unfair, unjust, or plain wrong, we are judging God's rule of providence - arguing with our Maker. The familiar metaphor of potter and clay is used to drive the point home: we have NO RIGHT to question or argue with Him. I like the wording of the HCSB here - how ABSURD for a child to question his birth, as if his parents didn't do it right.

Isaiah 45:11-13 *This is what the LORD, the Holy One of Israel and its Maker, says: "Ask Me what is to happen to My sons, and instruct Me about the work of My hands. I made the earth, and created man on it. It was My hands that stretched out the heavens, and I commanded all their host. I have raised him up in righteousness, and will level all roads for him. He will rebuild My city, and set My exiles free, not for a price or a bribe," says the LORD of Hosts.*

YHWH builds on verse 10, turning it around, as that the Holy One of Israel, the One who is its Maker, asking Israel to tell Him about His work. He is the Creator of all things and all people; He stretched out the heavens and will one day roll them up like a scroll! He has raised up Cyrus to rebuild His city and He is telling Israel not to bark at the idea of a pagan king doing them a favor. All of this is the Lord's doing - is it marvelous in your eyes? It should be!

I'll stop here and pick the second half of this chapter later. Think about what God has revealed here in this passage. He is so far more than we can comprehend, God help us to not imagine any less than we're able.

Isaiah 45, part 2: One Savior

Isaiah 45:14 *This is what the LORD says: The products of Egypt and the merchandise of Cush and the Sabeans, men of stature, will come over to you and will be yours; they will follow you, they will come over in chains and bow down to you. They will confess to you: God is indeed with you, and there is no other; there is no other God.*

The God of Israel is the only God; everything else that claims deity is the work of man's hands and is a fraud. In this verse, God is addressing the elect among the nation of Israel - at no time in her history did the nations come to national Israel in this fashion, but at the end of time all nations will be in chains and the redeemed will participate in judging them (1 Cor 6:2).

Isaiah 45:15-17 *Yes, You are a God who hides Himself, God of Israel, Savior. All of them are put to shame, even humiliated; the makers of idols go in humiliation together. Israel will be saved by the LORD with an everlasting salvation; you will not be put to shame or humiliated for all eternity.*

This appears to be Isaiah speaking, saying the God who saves Israel hides Himself. By this, he means that God cannot be truly discerned by natural man; for general revelation is merely in part and God must open eyes and ears before mortal man sees Him. All who rebel against Him will be humiliated along with idolaters. In another stark contrast, elect Israel will be redeemed with an everlasting salvation no shame or humiliation for those who have refuge in Christ.

Isaiah 45:18-19 *For this is what the LORD says— God is the Creator of the heavens. He formed the earth and made it. He established it; He did not create it to be empty, [but] formed*

172

it to be inhabited— "I am Yahweh, and there is no other. I have not spoken in secret, somewhere in a land of darkness. I did not say to the descendants of Jacob: Seek Me in a wasteland. I, Yahweh, speak truthfully; I say what is right."

YHWH declares that He is the Creator of heaven and earth, with the full intention that it would be full of life. Consider what this means. Think of the most complex, intricate mechanism man has "created" and compare with the glorious expanse and complexity of the universe! I put "created" in quotes because man can create nothing - everything man invents or develops is nothing more than rearranging what God has created. An old joke has a Texas A&M scientist working in the lab to "create" life and he succeeds! He shakes his fist at the heavens and tells God all about it. God condescends to talk with the creature and asks him to explain how he did it. "First thing I did," he said, "was to grab a little dirt." "Oh no!" said YHWH. "You must make your own dirt!" That's the point - God formed, created, and established the universe with the plan to fill it full of life. Ex nihilo!

There is NO ONE like unto Him, all the prophets of Baal are less than dust. All creation testifies of His glory, this was not done in secret, not in a corner of darkness as many cult religions do. He does not tell His people to go into the desert and find Him gazing at their navels; He calls His people to come to Him directly - this is the only true religion.

Isaiah 45:20-24a *Come, gather together, and draw near, you fugitives of the nations. Those who carry their wooden idols, and pray to a god who cannot save, have no knowledge. Speak up and present [your case]— yes, let them take counsel together. Who predicted this long ago? Who announced it from ancient times? Was it not I, Yahweh? There is no other God but Me, a righteous God and Savior; there is no one except Me. Turn to Me and be saved, all the ends of the earth. For I am God, and there is no other. By Myself I have sworn; Truth has gone from My mouth, a word that will not be revoked: Every knee will bow to Me, every tongue will swear allegiance. It will be said to Me: Righteousness and strength is only in the LORD.*

This passage is a call to the elect from all four corners of the earth, fugitives of every nation. Those not called have no saving knowledge and continue in their idolatry. They are commanded to present themselves, take counsel, and speak up for themselves; another court room scene for the judgment that will take place. God taunts these reprobates, asking them who prophesied these events, announced them in ancient times?

Then He answers them: It was I, YHWH! There is no God but YHWH; He is the righteous Savior and (in case you missed it) there is no one other than Him! *Turn to Me and be saved, all the ends of the earth* - His saving call goes out to all the elect. He has sworn by an irrevocable oath that every knee will bow and every tongue confess allegiance to Him; for in Him ONLY is righteousness and strength. Now it's a fact that on judgment day every deed by man is judged (Matt 16:27) and every one will bow and confess Christ as Lord. Paul cited this verse this to describe the Lord Jesus in two of his letters, Phil 2:11 (every tongue should confess that Jesus Christ is Lord, to the glory of God the Father) and Rom 14:11 (speaking of Christ: *For it is written: As I live, says the Lord, every knee will bow to Me, and every tongue will give praise to God*). But on that great and terrible day, only the redeemed will confess allegiance to Him. This is how we know this part of Isaiah is about spiritual redemption, not geographical redemption.

Isaiah 45:24b-25 *All who are enraged against Him will come to Him and be put to shame. All the descendants of Israel will be justified and find glory through the LORD.*

A final stark contrast as this chapter closes: All who war against God will come to Him and be ruined. All the descendants of Israel (according to the promise, not the flesh) will be justified and be glorified in the Lord. Again, it seems like Paul was thinking of this when he wrote this: *For while we were still helpless, at the appointed moment, Christ died for the ungodly. For rarely will someone die for a just person—though for a good person perhaps someone might even dare to die. But God proves His own love for us in that while we were still sinners, Christ died for us! Much more then, since we have now been declared righteous by His blood, we will be saved through Him from wrath. For if, while we were enemies, we were reconciled to God through the death of His Son, [then how] much more, having been reconciled, will we be saved by His life! And not only that, but we also rejoice in God through our Lord Jesus Christ. We have now received this reconciliation through Him.* (Romans 5:6-11)

We have no boast in anything we've done or in our person. We were part of those who are enraged against God. But if you are in Christ, you are one He called to and justified and will glorify. Oh dear brothers and sisters - resist thinking you chose God or that He chose you because He saw something of value in you. We were helpless - unable to help ourselves; we were His enemies - thinking we didn't need His grace. But He has declared us righteous because Christ died for us - not because we've done anything to help our cause. Rejoice in Christ, boast of Him! Jesus is Lord of all and He ALONE save sinners from the wrath that is certainly coming for those who are not at peace with the Father.

Isaiah 46 - The Great I AM.

Building on chapter 45's ending section on Salvation by God alone, chapter 46 is a treatise on how God is not like anything or anyone else. He has made these assertions before, but we need to be reminded of them because we tend to make much of self and little of God. Peter opens his second letter with a description of the characteristics of Christians and then says, *Therefore I will always remind you about these things, even though you know them and are established in the truth you have.* (2 Peter 1:12) So let's bear with Isaiah as he reminds us of what we've already been taught.

Isaiah 46:1-2 *Bel crouches; Nebo cowers. Their idols are consigned to beasts and cattle. The [images] you carry are loaded, as a burden for the weary [animal]. The gods cower; they crouch together; they are not able to rescue the burden, but they themselves go into captivity.*

"Bel" is likely a reference to the chief god of Babylon, Marduk. Nebo was Marduk's son - the god of wisdom and scribes. The idols made to represent these demonic gods would have been large and heavy, hence the need of animals who were wore down from transporting them. Note God's perspective of these gods: they cower and crouch in fear, they cannot bear the burden of the idols but are carried away by whoever conquers Babylon.

Isaiah 46:3-4 *Listen to Me, house of Jacob, all the remnant of the house of Israel, who have been sustained from the womb, carried along since birth. I will be the same until [your] old age, and I will bear [you] up when you turn gray. I have made [you], and I will carry [you]; I will bear and save [you].*

YHWH now turns His attention to the elect in ethnic Israel, the remnant of Jacob and Israel - those whom He had sustained from conception (actually, from before the foundation of the world!) and carried them along in His protection. He does not change, He is the faithful One! As I've grown older and my beard turned gray, I like this verse more. God will bear us up when we are weak (even when we are young and strong, we are weak!); He made us, He will carry us (no mundane beasts of burden!); He will save us! This is all of God - doing what no man or god of man can do. And it is marvelous in our eyes!

Isaiah 46:5-7 *Who will you compare Me or make Me equal to? Who will you measure Me with, so that we should be like each other? Those who pour out their bags of gold and weigh out silver on scales— they hire a goldsmith and he makes it into a god. Then they kneel and bow down to it. They lift it to their shoulder and bear it along; they set it in its place, and there it stands; it does not budge from its place. They cry out to it but it doesn't answer; it saves no one from his trouble.*

Here we see the futility of idol worship, which goes way beyond the idols described here. These are examples from history, idols that folk were used to seeing and hearing about. In our day, we don't call them idols, but we have standard of living, spouse, kids, dogs, motorcycles - all sorts of acceptable things that tend to take up space they aren't meant to! As it was with Baal, idols made of gold or other things within creation tend to be expensive in more ways than one and they cannot bear their own load. These lesser things cannot hear, cannot speak, cannot save anyone from trouble. YHWH, on the other hand, hears all things, spoke the universe into existence, and saves people from their sin!

Isaiah 46:8-10 *Remember this and be brave; take it to heart, you transgressors! Remember what happened long ago, for I am God, and there is no other; [I am] God, and no one is like Me. I declare the end from the beginning, and from long ago what is not yet done, saying: My plan will take place, and I will do all My will.*

Short and simple - remember these things about God, take them to heart, and be brave - fear not, only believe! When the women went to the tomb and found it empty, Luke's account reveals the angels of God telling them to remember what Jesus had spoken to them; and they remembered His words! (Luke 24:1-8). We will be prone to fear and anxiety if we do not remember what God has spoken to us. He alone is God, everything else is a mere god. No one is like Him - one of the problems ethnic Israel had was to forget what God was really like. Forgetting this makes falling into sin all the easier. They engaged in a long list of sin; at the end of which, we read, *These things you have done, and I have been silent; you thought that I was one like yourself. But now I rebuke you and lay the charge before you.* (Psalm 50:21, ESV) Bear in mind what you know to be true about God - it will help keep one holy and humble.

God declares the end from the beginning, while we cannot even say we'll live and go a town and conduct business tomorrow unless God wills it. Without comparison to anything in creation, the Creator plans it and does it. His will is certain; He will do ALL His will. I cannot see how any man can think himself able to "ask Jesus into his heart" when - not only is natural man unable to do anything good - natural man does not have the will to make anything happen (James 4:13-15). Unless God wills it, it cannot be done!

Isaiah 46:11-13 *I call a bird of prey from the east, a man for My purpose from a far country. Yes, I have spoken; so I will also bring it about. I have planned it; I will also do it. Listen to me, you hardhearted, far removed from justice: I am bringing My justice near; it is not far away, and My salvation will not delay. I will put salvation in Zion, My splendor in Israel.*

The note in my study Bible says the bird of prey is Cyrus; those with an earthly hermeneutic might agree. I rather think of this passage, among others: Revelation 19:17-18 *Then I saw an angel standing on the sun, and he cried out in a loud voice, saying to all the birds flying high overhead, "Come, gather together for the great supper of God, so that you may eat the flesh of kings, the flesh of commanders, the flesh of mighty men, the flesh of horses and of their riders, and the flesh of everyone, both free and slave, small and great."* These birds of prey are God's judgment on the world - the people described are those mentioned in Rev 6:15 who wanted the mountains to fall on them to hide them from the wrath of the Lamb. While Cyrus was called and served God's purpose in the shadowlands, the light of eternity reveals a different scene.

178

A warning to those who consider Him not, who trust in the works of their hands and their own wisdom rather than trust in God's judgment. His justice is coming, the birds will eat the flesh of His enemies, no matter how strong or powerful they are. Salvation is of the Lord! Those in Zion will be saved - His glory and splendor will be displayed in Israel! The remnant will glorify the Son on that day!

Hebrews 4:6-7 *Since it remains for some to enter it, and those who formerly received the good news did not enter because of disobedience, again, He specifies a certain day—today—speaking through David after such a long time, as previously stated: Today, if you hear His voice, do not harden your hearts.*

Isaiah 47 - God's Judgment on Babylon.

Once again, I think the KJV editors had a better grasp on the main theme of the chapter. The HCSB and ESV have The Fall or Humiliation of Babylon. God's judgment is the cause of the fall or humiliation and it's better for us to see Him as the reason these things happen.

Isaiah 47:1-4 *Go down and sit in the dust, Virgin Daughter Babylon. Sit on the ground without a throne, Daughter Chaldea! For you will no longer be called pampered and spoiled. Take millstones and grind meal; remove your veil, strip off [your] skirt, bare your thigh, wade through the streams. Your nakedness will be uncovered, and your shame will be exposed. I will take vengeance; I will spare no one. The Holy One of Israel is our Redeemer; Yahweh of Hosts is His name.*

Babylon is often used in Scripture to depict the system of the world; but Babylon was a real nation. This is the pattern of types and anti-types; contrary to metaphors, types are always actual, real historical things or people. In this chapter, it's the type, the nation of Babylon that is being judged by God.

Here, Babylon is mockingly called a virgin daughter who is told to sit on the ground. Mighty Babylon the great will be humiliated, no longer treated like royalty but required to work the mills. No longer mighty and ruling in luxury, Babylon will be unveiled, stripped naked, and exposed for all to see. None will be spared. Chaldea was a tribe in southern Babylon that spoke Aramaic that ruled the nation from 626 - 586 BC. All that happens is because the Holy One of Israel - redeemer of sinners, YHWH of Hosts has spoken it. Nothing is "left to chance."

Isaiah 47:5-7 *Daughter Chaldea, sit in silence and go into darkness. For you will no longer be called mistress of kingdoms. I was angry with My people; I profaned My possession, and I placed them under your control. You showed them no mercy; you made your yoke very heavy on the elderly. You said, 'I will be the mistress forever.' You did not take these things to heart or think about their outcome.*

The powerful tribe of Babylon is told to sit in silence in darkness; no longer mistress of kingdoms, she is brought low, taken prisoner. God was angry with His people, ethnic Israel; He ordered the pagan nations to punish them, placing His covenant people under their rule for the chastisement He deemed necessary. Babylon went "above and beyond" the mission, displaying natural man's depravity without restraint. Babylon imposed heavy burdens on the old people in Israel, thinking she would remain the mistress of kingdoms always. Kings were known for having many wives and mistresses and concubines. A good mistress would be well taken care of. But Babylon did not take to heart what YHWH had told her not considered the consequences of her cruelty.

Isaiah 47:8-10 *So now hear this, lover of luxury, who sits securely, who says to herself, 'I exist, and there is no one else. I will never be a widow or know the loss of children.' These two things will happen to you suddenly, in one day: loss of children and widowhood. They will happen to you in their entirety, in spite of your many sorceries and the potency of your spells. You were secure in your wickedness; you said, 'No one sees me.' Your wisdom and knowledge led you astray. You said to yourself, 'I exist, and there is no one else.'*

Deeper into the humiliation of Babylon as she sees herself as one who deserves luxury, is alone wise and powerful, and will never suffer loss. God demands to be heard, even of this stiff-necked nation. Two things will take place suddenly - the loss of the two things Babylon thought she would never loose. None of Babylon's magic, no false security in luxury could withstand the judgment and loss delivered by the Holy One of Israel. Babylon thought she could hide her sins, being wise in her own estimation, thinking she was above the fray of the "common folk." We know from Scripture that nothing is hid from God, that none are wise that trust in self. In the ancient near east, being a woman without husband or children was a most vulnerable person. Even as the most powerful nation in the world at one time, Babylon was as a childless widow in contrast to almighty Creator and Judge, YHWH of Hosts!

Isaiah 47:11-15 *But disaster will happen to you; you will not know how to avert it. And it will fall on you, but you will be unable to ward it off. Devastation will happen to you suddenly and unexpectedly. So take your stand with your spells and your many sorceries, which you have wearied yourself with from your youth. Perhaps you will be able to succeed; perhaps you will inspire terror! You are worn out with your many consultations. So let them stand and save you— the astrologers, who observe the stars, who predict monthly what will happen to you. Look, they are like stubble; fire burns them up. They cannot deliver themselves from the power of the flame. This is not a coal for warming themselves, or a fire to sit beside! This is what they are to you— those who have wearied you and have traded with you from your youth— each wanders on his own way; no one can save you.*

When God moves against a people, nothing they can do will avert it - no magic, no human goodness, no "life coaches". Judgment is coming and it will go according to God's predetermined plan. It will come quickly and when the people think all is well - when preachers preach "peace, peace!" where there is no peace.

God taunts Babylon, telling her to gather all her magic (that were wearisome to keep up) and try to stand and succeed. Gather the astrologers and watch their charts and prophecies burn. No demonic magic, no pagan religion, no self-important people can deliver themselves from God's judgment fire! God's judgment is not something man can handle, like a campfire. When judgment comes, each of these powerful men who could provide no aid will abandon Babylon, each seeing to his own interests - unable and disinterested in saving Babylon.

Now let's see how this type is fulfilled at the end of the age.

Revelation 18:9-11 *The kings of the earth who have committed sexual immorality and lived luxuriously with her will weep and mourn over her when they see the smoke of her burning. They will stand far off in fear of her torment, saying: Woe, woe, the great city, Babylon, the mighty city! For in a single hour your judgment has come.* The merchants of the earth will also weep and mourn over her, because no one buys their merchandise any longer—Revelation 18:15-20 *The merchants of these things, who became rich from her, will stand far off in fear of her torment, weeping and mourning, saying: Woe, woe, the great city, dressed in fine linen, purple, and scarlet, adorned with gold, precious stones, and pearls, for in a single hour such fabulous wealth was destroyed! And every shipmaster, seafarer, the sailors, and all who do business by sea, stood far off as they watched the smoke from her burning and kept crying out: "Who is like the great city?" They threw dust on their heads and kept crying out, weeping, and mourning: Woe, woe, the great city, where all those who have ships on the sea became rich from her wealth, for in a single hour she was destroyed. Rejoice over her, heaven, and you saints, apostles, and prophets, because God has executed your judgment on her!*

Verse 21 tells us a mighty angel threw a large millstone into the sea (which represents the people of the world). Recall how Babylon was told to pick up a millstone in verse 2?

Everything we've read in Isaiah 47 regarding the actual nation of Babylon took place in history, and foreshadowed God's judgment on the system of the world.

Brothers and sisters, we cannot afford to deceive ourselves, thinking we can hide things from God, thinking we will always sit in the lap of luxury, that we'll know when bad times are coming. Whether it's the stock market, disease, or death - we do not know what tomorrow holds. If we know who holds tomorrow in His hands, we will be fine. This world is not our home - let's not act like it is. That's how Babylon behaved.

1 Peter 2:16-17 *As God's slaves, [live] as free people, but don't use your freedom as a way to conceal evil. Honor everyone. Love the brotherhood. Fear God. Honor the Emperor.*

Trust the King - not your ability to follow Him.

Isaiah 48 - Israel Refined for God's Glory.

This time, the ESV gives us the best view of the text with its title. The HCSB has "Israel Must Leave Babylon" and the KJV has too many words to be repeated here. God will refine Israel for His glory - that is what we will see.

Isaiah 48:1-2 *Listen to this, house of Jacob— those who are called by the name Israel and have descended from Judah, who swear by the name of Yahweh and declare the God of Israel, [but] not in truth or righteousness. For they are named after the Holy City, and lean on the God of Israel; His name is Yahweh of Hosts.*

Ethnic Israel had a long-standing problem of putting confidence in the flesh - they were children of Abraham, thought themselves the true worshipers of YHWH even though they broke His covenant and lusted after the things the pagan nations had that were forbidden to them. Repeatedly God tells them He finds their religion tedious and putrid. Having a name from God ethnic Israel thought they could pay lip service to Him.

Isaiah 48:3-5 I declared the past events long ago; they came out of My mouth; I proclaimed them. Suddenly I acted, and they occurred. Because I know that you are stubborn, and your neck is iron and your forehead bronze, therefore I declared to you long ago. I announced it to you before it occurred, so you could not claim, 'My idol caused them; my carved image and cast idol control them.'

The "past events" were the previous judgments YHWH caused to rain down on Israel. These didn't happen out of national envy - this was God's plan, acting without notice to man so it seemed sudden. Why did He do this? National Israel was stubborn and stiff-necked and hard-headed - they were told this multiple times by numerous prophets. To make sure they wouldn't think too little of their misfortune, God declared His judgment to them a long time prior so they would not blame it on things they made with their hands. They had not offended mute, dumb gods; they had rebelled against Creator God who had formed them into a nation for His own redemptive purposes.

Isaiah 48:6-11 You have heard it. Observe it all. Will you not acknowledge it? From now on I will announce new things to you, hidden things that you have not known. They have been created now, and not long ago; you have not heard of them before today, so you could not claim, 'I already knew them!' You have never heard; you have never known; For a long time your ears have not been open. For I knew that you were very treacherous, and were known as a rebel from birth. I will delay My anger for the honor of My name, and I will restrain Myself for your benefit and [for] My praise, so that you will not be destroyed. Look, I have refined you, but not as silver; I have tested you in the furnace of affliction. I will act for My own sake, indeed, My own, for how can I be defiled? I will not give My glory to another.

Their God and King changes tone and bids His people to listen to Him. Something new will take place, things they have not seen, things created NOW. This was done so national Israel would not think to themselves, "Oh yeah - I remember these things that Moses mentioned!" As Isaiah was told in his commissioning, in chapter 6, this people would have ears that would not listen; hardened because they were deceitful (see Amos 8 wherein they anticipated the end of the Sabbath so they could cheat people in the marketplace) and rebellious (as were we - see Romans 5). Yet YHWH was patient with national Israel, exercising restraint for their benefit and His praise. Their long exile in Babylon would end, having served to refine and purify and test them. God sent them to exile and He would redeem from exile for His sake - see Numbers 14:13-14 where Moses pleads with God to not destroy the people for the sake of His name. We are not to seek God's favor merely for our benefit, but that He would be honored in whatever He does for us. YHWH will not be defiled by His actions - His motives are pure and His jealously for His glory is righteous. He will not share that with ANYONE.

Isaiah 48:12-15 *Listen to Me, Jacob, and Israel, the one called by Me: I am He; I am the first, I am also the last. My own hand founded the earth, and My right hand spread out the heavens; when I summoned them, they stood up together. All of you, assemble and listen! Who among the idols has declared these things? The LORD loves him; he will accomplish His will against Babylon, and His arm [will be against / the Chaldeans. I—I have spoken; yes, I have called him; I have brought him, and he will succeed in his mission.*

My tendency is to say, "This reference to Jacob and Israel refers to the elect, the remnant and not to the nation." But the context here does not allow that. God continues to call to His ethnic people, the community He formed. Note how He refers to Himself here, as the first and last and recall how Jesus described Himself - Rev 1:8 *"I am the Alpha and the Omega," says the Lord God, "the One who is, who was, and who is coming, the Almighty."* Jesus alludes to this passage to make clear He is God, "alpha" and "omega" being the first and last letters of the Greek alphabet. He is the One who made all things, caused them to bow to His will (see Col 1:16-17); the people that He made and called together and gave His law to are commanded to gather themselves up and pay attention. No gods of Baal or Dagon can do this!

One that YHWH loves will do His will and overthrow Babylon and Chaldea. The word rendered love in English is a Hebrew word (ahab) which means "kind affection". Every commentary I was able to consult agree that the one described here is Cyrus. It was the Medes and Persians that overthrew Babylon after Belshazzar was weighed in the balance and found wanting. It was during the first year of Cyrus' reign that Daniel was released from Babylon (Dan 1:21). Cyrus was king of Persia and Daniel prospered under the rule of Darius and Cyrus (Dan 6:28). Cyrus would triumph over Babylon and Chaldea because it was the mighty arm of the Lord that was holding Cyrus up to do His good pleasure.

Matthew Poole had the best summary of why we see Cyrus as the one God loved: "Now God loved Cyrus, not with a special, and everlasting, and complacential love, for he was a heathen, and had some great vices as well as virtues; but with that general love and kindness which God hath for all his creatures, as is observed in Psalm 145:9; and moreover with that particular kind of love which God hath for such men as excel others in any virtues, as Cyrus did; in which sense Christ loved the young man, Mark 10:21; and with a love of good-will and beneficence. God had such a kindness for him, as to make him a most glorious and victorious general and king, and the great instrument for the deliverance of his own people."

Isaiah 48:16 *"Approach Me and listen to this. From the beginning I have not spoken in secret; from the time anything existed, I was there." And now the Lord GOD has sent me and His Spirit.*

This verse stands as a reminder that it is God who commands His people come near and listen, He is the only One who was before time. And He works through means, which includes His called out ones - prophets and preachers who proclaim His Truth, by His Spirit.

Isaiah 48:17-19 *This is what the LORD, your Redeemer, the Holy One of Israel says: I am Yahweh your God, who teaches you for [your] benefit, who leads you in the way you should go. If only you had paid attention to My commands. Then your peace would have been like a river, and your righteousness like the waves of the sea. Your descendants would have been as [countless] as the sand, and the offspring of your body like its grains; their name would not be cut off or eliminated from My presence.*

Again, YHWH declares Who He is so this stiff-necked, hard-headed people will listen. None but God is their redeemer, their Holy One who teaches them and leads them. If they had not been stiff-necked and hard-hearted they would have heard and obeyed Him, and they would have "peace like a river." We are all familiar with that phrase, from a hymn. Such peace only comes to those who have had their ears opened to the gospel of grace and walk as children of the light. It is these true children of God that have an alien righteousness that flows like the sea. If national Israel had not been stiff-necked and hard-hearted they would have countless offspring and not cut off by God. The promise to Abram would be fulfilled in a people not stiff-necked nor hard-hearted, a people given new hearts of flesh and a willing, humble soul that rejoices in the blessedness bestowed upon them by their Redeemer. The kingdom was taken from national Israel and given to spiritual Israel (Matt 21:43).

Isaiah 48:20-22 *Leave Babylon, flee from the Chaldeans! Declare with a shout of joy, proclaim this, let it go out to the end of the earth; announce, "The LORD has redeemed His servant Jacob!" They did not thirst when He led them through the deserts; He made water flow for them from the rock; He split the rock, and water gushed out. "There is no peace for the wicked," says the LORD.*

There is irony here. It was God Who sent Israel to Babylon, telling them to prosper there (see Jeremiah 29:7) and now He tells them to flee that nation; and He will make their return from exile possible. That is the whole point of this discourse - God rules history, the means and the metanarrative. All the earth will hear how the Holy One of Israel had redeemed them from Babylon! He reminds that He had taken care of them in the wilderness, referring to that rock that was Christ (1 Cor 10:4). Here we see the anti-type as the type is being prepared for temporal redemption, those who drink living water will experience spiritual, eternal redemption. Another stark contrast that Isaiah is so fond of: Those wicked persons that remain stiff-necked and hard-hearted will have no peace. Only those called out of darkness into the kingdom of His glorious light will experience peace like a river. YHWH says this, man cannot overthrow it.

Isaiah 49: The Servant Brings Salvation.

I enjoy seeing how various translations title chapters. I have the HCSB above; the ESV calls this chapter "The Servant of the Lord" and the KJV has it "Christ, being sent to the Jews, complains of them." We certainly read of Jesus rebuking the Jewish leaders during His earthly ministry. You decide if this chapter has Him complaining about them.

I haven't been leaning on commentaries much during this walk through Isaiah, but I see what John Gill said every once in a while. He agrees with me that this chapter is a prophecy about the Lord Christ; it begins the section in this book about the suffering Servant.

Isaiah 49:1-3 *Coastlands, listen to me; distant peoples, pay attention. The LORD called me before I was born. He named me while I was in my mother's womb. He made my words like a sharp sword; He hid me in the shadow of His hand. He made me like a sharpened arrow; He hid me in His quiver. He said to me, "You are My Servant, Israel; I will be glorified in him."*

The first three verses identify who is being called: distant people- Gentiles; that this Servant was called by God before He was born (Jesus - eternally with the Father); and was named while in the womb (see Matt 1:21). The Servant was like an arrow crafted by the Father, hidden until the fullness of time when He would come as a man to fulfill the Father's will and glorify Him in all He did.

Some will say that these terms are applied to mortals in Scripture - true enough! But recall that this book is a vision given to Isaiah (first verse) and types that were true in the time of the author find their fulfillment in the spiritual reality that was to come - in the person of Christ or in the consummation of the ages when He returns the second time.

Isaiah 49:4-5 *But I myself said: I have labored in vain, I have spent my strength for nothing and futility; yet my vindication is with the LORD, and my reward is with my God. And now, says the LORD, who formed me from the womb to be His Servant, to bring Jacob back to Him so that Israel might be gathered to Him; for I am honored in the sight of the LORD, and my God is my strength.*

Jesus, speaking of the reception He would have among His own people. This aligns with His lament about the leaders of that people - *Jerusalem, Jerusalem! She who kills the prophets and stones those who are sent to her. How often I wanted to gather your children together, as a hen gathers her chicks under her wings, yet you were not willing!* (Matt 23:37). He worked signs and wonders among them and yet, they demanded He be crucified and the murderer released. And for the glory of His Father's approval, Christ went to the cross on behalf of His sheep, bringing the elect from near (Israel) and far (Gentiles) back to the sheepfold of God. His strength was to do the Father's will and in Him God the Father was delighted. It was the Holy Spirit that conceived Christ in the womb of Mary for this very purpose!

Isaiah 49:6-7 *He says, "It is not enough for you to be My Servant raising up the tribes of Jacob and restoring the protected ones of Israel. I will also make you a light for the nations, to be My salvation to the ends of the earth." This is what the LORD, the Redeemer of Israel, his Holy One, says to one who is despised, to one abhorred by people, to a servant of rulers: "Kings will see and stand up, and princes will bow down, because of the LORD, who is faithful, the Holy One of Israel—and He has chosen you."*

We read here the Father telling the Son something they both already knew, but ethnic Israel would have a long time failing to understand this. The Son would redeem people from all of ethnic Israel, He would also be a light unto the nations, redeeming people from the far corners of the planet in every generation. The emphasis here is to remind the Jewish people that "their" God would save people from every nation. Jesus came to His own, the Jewish people, but they did not receive Him - He was mocked, ridiculed, and put to death by them. He came to serve those He would save and would be renowned throughout the world as the chosen One, the promised One, the only Son of the one true God.

Isaiah 49:8-12 *This is what the LORD says: I will answer you in a time of favor, and I will help you in the day of salvation. I will keep you, and I will appoint you to be a covenant for the people, to restore the land, to make them possess the desolate inheritances, saying to the prisoners: Come out, and to those who are in darkness: Show yourselves. They will feed along the pathways, and their pastures will be on all the barren heights. They will not hunger or thirst, the scorching heat or sun will not strike them; for their compassionate One will guide them, and lead them to springs of water. I will make all My mountains into a road, and My highways will be raised up. See, these will come from far away, from the north and from the west, and from the land of Sinim.*

This segment highlights YHWH's declaration that He will be help to His Son in the day of salvation, when the Messiah would suffer for us. He would appoint the Son to be a covenant for us which would provide homes in the heavenly land, where prisoners were free, and the people would have neither hunger nor thirst. The Lamb of God will guide them to His sheepfold, providing springs of water and smooth ways for all the elect to come from all four corners of the world.

Isaiah 49:13 *Shout for joy, you heavens! Earth, rejoice! Mountains break into joyful shouts! For the LORD has comforted His people, and will have compassion on His afflicted ones.*

At the good news in verses 8-12, the people and heavenly hosts have every good reason to shout for joy and rejoice with gladness! YHWH has comforted His people with the Lamb - has compassion on His afflicted ones, those who are poor in spirit.

Isaiah 49:14-21 *Zion says, "The LORD has abandoned me; The Lord has forgotten me!" "Can a woman forget her nursing child, or lack compassion for the child of her womb? Even if these forget, yet I will not forget you. Look, I have*

191

inscribed you on the palms of My hands; your walls are continually before Me. Your builders hurry; those who destroy and devastate you will leave you. Look up, and look around. They all gather together; they come to you. As I live"— [this is] the LORD's declaration— "you will wear all your children as jewelry, and put them on as a bride does. For your waste and desolate places and your land marked by ruins— will now be indeed too small for the inhabitants, and those who swallowed you up will be far away. Yet as you listen, the children that you have been deprived of will say, 'This place is too small for me; make room for me so that I may settle.' Then you will say within yourself, 'Who fathered these for me? I was deprived of my children and unable to conceive, exiled and wandering— but who brought them up? See, I was left by myself— but these, where did they come from?'"

The ones chosen by God whine that He has abandoned them, forgotten them. He answers, using striking metaphors to drive the point home. God further declares that they - the redeemed - will have countless children. Recall the promise to Abram - he would be the father of many nations. We are children of Abraham if we have faith in Christ; many children has father Abraham! In the agrarian life of the ancient near east, having many children insured wealth - this is the reason the people were whining and it's the reason God uses the metaphors He does to assure them they have not been abandoned.

Isaiah 49:22-23 *This is what the Lord GOD says: Look, I will lift up My hand to the nations, and raise My banner to the peoples. They will bring your sons in their arms, and your daughters will be carried on their shoulders. Kings will be your foster fathers, and their queens your nursing mothers. They will bow down to you with their faces to the ground, and lick the dust at your feet. Then you will know that I am Yahweh; those who put their hope in Me will not be put to shame.*

When a prophet declares "this is what the Lord God says" - pay close attention! That is the point. Nothing new being presented here - God will call to the nations and bring children of Abraham to Zion. The people listed - sons, daughters, kings, queens, foster fathers, and nursing mothers - all serve one another in the New Covenant. Once proud people would humble themselves before other saints - and all would then know the Savior, being found in Him would be a refuge on the day when people seek a hiding place apart from Christ.

Isaiah 49:24-26 *Can the prey be taken from the mighty, or the captives of the righteous be delivered? For this is what the LORD says: "Even the captives of a mighty man will be taken, and the prey of a tyrant will be delivered; I will contend with the one who contends with you, and I will save your children. I will make your oppressors eat their own flesh, and they will be drunk with their own blood as with sweet wine. Then all flesh will know that I, Yahweh, am your Savior, and your Redeemer, the Mighty One of Jacob."*

YHWH brings up these questions because, like people today, people then had worries that they might not be secure, safe in His care. Again, reminiscent of the promise to Abraham - *I will bless those that bless you, I will curse those that curse you.* The battle against our enemies belongs to the Lord. They will be soundly defeated so that all flesh will that YHWH is the savior of His people, their Redeemer, the Mighty One that none can withstand.

Child of God - do not doubt the saving and keeping power of God regarding His chosen ones. Jesus is faithful even when we are faithless. Faith in Him works itself out by daily trusting in Him. This day - do you trust in Christ? He is surety for all who trust in Him.

Isaiah 50 - Israel's Sin and the Obedient Servant.

The ESV wins the title for this chapter; the HCSB has none. This chapter opens with YHWH asking Israel to produce evidence to support their complaints of being abandoned by God.

Isaiah 50:1-3 *This is what the LORD says: Where is your mother's divorce certificate that I used to send her away? Or who were My creditors that I sold you to? Look, you were sold for your iniquities, and your mother was put away because of your transgressions. Why was no one there when I came? Why was there no one to answer when I called? Is My hand too short to redeem? Or do I have no power to deliver? Look, I dry up the sea by My rebuke; I turn the rivers into a wilderness; their fish rot because of lack of water and die of thirst. I dress the heavens in black and make sackcloth their clothing.*

YHWH asks Israel, where is your mother's divorce certificate? This appears to refer to Zion as Israel's mother. The Mosaic Law (Deut 24:1-3) mandated a certificate when a man divorced his wife. While God had put her away because of Israel's transgressions (this word refers to violations of the law given to them), He asks where are the creditors - which would be the case IF they had been sold to settle a debt. They were sold because of their iniquities, their depraved acts. There is no one to validate Israel's contention - these acts were from God's hands and only His hands can redeem and deliver Israel.

YHWH reminds Israel of His redemption from Egypt by referring to the dry seabed (Ex 14:21); He points them to the end of the age by providing a peek into the judgment that will come on the world (Rev 6:12). This sets the stage for the Servant to be announced. Sin has been dealt with - Israel has no hope unless God Himself does something.

Isaiah 50:4-5 *The Lord GOD has given Me the tongue of those who are instructed to know how to sustain the weary with a word. He awakens [Me] each morning; He awakens My ear to listen like those being instructed. The Lord GOD has opened My ear, and I was not rebellious; I did not turn back.*

The Servant speaks, declaring that He has been given wise speech that will give hope to the weary; ears to hear wisdom from the Father. God has done this for a humble, obedient Servant who does the way He is instructed (see John 8:29).

Isaiah 50:6-7 *I gave My back to those who beat Me, and My cheeks to those who tore out My beard. I did not hide My face from scorn and spitting. The Lord GOD will help Me; therefore I have not been humiliated; therefore I have set My face like flint, and I know I will not be put to shame.*

Read the gospel accounts of the punishment meted out by the Romans (Mark 14:65; 15:19; etc.) and see the fulfillment of this account. Imagine the face of a man whose beard has been ripped from his flesh. Not seemly, someone no one would want to look at. The Creator spurned and beaten and mocked by the creature. As Peter declared in Acts 2:22-24, all this was God's predetermined plan.

The Son relied upon the Father's help, who for the joy that lay before Him endured the cross and despised the shame and has sat down at the right hand of God's throne. Not humiliated, but glorified! This confidence in the Father was why the Servant could set His course for the cross and know He would not be put to shame. Flint is a hard rock, used to makes sparks to start a fire. There is a fire of judgment coming and all who are in Christ will not be put to shame. But woe be those who know Him not!

Isaiah 50:8-9 *The One who vindicates Me is near; who will contend with Me? Let us confront each other. Who has a case against Me? Let him come near Me! In truth, the Lord GOD will help Me; who will condemn Me? Indeed, all of them will wear out like a garment; a moth will devour them.*

The Servant alludes to Psalms 118:6, which Paul cited in Romans 8:31. *If God is for us, who can stand against us? If God is our advocate, who can lay a charge against us?* (see Romans 8:33) Our trust and confidence ought to be as that of the Servant - trusting in God for help, knowing nothing can condemn us (Romans 8:1). All who rail against the Servant and His body will wear out like a garment (like the Old Covenant - Heb 8:13) and moth-eaten (Job 12:38). These two signs indicated poverty - physical poverty for national Israel, spiritual poverty for those not in Christ.

Isaiah 50:10-11 *Who among you fears the LORD, listening to the voice of His Servant? Who [among you] walks in darkness, and has no light? Let him trust in the name of Yahweh; let him lean on his God. Look, all you who kindle a fire, who encircle yourselves with firebrands; walk in the light of your fire and in the firebrands you have lit! This is what you'll get from My hand: you will lie down in a place of torment.*

Two types of people are addressed here: those who fear YHWH and listen to the Servant and those who walk in darkness and have no light. Note this: the right fear of God results in listening to what the Son has said and walking in obedience, in the light. Those who walk in the darkness know Him not. I think John picked up on this light/dark idea: 1 John 2:9-11 *The one who says he is in the light but hates his brother is in the darkness until now. The one who loves his brother remains in the light, and there is no cause for stumbling in him. But the one who hates his brother is in the darkness, walks in the darkness, and doesn't know where he's going, because the darkness has blinded his eyes.* Walking in darkness is being apart from the grace of God in Christ. Walking in the light is being obedient to Him - love does not cause a brother to stumble.

Let the one who walks in darkness learn to trust in and lean on YHWH. None other than Him is trustworthy! Poor sinner

- look unto Christ! He is the only One and only Way to bring peace with God!

If you don't, you will be like those who are content with a small fire that they lit and control - thinking the warmth of the flame will protect against evil. As when Lot fled to the wrong side of the valley, away from uncle Abraham and the covenant people of God, sin went with him - so it is with those who think a few burning sticks will protect them, think their own efforts can bring them peace. They will not be protected from the One they refuse to submit to. They will be made to lie down in a place of torment, submitted to the fires of hell they cannot control, which will endlessly consume them rather than protect them.

Oh sinner - consider this! Judgment is coming. You have been storing up God's wrath since your birth. Look to the Servant, the God-man Jesus, Who is the Christ!

Isaiah 51 - From Abraham to Christ, Salvation for Zion.

We learned about the obedient Servant in chapter 50; we now see the large back-story of redemption from Abraham to Christ. Isaiah speaks first, calling his kinsmen of the flesh to remember how the promise made to Abram would be fulfilled; God then speaks reminding Israel and us that He is truly, completely sovereign over everything.

Isaiah 51:1-3 *Listen to Me, you who pursue righteousness, you who seek the LORD: Look to the rock from which you were cut, and to the quarry from which you were dug. Look to Abraham your father, and to Sarah who gave birth to you in pain. When I called him, he was only one; I blessed him and made him many. For the LORD will comfort Zion; He will comfort all her waste places, and He will make her wilderness like Eden, and her desert like the garden of the*

LORD. Joy and gladness will be found in her, thanksgiving and melodious song.

There will be people who seek after what they think is God in every culture. Isaiah tells his kinsmen to see things correctly: they were nothing, raw material that God culled from the debris of mankind. Just like Abraham. There were nine generations between Adam and Noah; ten generations stood between Noah and the next Adam – Abram. Out of this sea of humanity, the world lost in re-learning how to communicate and rediscover their place, one genealogy is highlighted and traced down to a solitary man God would call to stand as the father of many nations; and the father of all the redeemed.

Just as God had blessed Abraham and made him many, so He will bless Zion - transforming her waste places, her wilderness, and her desert into comfortable, lush gardens where joy and gladness will be found; giving them cause to rejoice with thanksgiving and song. Since we know all good things come from God, do we give thanks to Him when we prosper; do we sing praises to Him for His kindness to us?

Isaiah 51:4-6 *Pay attention to Me, My people, and listen to Me, My nation; for instruction will come from Me, and My justice for a light to the nations. I will bring it about quickly. My righteousness is near, My salvation appears, and My arms will bring justice to the nations. The coastlands will put their hope in Me, and they will look to My strength. Look up to the heavens, and look at the earth beneath; for the heavens will vanish like smoke, the earth will wear out like a garment, and its inhabitants will die like gnats. But My salvation will last forever, and My righteousness will never be shattered.*

God now speaks, calling His people, His nation to listen closely to His instructions - words from Himself and not from false prophets, even if they are our favorite people. When God speaks, it is with authority. He will bring salvation to His own and justice to the nations, which will be a light in the darkness that they naturally crave. The arm of the Lord God is strong to save His people and strong to judge the nations. There is no hope apart from Him, so all who desire Him, have been called by Him, place their hope in Him; trusting His arm to bring salvation.

The end of this creation was declared long before Isaiah's time; he alluded to this passage: Psalm 102:25-26 *Long ago You established the earth, and the heavens are the work of Your hands. They will perish, but You will endure; all of them will wear out like clothing. You will change them like a garment, and they will pass away.* This aligns with what Peter tells us of the end of this age: *But the Day of the Lord will come like a thief; on that [day] the heavens will pass away with a loud noise, the elements will burn and be dissolved, and the earth and the works on it will be disclosed. Since all these things are to be destroyed in this way, [it is clear] what sort of people you should be in holy conduct and godliness as you wait for and earnestly desire the coming of the day of God. The heavens will be on fire and be dissolved because of it, and the elements will melt with the heat. But based on His promise, we wait for the new heavens and a new earth, where righteousness will dwell.* (2 Peter 3:10-13)

In Isaiah, God spoke that His salvation and His righteousness will last forever - those who are saved inherit the new earth where His righteousness dwells. Fear not what Peter describes if you be in Christ. If you are not known by Him, do not deceive yourself - there is no other refuge.

Isaiah 51:7-8 *Listen to Me, you who know righteousness, the people in whose heart is My instruction: do not fear disgrace by men, and do not be shattered by their taunts. For the moth will devour them like a garment, and the worm will eat them like wool. But My righteousness will last forever, and My salvation for all generations.*

God speaks to those who know Him, reminding all of us to not fear man - his arm is short and God can defeat them with mundane things. All flesh is like grass and withers and dies, eaten by moth and worms. BUT GOD and His righteousness will never end, He is stronger than all He has created; those He saves will never perish.

Isaiah 51:9-11 *Wake up, wake up! Put on the strength of the LORD's power. Wake up as in days past, as in generations of long ago. Wasn't it You who hacked Rahab to pieces, who pierced the sea monster? Wasn't it You who dried up the sea, the waters of the great deep, who made the sea-bed into a road for the redeemed to pass over? And the redeemed of the LORD will return and come to Zion with singing, crowned with unending joy. Joy and gladness will overtake [them], and sorrow and sighing will flee.*

Israel pleads with God to WAKE UP! This is a plea to God by His covenant people, asking Him to reveal and use His strength, to put on the strength of His power. This reminds me of the apostle's instruction for us to put on the full armor of God. No mortal can rely on his own strength, though he may have done mighty deeds when he was younger. Man cannot defeat nature, cannot rule the sea, or push the sea back to allow dry passage. God does these things, as we read in Psalm 89:9-10 *You rule the raging sea; when its waves surge, You still them. You crushed Rahab like one who is slain; You scattered Your enemies with Your powerful arm.* Very similar language to what Isaiah used - the prophet was familiar with the Psalms. When the redeemed of YHWH remember His mighty deeds we will be refreshed, encouraged, and we should gather together as His chosen ones singing with joy and gladness - for sorrow will flee from us as we draw close to Him.

Isaiah 51:12-16 *I—I am the One who comforts you. Who are you that you should fear man who dies, or a son of man who is given up like grass? But you have forgotten the LORD, your Maker, who stretched out the heavens and laid the foundations of the earth. You are in constant dread all day long because of the fury of the oppressor, who has set himself to destroy. But where is the fury of the oppressor? The prisoner is soon to be set free; he will not die [and go] to the Pit, and his food will not be lacking. For I am Yahweh your God who stirs up the sea so that its waves roar— His name is Yahweh of Hosts. I have put My words in your mouth, and covered you in the shadow of My hand, in order to plant the heavens, to found the earth, and to say to Zion, "You are My people."*

God answers. There is so much here that we ought to ponder, devotedly and slowly. Have we lived so long as to have grown accustomed to the GLORY of being raised up in Christ? He alone comforts us - why do we forget Him? How can we forget Him, when we see the heaven and earth before us? Saints - do not live in dread because of what those of this world can do us. We are prisoners who have been set free, not destined for the pit; well fed and cared for. See Psalms 118:6, 1 Peter 1:24, Amos 9:6, Psalms 107:25, and Jeremiah 31:35; all of which declare the glorious might of God over all His creation and reveal us to nothing but dust.

Ponder who He is and what He has done for us. He has given us His Word and provided refuge for us in the strength of His hand. He will stretch out a new heavens and bring about a new earth and He will declare to His redeemed "You are My people!" We who were not His people are called His people! Please let that sink into your soul. If you are in Christ - that in itself a thought that ought to undo each of us - then you are His people. None of us deserve this status - we were not His people by birth, though His elect were marked out for salvation before time. You and I lived as though we should just eat and drink for tomorrow we wake up and do it again. BUT GOD, Who is rich in mercy, reached out at a point in time and gave you life, spiritual life; life that was grounded in God and able to see Him. His people. Oh how wonderful! Don't EVER get accustomed to being in Christ!

Isaiah 51:17-20 *Wake yourself, wake yourself up! Stand up, Jerusalem, you who have drunk the cup of His fury from the hand of the LORD; you who have drunk the goblet to the dregs— the cup that [causes people] to stagger. There is no one to guide her among all the children she has raised; there is no one to take hold of her hand among all the offspring she has brought up. These two things have happened to you: devastation and destruction, famine and sword. Who will grieve for you? How can I comfort you? Your children have fainted; they lie at the head of every street like an antelope in a net. They are full of the LORD's fury, the rebuke of your God.*

Isaiah the prophet now speaks again to his kinsmen, urging them to wake up! By their long record of disobedience, they have been putting God to the test, storing up wrath. See how this reflects what the pagan nations do: This is what the LORD, the God of Israel, said to me: *Take this cup of the wine of wrath from My hand and make all the nations I am sending you to, drink from it. They will drink, stagger, and go out of their minds because of the sword I am sending among them.* (Jeremiah 25:15-16)

Drunkards have need of help to raise their children and they often cannot find it. Devastation and destruction, famine and death come upon drunks who have no one to grieve for them. So it is with those who are drunk on their rebellion, no comfort for them; no direction - like a beast caught in a net. These people, who are NOT called His people, are the object of YHWH's fury and His rebuke. At this, the mountains will flee! Oh sinner! While you have breath, cry out to your Creator for mercy!

Isaiah 51:21-23 *So listen to this, afflicted and drunken one— but not with wine. This is what your Lord says— Yahweh, even your God, who defends His people— "Look, I have removed the cup of staggering from your hand; that goblet, the cup of My fury. You will never drink it again. I will put it into the hands of your tormentors, who said to you: Lie down, so we can walk over you. You made your back like the ground, and like a street for those who walk on it.*

God calls to His people who have been drunk on their rebellion; He first reminds them Who He is: YHWH their God who defends His people. He takes away their love for rebellion, the cup of His fury. All who have been redeemed can never be exposed to His wrath. Those who will not be called "His people" will be made to drink the cup of His fury (as we read in Jeremiah, earlier). Those who have tormented His people will be made like a road His people walk on. This should remind you of the highway to Zion we've read about. Birds of prey will feast on them, no one will save them. They are not "His people."

Saints - being in union with Christ is our security. Because of that union, we who were once not called "His people" are now, truly His people. Rejoice if you are His people. Cry out for mercy if you are not.

Isaiah 52 - YHWH's Promised Redemption.

Nearly 900 years ago, Stephen Langton divided the Bible up into chapters. His decision as to where chapters 52 and 53 of Isaiah are divided is one of those things that make you go "hmmm." This study will go through chapter 52 and verse 12; the last three verses belong to chapter 53.

Isaiah 52:1-2 *Wake up, wake up; put on your strength, Zion! Put on your beautiful garments, Jerusalem, the Holy City! For the uncircumcised and the unclean will no longer enter you. Stand up, shake the dust off yourself! Take your seat, Jerusalem. Remove the bonds from your neck, captive Daughter Zion.*

This passage starts off with yet another call for national Israel to WAKE UP! They are told to straighten up, recall to Whom they belong. For those that do not belong to God will be kept out. Recall to Whom you belong, get out of the dust and be seated in the heavenlies with Christ Jesus (Eph 2:4-7)! Those led off to captivity would be set free. Lo, we who have been captive to sin since our birth have BEEN set free by the promised One!

Isaiah 52:3-6 *For this is what the LORD says: "You were sold for nothing, and you will be redeemed without silver." For this is what the Lord GOD says: "At first My people went down to Egypt to live there, then Assyria oppressed them without cause. So now what have I here"— [this is] the LORD's declaration— "that My people are taken away for nothing? Its rulers wail"— [this is] the LORD's declaration— "and My name is continually blasphemed all day long. Therefore My people will know My name; therefore [they will know] on that day that I am He who says: Here I am."*

Israel was banished to Babylon without price; she will be redeemed without price. Indeed, king Cyrus of Persia would pay dearly to have the Jewish people resettle in Jerusalem and rebuild her. The history of national Israel started with slavery to Egypt, and God redeemed them without pay, as Egypt paid dearly to send them away. Assyria had been used by God so many times to punish rebellious Israel, yet they had no justifiable reason for their actions. Now Babylon will take Israel into exile and this is YHWH's declaration - His people are taken away without payment and their rulers wail, for their life of comfort and luxury had been taken from them. This is YHWH's declaration, those people who looked to their creature comforts would profane His name and blaspheme Him, forgetting Who had redeemed them from Egypt and for Whose reputation.

We who have been redeemed from a life of sin must never forget Who purchased us and for what reason He did so. Not for our sake, were we chosen - before anyone was born. For the sake of His name and the glory He alone deserves has anyone been raised up from death unto life. National Israel was redeemed from fleshly slavery and would be again; spiritual Israel is being redeemed from sin, gaining spiritual freedom, and reconciliation with God. The last verse in this section reminds us that is His desire - for His people know Him rightly. Not as the pagans and demons know OF Him, but truly to know Him as He knows us. And so we will, by the work of the Son.

Isaiah 52:7-10 *How beautiful on the mountains are the feet of the herald, who proclaims peace, who brings news of good things, who proclaims salvation, who says to Zion, "Your God reigns!" The voices of your watchmen— they lift up their voices, shouting for joy together; for every eye will see when the LORD returns to Zion. Be joyful, rejoice together, you ruins of Jerusalem! For the LORD has comforted His people; He has redeemed Jerusalem. The LORD has displayed His holy arm in the sight of all the nations; all the ends of the earth will see the salvation of our God.*

You ought to remember Paul's use of verse 7 in letter to the Romans, chapter 10. One who heralds good news is write it larger and run with the message so all can see it. Salvation is because God reigns - if He was the impotent god of so much bad theology, He would not be able to save; He would TRY to make salvation possible. To quote a line from a movie - that would be a "puny god." The watchmen who shout out with joy have a job to stay alert and let the city know when a messenger or an enemy approaches. Ezekiel has a couple of chapters devoted to these watchmen and we see in his writings (chapters 33 & 34) what their duties are and we'll find out how that relates to the charge elders in the New Covenant.

When Christ returns, when YHWH returns to Zion, everyone to the ends of the earth will know He has redeemed His people. We will rejoice with great joy to see Him, though everything of this realm is in ruins. Our time of toil and sweat and suffering will end. His strong arm will comfort His people and bring dismay to those who continue in their rebellion.

Isaiah 52:11-12 *Leave, leave, go out from there! Do not touch anything unclean; go out from her, purify yourselves, you who carry the vessels of the LORD. For you will not leave in a hurry, and you will not have to take flight; because the LORD is going before you, and the God of Israel is your rear guard.*

When national Israel is redeemed from Babylon and Persia, they will not be in a hurry as when they left Egypt. So it will be when He returns to gather all His redeemed unto Himself - no hurry on our part for YHWH goes before us, making our way straight and smooth. And He is our rear guard as well, making sure the slowest among us is not left behind.

All is from God, for God, and to God. We who are His will rejoice and praise Him for the mercy He has poured out on us. Again, take not for granted your standing with YHWH - we cannot stand of our own strength. He will hold us up - if we are His. Do you know Him?

Isaiah 53 - The Suffering Servant.

As I mentioned above, the last three verses of chapter 52 fit with the theme of chapter 53 better than they fit with chapter 52. The ESV and HCSB have a subtitle above chapter 52:13 referring to the suffering Servant, which is the theme of chapter 53. John Gill agrees with me on this - he was a pretty good nut.

Isaiah 52:13-15 *See, My Servant will act wisely; He will be raised and lifted up and greatly exalted. Just as many were appalled at You— His appearance was so disfigured that He did not look like a man, and His form did not resemble a human being—so He will sprinkle many nations. Kings will shut their mouths because of Him, For they will see what had not been told them, and they will understand what they had not heard.*

The Servant will act wisely - none as wise as Christ Jesus; His wisdom is spoken of in Proverbs and Ecclesiastes. Just as the serpent was raised up in the wilderness, so will the Son of man be lifted up and be glorified by the Father. In spite of how God views His Son, man was appalled at His appearance - so marred by the creature was the Creator that He no longer appeared as a man. A couple of chapters back we read of how part of this took place: Isaiah 50:6 *I gave My back to those who beat Me, and My cheeks to those who tore out My beard. I did not hide My face from scorn and spitting.* In his excellent book, *The Simple Gospel*, Jon Caldwell has a chapter on the Shroud of Turin in which he comments on this verse: "The Hebrew word למרטים (L'Maratiym), which is translated "plucked off the hair," literally means "to make bald." Jesus Christ didn't just have a tuft of His beard pulled out; His entire beard was plucked from His face!" Jewish men weren't supposed to even trim their beards. To be bald-faced was a mark of shame and/or mourning. See Isaiah 151-2 for Hebrew shaving their head and beards in mourning; see Jeremiah 48:37 for Gentiles being shaved head and face as a sign of defeat. Jesus appeared as one defeated, mourning His circumstance. We know His vision was fixed on the glory that awaited Him beyond the cross as He entrusted Himself to the trustworthy Judge.

And so even though He appeared to be shamefully defeated, He would sprinkle many nations - as the Hebrews would sprinkle blood on the altar (Lev 4:6, 17) or water on an unclean person to cleanse him (Numbers 19:18-21), yet with a more sure sacrifice that would ensure the redemption of every chosen one.

Kings will be silent, they will see what had not been told to them, they will understand that which they had not heard. Because of their response, we see these "kings" as representative of Gentiles who, as Paul mentioned, did not have the oracle of God - the advantage was to the Jews (Romans 3:1-2). But when Christ came, He was displayed to all and His disciples went forth with His gospel and these "wise men" had their minds and hearts opened to comprehend that which had been a mystery prior to the fullness of time. Now the high and mighty men are low and humble, see Him as He is - God in human flesh, beaten and tortured by those He created, suffering the wrath of God for those He came to save. How can we not be in awe of Him!

Isaiah 53:1 *Who has believed what we have heard? And who has the arm of the LORD been revealed to?*

This question reveals what we read about everywhere: only a remnant will be saved. As man sees it, not many hear and believe. Isaiah was told he would preach to a people that would not understand or see rightly. So WHO would believe what Isaiah had heard, to whom has He revealed His strong arm of salvation? We've read much in Isaiah about the strong arm of God; it was His arm that brought Israel out of Egypt in victory; Mary's song in Luke 1 testifies, *He has done a mighty deed with His arm; He has scattered the proud because of the thoughts of their hearts.* Whether it's salvation or judgment, the strong arm of the Lord prevails over the hearts and souls of every man.

Isaiah 53:2-3 *He grew up before Him like a young plant and like a root out of dry ground. He didn't have an impressive form or majesty that we should look at Him, no appearance that we should desire Him. He was despised and rejected by men, a man of suffering who knew what sickness was. He was like someone people turned away from; He was despised, and we didn't value Him.*

Recall that Isaiah lived and wrote more than 700 years before Christ; long before the Romans had invented crucifixion as the most cruel way possible to kill a man. Jesus the man grew up as a human, learned obedience; was brought out of Egypt to live in the backwater town of Nazareth. As a child and young man, Jesus was nothing to look at - reminiscent of David in comparison to his brothers. When those who despised Him rejected Him and demanded He be crucified, claiming they had no king but Caesar, that His blood be on them AND their children (Matt 27:25) - He was beaten, scourged, mocked, and hung on the tree. While every man who was crucified suffered, Jesus was not merely a man and His suffering was vastly worse than those on either side of Him. As Isaiah 50:6 portrayed, He was beaten so badly He was difficult to look upon. And He suffered the wrath of God due us: God made Him, who knew no sin, to be a sin offering for us so we would have the righteousness of Christ (2 Cor 5:21). Thousands who were in Jerusalem for the Jewish rites came by to see the site - and they mocked Him and shouted for Him to save Himself if He was God, proving He was right when He said Satan was their father. They said the same thing Satan had spoken to Jesus. Only a few saw Him for what He is - the Roman centurion, who had seen the horrible butchery of war was struck with true awe as he beheld the Son of God. Saints - are you still in awe of Who He is? Let us encourage one another to see Him rightly and behold Him in His majesty, for a savior that does not inspire such a response is not a Savior.

Isaiah 53:4-6 *Yet He Himself bore our sicknesses, and He carried our pains; but we in turn regarded Him stricken, struck down by God, and afflicted. But He was pierced because of our transgressions, crushed because of our iniquities; punishment for our peace was on Him, and we are healed by His wounds. We all went astray like sheep; we all have turned to our own way; and the LORD has punished Him for the iniquity of us all.*

> Stricken, smitten, and afflicted,
> See Him dying on the tree!
> 'Tis the Christ by man rejected;
> Yes, my soul, 'tis He, 'tis He!
> 'Tis the long-expected prophet,
> David's Son, yet David's Lord;
> By His Son, God now has spoken
> Tis the true and faithful Word.

Great hymns and spiritual songs will point us to the biblical Christ, reveal natural man's true condition, and humble the child of God. When God in human flesh submitted Himself to the varied punishments meted out by man, this was to show man something of the suffering He would undergo. But the deepest stroke that pierced him was the stroke that Justice gave. And man looked upon the Lam of God as He hung on judgment's tree and most saw Him as deserving it.

But, Isaiah reminds us, He was pierced for OUR transgressions - He had none of His own! He who had NO SIN was MADE SIN so we might become the righteousness of God! The punishment He received brought us peace with God - for no sinful creature can approach Him. None but those clothed in the righteousness of Christ can approach, can have peace with the Father. Because the Son was stricken, smitten, and afflicted for us! The healing He provides is the glorious truth of our sin being put away. A pox on all who claim He suffered to cure ailments of the flesh! Eternal life if the healing He brings!

To whom did He give this healing? Not to the self-righteous (as if there were any!) but to the wretched! Like stupid sheep we wandered, seeking our own way. The only way we could be made right with God is for God to be punished in our place.

> Ye who think of sin but lightly,
> Nor suppose the evil great
> Here may view its nature rightly,
> Here its guilt may estimate.
> Mark the sacrifice appointed,
> See who bears the awful load;
> 'Tis the Word, the Lord's Anointed,
> Son of Man and Son of God.

Isaiah 53:7-9 *He was oppressed and afflicted, yet He did not open His mouth. Like a lamb led to the slaughter and like a sheep silent before her shearers, He did not open His mouth.*

He was taken away because of oppression and judgment; and who considered His fate? For He was cut off from the land of the living; He was struck because of my people's rebellion. They made His grave with the wicked and with a rich man at His death, although He had done no violence and had not spoken deceitfully.

Read 1 Peter 2:18ff to see the Apostle's treatment of this passage, applying it to the Christian life. The suffering of Christ is not merely and account of His death, it stands as the historical PROOF of God's redeeming love for His own and justice for the rebels, at such a great cost.

How quick are we to defend ourselves when someone maligns us? We often deserve to be maligned and are overly self-defensive. The Creator being maligned by the creature! And He did not defend Himself, did not seek to avoid OUR punishment. Most people then - and now - fail to comprehend the necessity of the crucifixion; by human wisdom, it was "cosmic child abuse" (Sarah Young used this term in her heretical book, The Shack).

Cut off from the land of the living - this term "cut off" refers to covenantal punishment, being separated from the community. Jesus died, didn't swoon. Jesus, the God-man, died - was cut off from the land of the living. This was because His people - recall that phrase? - had rebelled against His rule. We, like the rest, were children of wrath until His Spirit gave us life.

The Lord of glory was laid in a tomb as if He were nothing more than a dead man. Yet it was a rich man (a king who was made to see Him rightly?) that gave Him the tomb. All of this took place - the trial, the mocking, the scourging, the crucifixion, the wrath of God - even though He had done no violence, had spoken no deceit. These two things are the hallmark of rebels; they oppress the poor and deceive many in the marketplace. Things the Hebrew nation was noted for.

Isaiah 53:10-12 *Yet the LORD was pleased to crush Him severely. When You make Him a restitution offering, He will see [His] seed, He will prolong His days, and by His hand, the LORD's pleasure will be accomplished. He will see [it] out of His anguish, and He will be satisfied with His knowledge. My righteous Servant will justify many, and He will carry their iniquities. Therefore I will give Him the many as a portion, and He will receive the mighty as spoil, because He submitted Himself to death, and was counted among the rebels; yet He bore the sin of many and interceded for the rebels.*

But because God set His redeeming love on His chosen ones, it PLEASED HIM to punish Jesus for our sins. It was, as the HCSB put it, SEVERE. God the Father made Him the Son a restitution offering to buy back His chosen ones. The Son was one with the Father before the cross and would be greatly glorified to be reunited with Him AFTER His work was accomplished (Heb 12:2).

From before time, the Godhead knew who the saints would be, the Son knew His seed - a large number of people from every nation, tribe, and language. Though low in the grave He lay, up from the grave He arose to an indestructible, eternal life - all according to the Father's will and for His glory, which He will not share with another. There is no doubt we benefit greatly from the entire plan of redemption as it applied to us. But do not lose sight of this fact: the first and primary reason for all of creation and whatever end each bit of it faces is to bring GLORY to the Father, GLORY to the Son, Glory to the Spirit - three in one! (tip of the hat to Shai Linne)

The Son would see all this afore (recall Heb 12:2) and be satisfied in doing the Father's will (He came for this purpose - John 6:38). The righteous, obedient Servant HAS justified many, He carried their sins to the cross (Col 2:14), and He was given the many - the justified ones - as a portion, a reward, a spoil.

212

Consider this, saints: Jesus the good shepherd was sent to seek and save that which was lost. He will bring every lost sheep into the sheepfold of God the Father - an offering to Him. And the Father gives back to the Son all those He purchased from hell as a reward for His faithful obedience! He submitted Himself to death, even death on the cross; earning that which was His from before time - the glory He had before the world existed (John 17:4-5).

The Son was counted among the rebels - scourged, beaten, and crucified; in so doing He bore the sin of many - His people - and interceded for the rebels that were chosen.

Dear brothers and sisters, I have no words to describe the horror of our sins, the heinous price paid by the Lord Jesus to buy us off sin's slave market. How often I fail to consider these things as I go through one mundane day after another. YET - these things Isaiah recorded ARE TRUE and were written for our instruction. Let us lay them up in our hearts and mediate thereupon, encouraging one another to look unto Christ daily and not think of sin lightly. We have a sure foundation, a secure refuge from the storm in Christ Jesus.

Here we have a firm foundation,
Here the refuge of the lost;
Christ's the Rock of our salvation,
His the name of which we boast.
Lamb of God, for sinners wounded,
Sacrifice to cancel guilt!
None shall ever be confounded
Who on him their hope have built.

Isaiah 54 - YHWH's covenant of peace.

One thing we can know for sure, regarding this chapter: it begins with a promise that IS fulfilled spiritually. The first verse is quoted by Paul in Gal 4:27 in his defense of the New

Covenant, wherein he describes Jerusalem from above as freedom - freedom from the slavery of sin!

Isaiah 54:1 *"Rejoice, childless one, who did not give birth; burst into song and shout, you who have not been in labor! For the children of the forsaken one will be more than the children of the married woman," says the LORD.*

While the redeemed in national Israel were never more than a mere remnant, causing Hagar to be seen as more fruitful and Sarah to be seen as childless, the children from above are delivered without labor by man or woman but are born from above! This is God's doing and it is marvelous in our eyes!

Isaiah 54:2-3 *Enlarge the site of your tent, and let your tent curtains be stretched out; do not hold back; lengthen your ropes, and drive your pegs deep. For you will spread out to the right and to the left, and your descendants will dispossess nations and inhabit the desolate cities.*

This language of enlarge the tent site, moving the pegs, etc. is a word picture built on literal meaning. For as this Bedouin people would need to do these things to accommodate a larger community, God speaks here of that community born of the Spirit. In similar language James quotes from Amos 9 and Isaiah 45, saying that David's tent had been rebuilt and set up again to accept the Gentiles who are called by God (Acts 15:15-18). God's redemptive plan has always included those who were excluded from the covenant with national Israel. The redeemed Jews would enlarge and rebuild their tents to welcome these new brothers and sisters who had been far off and excluded from the citizenship of Israel, and foreigners to the covenants of promise, without hope and without God in this world (Eph 2:12). The cities that were desolate would now be home children of the King!

Isaiah 54:4-8 *"Do not be afraid, for you will not be put to shame; don't be humiliated, for you will not be disgraced. For you will forget the shame of your youth, and you will no longer remember the disgrace of your widowhood. Indeed,*

214

your husband is your Maker— His name is Yahweh of Hosts— and the Holy One of Israel is your Redeemer; He is called the God of all the earth. For the LORD has called you, like a wife deserted and wounded in spirit, a wife of one's youth when she is rejected," says your God. "I deserted you for a brief moment, but I will take you back with great compassion. In a surge of anger I hid My face from you for a moment, but I will have compassion on you with everlasting love," says the LORD your Redeemer.

All who have saving faith in the Son have no reason to live in fear - their sins have been forgiven and He will remember them no longer. Those foolish and shameful things we did in former times, when we walked according to the prince of the power of the air no longer stain our account. In the ancient near-east, widows were vulnerable, as they could not own property. It was risky to be without a husband, just as it is risky to be without YHWH. For the chosen ones, the Creator is our husband - YHWH of hosts - the Holy One of Israel - the God of all the earth! He has stooped low and gather up poor souls from desolate areas to be His prized possessions.

National Israel would feel like a deserted wife, wounded by rejection of her husband - for God deserted national Israel for a time; 70 years in this case. Israel would be in bondage a far shorter time than when in Egypt. But for those taken into bondage by Babylon, it was a far great distress. All their history as God's covenant people was under their belt. They had grown accustomed to being the apple of His eye. The length of their exile was pegged to the yearly Sabbath they had forsaken. Jeremiah prophesied this, as we read in Jer. 25:11-12; 29:10-14 *This whole land will be a desolation and a horror, and these nations will serve the king of Babylon seventy years. 'Then it will be **when seventy years are completed I will punish the king of Babylon** and that nation,' declares the LORD, 'for their iniquity, and the land of the Chaldeans; and I will make it an everlasting desolation... "For thus says the LORD, **'When seventy years have been completed for Babylon, I will visit you and fulfill***

215

My good word to you, to bring you back to this place. *'For I know the plans that I have for you,' declares the LORD, 'plans for welfare and not for calamity to give you a future and a hope. 'Then you will call upon Me and come and pray to Me, and I will listen to you.* *'You will seek Me and find Me when you search for Me with all your heart.* *'I will be found by you,' declares the LORD, 'and I will restore your fortunes and will gather you from all the nations* *and from all the places where I have driven you,' declares the LORD, 'and I will bring you back to the place from where I sent you into exile.'*

Yet He was still Israel's redeemer, for her time had not yet come. History was unfolding precisely according to the plan laid out before time was spoken into existence. The time would come for the kingdom to be taken from national Israel and given to another nation bearing fruit (Matt 21:43) - but that time was not during Isaiah's day.

Isaiah 54:9-10 *"For this is like the days of Noah to Me: when I swore that the waters of Noah would never flood the earth again, so I have sworn that I will not be angry with you or rebuke you. Though the mountains move and the hills shake, My love will not be removed from you and My covenant of peace will not be shaken," says your compassionate LORD.*

This is the promise to all who are called, not a promise to the nation-state of Israel. Jesus, the Holy One of Israel, saves all who have been appointed unto eternal life, from every nation, tribe, and tongue. This redemption is as the waters of Noah to me, says the Lord of Hosts. Author Hal Brunson observed:

> this points backwards, not merely to the language and theology of the slaughtered and speechless Lamb, but even to the very moment at which God would impute the transgressions of His people to their Savior and His righteousness to them. *"This"*, God says, *"is as the waters of Noah to me"* -

> *"this"* - His being *"despised and rejected of men"*; "this is as the waters of Noah – His identity as *"a man of sorrows, and acquainted with grief"*; His *"bearing our griefs and carrying our sorrows"*; the Savior *"stricken, smitten of God, and afflicted ... wounded for our transgressions, bruised for our iniquities, chastised for our peace, and striped for our healing"* - *"This is as the waters of Noah to me"* - His oppression, His affliction, His slaughtering, His substitutionary imprisonment within the iron bars of injustice, His burial with the wicked in the grave of hell's billows: *"This"*, says the Almighty, *"is as the waters of Noah to me.*[1]

This is the testimony of God and cannot be erased. National Israel would be ransomed without money, but that would be to serve as a type of the redemption God has planned for His spiritual children. Though mountains be moved and hills shaken (reminds me of the ending of Rev 6) God's love will not be removed from His sheep - because they are in His covenant of peace, that promise to Abraham in Gen 12 which finds fulfillment in the New Covenant. This is the word of the living God Who has compassion on His own.

Isaiah 54:11-15 *Poor [Jerusalem], storm-tossed, and not comforted, I will set your stones in black mortar, and lay your foundations in sapphires. I will make your fortifications out of rubies, your gates out of sparkling stones, and all your walls out of precious stones. Then all your children will be taught by the LORD, their prosperity will be great, and you will be established on [a foundation of] righteousness. You will be far from oppression, you will certainly not be afraid; you will be far from terror, it will certainly not come near*

---

1. Brunson, Hal, *The Rickety Bridge and the Broken Mirror,* page 60

you. If anyone attacks you, it is not from Me; whoever attacks you will fall before you.

Poor storm-tossed, pagan assaulted temporal, earthly Jerusalem. Though many a Jew anticipated the return of earthly Jerusalem to earthly glory, such was never realized. Because the purpose all along was for that city to serve as a shadow or type of the heavenly Jerusalem, that city from above, which is and always was the goal of YHWH. The description of the foundation and gates and walls harkens to what we read in Revelation 21. All of the children of promise will be taught by God, they will all know Him and not need to be told, "Know the Lord." (Jer 31:34). All in this kingdom will be prosperous - but not in the way the Jewish men thought; in righteousness that is of God Himself. No poverty, no fear of man, for God will defend His own. Part of the promises made to the patriarchs is almighty God's promise to protect and defend His people and take retribution out on those who attack them. This becomes all the more sweet to those of us who have been adopted into His family and are called His temple and His body. Let us see how this protection of God is portrayed for Israel – the Israel of God.

Abram. Genesis 12:2 & 3: *I will make of you a great nation, and I will bless you and make your name great, so that you will be a blessing. I will bless those who bless you, and him who dishonors you I will curse, and in you all the families of the earth shall be blessed.*

Jacob. Genesis 27:29: *Let peoples serve you, and nations bow down to you. Be lord over your brothers, and may your mother's sons bow down to you. Cursed be everyone who curses you, and blessed be everyone who blesses you!*

Israel. Numbers 24:8 & 9: *God brings him out of Egypt and is for him like the horns of the wild ox; he shall eat up the nations, his adversaries, and shall break their bones in pieces and pierce them through with his arrows. He crouched, he lay down like a lion and like a lioness; who will rouse him* *up? Blessed are those who bless you, and cursed are those who curse you.*

True Israel. 1 Corinthians 3:16-17: *Do you not know that you are God's temple and that God's Spirit dwells in you? If anyone destroys God's temple, God will destroy him. For God's temple is holy, and you are that temple.*

Re-read verse 15 in our chapter: *If anyone attacks you, it is not from Me; whoever attacks you will fall before you.* I pray we have more clarity about God's purpose and intent about protecting and caring for those who were not His people but now ARE His people.

Isaiah 54:16-17 *Look, I have created the craftsman who blows on the charcoal fire and produces a weapon suitable for its task; and I have created the destroyer to cause havoc. No weapon formed against you will succeed, and you will refute any accusation raised against you in court. This is the heritage of the LORD's servants, and their righteousness is from Me." [This is] the LORD's declaration.*

These past two verses show us the futility of man thinking he can wage war against God. Like gods who cannot hear, think, or speak; these men are themselves not far different from the gods they serve. All these men who rage against God are His creatures, using material He created. They can kill one another but cannot prevail against the One Who rules all. How could a creature prevail against the Creator? Who can lay a charge against the elect - it is God Who justifies (Romans 8:33). It is Christ Jesus who intercedes as our advocate, our mediator. Further - He Who knew no sin became sin so we could have His righteousness! (2 Cor 5:21). This is the same message YHWH is telling His people in Isaiah's gospel. Same gospel - all is from God for His glory and our good.

Dear reader - are you His people, or are you those that are called NOT His people? There is no benefit to knowing about Him if you do not know Him, or rather be known by Him.

Indeed, the more knowledge without salvation the greater the judgment. Jesus is the only way to peace with God. Spurn Him not, harden not your heart. There is a day coming whence there will be no room for repentance.

Isaiah 55 - YHWH calls His people to Himself.

This chapter opens with what many call "an invitation" to come to salvation. Dear reader, the Sovereign God revealed to us in Scripture does not invite people to come to Him. We will see more of this, Lord willing, as we examine this chapter.

Isaiah 55:1-2 *Come, everyone who is thirsty, come to the waters; and you without money, come, buy, and eat! Come, buy wine and milk without money and without cost! Why do you spend money on what is not food, and your wages on what does not satisfy? Listen carefully to Me, and eat what is good, and you will enjoy the choicest of foods.*

Many people who claim the gospel is an offer turn to any of several places where God calls people to come to Him. In the first place, the English word, come, is an imperative - a command, as it is in Hebrew and Greek. When a mother tells her toddler "come here," she is not inviting him, she's not offering him the option; she's commanding him. When the queen of England bids an entertainer to sing for her, everybody calls it a "command performance" because the queen issued the "invitation." So many who call God sovereign posit Him as someone who offers and invites His creatures to come into His kingdom - as if He were less than the queen of England, less than a mother of small children.

How much more greater and grander and beyond our ability to comprehend is the Creator and Judge of all flesh? When the Lord of glory tells His chosen ones, "Come!" it is, as everyone who embraces the doctrines of grace knows, an irresistible call. When you and I preach the gospel, we try to persuade men - the general call we give (not knowing who

220

the elect are) can be resisted or accepted. Yet our words, our persuasive speech is not what saves anyone. The Spirit of God moves as does the wind - no man controls nor is able to know for sure where He goes (John 3:8). And He gives life to that which was dead, and those called by God to come are no more able to say yes or no than Lazarus was, being 4 days dead in the tomb. Jesus did not invite Lazarus to come forth, didn't offer him another few years in the flesh. He commanded Lazarus to come forth; and Lazarus did so.

Preach the gospel to every creature, we are told. Nothing about offering the kingdom to anyone. Nothing about inviting them - compel them to come, the master of the wedding feast said. How do we compel people to come to Christ? By being faithful with our proclamation of His gospel. It is the power of God unto salvation for those who are being saved. He compels His chosen ones to come to the wedding feast.

When YHWH calls people who are thirsty to come to the waters, He is calling His people to Himself; this is not analogous to the general call we as men - for we do not know who are His people until we see the fruit of repentance and faith. Those who answer the gospel call of men are being drawn by the irresistible call from God to come! This is the command, not an invitation, that brings life eternal.

All of His people will come to Him, in due time. And they will all drink from the fount of living water, buy wine and milk (representing spiritual and physical nourishment) without money. Just as national Israel was redeemed from Babylon without cost, spiritual Israel redeemed from sin and death can buy without cost - for the redeemer has paid it all.

Yet national Israel (always not far from view in Isaiah) is rebuked by the questions - "Why do you spend money on what is not food?" and "Why do you work hard to buy that which does not satisfy?" We should ask ourselves these questions. How much of what God has given us do we waste on that which is not good for our bodies and souls? God says to the Jewish nation and to us: Listen to me! I will provide that which is GOOD, the CHOICEST of foods! He gives to His people His Son, whose blood was shed and body broken to give us life eternal.

Isaiah 55:3-5 *Pay attention and come to Me; listen, so that you will live. I will make an everlasting covenant with you, the promises assured to David. Since I have made him a witness to the peoples, a leader and commander for the peoples, so you will summon a nation you do not know, and nations who do not know you will run to you. For the LORD your God, even the Holy One of Israel, has glorified you.*

Again, YHWH tells His people to listen closely and come close so they will have life eternal. The everlasting covenant with His people, based on the promises made to David; he was told he would always have a Son to sit on his throne (2 Sam 7:11b-12). David was prone to think in terms of his own fleshly lineage - this was the way of the culture he was in - but Nathan's prophecy was clear that this Son would be different. This Son would be a witness to and ruler of all people. The Jews would summon nations that did not "know" Israel nor her God. The apostles were such, those who went out to the nations with the gospel proclamation - for salvation is of the Jews, to the Jew first then the Gentile! And all who have been called of God will run to Him and His people, for the glory of God is displayed as He raises up those who were spiritually dead to new life in Christ!

Note this saints - all that is done in the redemption of sinners is primarily for the glory of God. The grand and glorious benefits we derive from being reconciled to God are secondary; what we called in the military "collateral benefits" - those which are caused by the primary mission or goal but are not the primary mission or goal. That primary goal is that God would be glorified in all of His creation.

Isaiah 55:6-11 *Seek the LORD while He may be found; call to Him while He is near. Let the wicked one abandon his way and the sinful one his thoughts; let him return to the LORD, so He may have compassion on him, and to our God, for He will freely forgive. "For My thoughts are not your thoughts, and your ways are not My ways." [This is] the LORD's declaration. "For as heaven is higher than earth, so My ways are higher than your ways, and My thoughts than your thoughts. For just as rain and snow fall from heaven and do not return there without saturating the earth and making it germinate and sprout, and providing seed to sow and food to eat, so My word that comes from My mouth will not return to Me empty, but it will accomplish what I please and will prosper in what I send it [to do]."*

The prophet calls to his kinsmen, come to YHWH today! Perhaps echoing the warning of Psalm 95 to not harden their hearts as in the days of the wilderness, Isaiah calls the wicked and sinful people to abandon their thoughts and action and seek YHWH Who will have compassion on all of His people - granting FORGIVENESS.

Who is this that forgives sin, punishing another for them? How foolish this reasoning is from a human perspective! Man is naturally hard-wired for self-justification, proving he is better than others. But the Creator and Judge of all flesh says His way of thinking is different than ours, His way of doing things is different than ours. One of the problems man has is to think too lowly of God, too highly of self. Psalm 50:21 is a good reminder that goes along with Isaiah's passage.

Look up at the stars - can you imagine the distance to them? Think about how difficult that would be without the data our modern instruments have made available to even grad school children. Far beyond our ability to think or imagine, God's ways and thoughts are beyond ours. When the angelic host declares He is thrice holy, this is what they meant; God is NOT LIKE His creation. All our inclinations to think we know better than God need to be nipped in the bud, repented of and burned up. "Mother Earth" does not control the weather; there is One Who does! It is YHWH, Creator, upholder, sustainer, king, and judge of all creation! He gave creation the covenant of Noah (Gen 9:9-17), promising life on earth to even the most reprobate person.

As the farmer learns to depend on the rain and snow to keep his soil fertile, producing much produce, so His people should depend on His Word to do likewise when we are faithful to proclaim to all people. He WILL redeem His people by the foolishness of our preaching and proclaiming His gospel. In this we CANNOT trust our ways or thoughts but must submit to Him.

Isaiah 55:12-13 *You will indeed go out with joy and be peacefully guided; the mountains and the hills will break into singing before you, and all the trees of the field will clap [their] hands. Instead of the thornbush, a cypress will come up, and instead of the brier, a myrtle will come up; it will make a name for Yahweh as an everlasting sign that will not be destroyed.*

Who goes out - regardless of circumstances - with joy and peace? Only those who have peace beyond human understanding, peace that brings comfort and assurance and JOY unbounded; not subject to whether we have electricity in the coldest storm on record. Creation rejoices when people are reconciled to God; the singing of mountains and clapping hands of trees reflects the joy in heaven as the angels rejoice over one lost sheep brought into the great shepherd's sheepfold.

On the new earth, the curse brought on creation by Adam's sin (Gen 3:17-18) is lifted and good trees sprout up in place of thorns and briers. This new creation testifies of YHWH even more than the current creation (Psalm 19:1; Romans 1:19-20), and the new creation - new heavens and earth - will never come to an end. For there will be no more sin or temptation on that new earth where righteousness dwells. Death came through sin and the death of sin will mean the end of death. All this is the work of God in Christ, who put sin and hell and death to death by His death in the flesh. And being raised up to an indestructible life, Christ Jesus gives us an indestructible sure hope of eternal life with Him.

Again - if you hear His voice, do not harden your heart. Repent and believe on the Christ. If you are His, consider Him as He is - not like us in His nature. He is God the Son who gave Himself as a sacrifice to give His people eternal life. Be in awe of Him and do not allow the mountains and trees to praise Him more than you - or I - do.

Isaiah 56 - Redemption for Foreigners and Eunuchs.

In this chapter, God speaks to those called "His people" and He speaks to those who are not "His people." In this first part we see salvation decreed for those who were His covenant people and those who were not His people; in the second part we see a rebuke of those who remain not His people.

Isaiah 56:1-2 *This is what the LORD says: Preserve justice and do what is right, for My salvation is coming soon, and My righteousness will be revealed. Happy is the man who does this, anyone who maintains this, who keeps the Sabbath without desecrating it, and keeps his hand from doing any evil.*

Notice the first thing YHWH speaks: preserve justice and do what is right. National Israel had practiced long and hard to disobey God, as we have seen previously in this study. The salvation decreed for national Israel here is not eternal life, but salvation from slavery in Babylon - as they had been redeemed from slavery to Egypt. The righteousness of God would be displayed as Cyrus funded the return to Jerusalem and the rebuilding of that city and its temple. Those Jews who had kept the Sabbath and refrained from evil would be rewarded. The weekly Sabbath was highlighted here because it was signaled by God as THE sign His covenant with the Hebrew nation: Exodus 31:12-14 *The LORD said to Moses:*

"Tell the Israelites: You must observe My Sabbaths, for it is a sign between Me and you throughout your generations, so that you will know that I am Yahweh who sets you apart. Observe the Sabbath, for it is holy to you. Whoever profanes it must be put to death. If anyone does work on it, that person must be cut off from his people."

We had previously read what Amos had said about Israel profaning the Sabbath. Nehemiah also made note of it - read Nehemiah 13:15-18. Not many kept the Sabbath - most of them looked forward to doing evil in the marketplace on the first day of the week, if they were kept from doing so on the Sabbath (as we read in Amos 8). The things God identified as special to Him, His covenant people repeatedly trampled. As we read in the gospel accounts, they aggressively promoted the minors and missed the point repeatedly. May it not be so with us!

Isaiah 56:3-8 *No foreigner who has joined himself to the LORD should say, "The LORD will exclude me from His people"; and the eunuch should not say, "Look, I am a dried-up tree." For the LORD says this: "For the eunuchs who keep My Sabbaths, and choose what pleases Me, and hold firmly to My covenant, I will give them, in My house and within My walls, a memorial and a name better than sons and daughters. I will give each [of them] an everlasting name that will never be cut off. And the foreigners who join themselves to the LORD minister to Him, love the name of Yahweh and become His servants, all who keep the Sabbath without desecrating it and who hold firmly to My covenant—I will bring them to My holy mountain and let them rejoice in My house of prayer. Their burnt offerings and sacrifices will be acceptable on My altar, for My house will be called a house of prayer for all nations." [This is] the declaration of the Lord GOD, who gathers the dispersed of Israel: "I will gather to them still others besides those already gathered."*

Foreigners and eunuchs were generally excluded from worship; but those who joined with ethnic Israel and kept the covenant were included. YHWH reminds Israel of this - these who were not His people became His people when they were circumcised and agreed to keep the Mosaic Covenant. These foreigners were entitled to all the benefits and privileges of that covenant - with security better than the Jews had, IF they kept the covenant. This is how we know this passage is "in the flesh" and refers to the Mosaic Covenant and is not the fulfillment picture of the New Covenant: all the blessings of this covenant are dependent upon the human participants keeping it, holding FIRMLY to it (twice YHWH uses that term here). We see God gathering the exiled Jews and those who were not His people - teaching the Jews that YHW was serious about the Abrahamic promise of gathering countless people from every nation as His children. This beautiful word picture no doubt filled the nation of Israel with joy and awe; but we know from Scripture they continued to see things through eyes of flesh and thought their temporal nation was the end-game YHWH had in mind, never really understanding that Gentiles would be JOINT heirs and not accepted foreigners. Since no one will be justified in the sight of God by keeping any law (Romans 3:20), the exhortations for keeping the law of the Mosaic Covenant cannot be that of finding eternal peace with God. The New Covenant is not dependent on anything man does - the blessings and inheritance is totally dependent on the work of Christ Jesus; the only faithful Son of Israel.

Isaiah 56:9-12 *All you animals of the field and forest, come and eat! Israel's watchmen are blind, all of them, they know nothing; all of them are mute dogs, they cannot bark; they dream, lie down, and love to sleep. These dogs have fierce appetites; they never have enough. And they are shepherds who have no discernment; all of them turn to their own way, every last one for his own gain. "Come, let me get [some] wine, let's guzzle [some] beer; and tomorrow will be like today, only far better!"*

This last part of the chapter is a rebuke to the faithless leaders of national Israel, echoing terms we read in the gospels -

blind guides, dogs, those seeking their own way, whose god is their bellies. Watchmen were supposed to keep a watch, warning the city of danger. Ezekiel, in chapter 34, devotes much effort at describing these responsibilities and Israel's failure to hold firmly and do them. People who are concerned and consumed with self will either be hopeless OR self-confident. These are described as blindly self-confident, with fierce appetites, seeking only their own gain - each one. These present the mindset Paul was warning against in 1 Cor 15:29-34, as some people were convinced the resurrection had already taken place and there was no longer any reason to be subject to the rule of God. *If the dead are not raised, let us eat and drink, for tomorrow we die! Do not be deceived: Bad company corrupts good morals. Come to your senses and stop sinning, for some people are ignorant about God. I say this to your shame.* (1 Cor 15:32b-34).

Brothers and sisters - let us be careful not to grow lax and drift into thinking we are doing good as we wander a crooked path of our desires. While we who are in Christ are kept by His Spirit and not our own work, none of us indwelt by His Spirit should be marked by a life of careless or deliberate sin. May God have mercy on us to keep us so we walk as children of the light! If you have not a desire to glorify Christ Jesus in your body, cry out for mercy and grace to do so. Do not be deceived, nothing done in the dark will remain hidden.

Isaiah 57 - No Peace for the Wicked.

As in much of Isaiah's writings - and, indeed, the whole of Scripture - this chapter presents a contrast between evil and righteous people. While we mainly see a focus on the promised Messiah as our hope, here the main focus is a warning to the wicked. The title for this chapter comes from the last verse thereof.

Isaiah 57:1-2 *The righteous one perishes, and no one takes it to heart; faithful men are swept away, with no one realizing that the righteous one is swept away from the presence of evil. He will enter into peace— they will rest on their beds— everyone who lives uprightly.*

In the world at large, when a righteous one dies, people don't mourn. As for the public record of what's happenin' now, they are swept into Orwell's "Memory Hole." What the wicked of the world cannot see is that being swept away from them into the first death brings rest and peace for the righteous. We know that all who live godly lives in Christ Jesus will face persecution. We know that the evil men rejoice when saints are killed. We also know we have a refuge in the risen Lord Jesus that protects us from the second death, bringing us peace and rest that the world cannot know.

Isaiah 57:3-5 *But come here, you sons of a sorceress, offspring of an adulterer and a prostitute! Who is it you are mocking? Who is it you are opening your mouth and sticking out your tongue at? Isn't it you, you rebellious children, you race of liars, who burn with lust among the oaks, under every green tree, who slaughter children in the wadis below the clefts of the rocks?*

Here's the first contrast of the destiny of the righteous with that of the wicked. The righteous enter into peaceful rest; the wicked are weighed and measured and found to be wanting. Look at all the descriptive words used here to describe the wicked and see how much of this evil is accepted as righteous in our culture right now. It's small talk when the Super Bowl's winning quarterback has a wife who's a witch; it's hushed up when a congressman has a mistress who's a communist Chinese spy. God is not mocked - nothing is hidden, nothing escapes. He asks these wicked people to examine themselves, to question what they are doing as He calls them rebellious liars and murderers of children. It's important to see that our nation is no different in its moral fiber than was national Israel - unregenerate people do wicked things!

Isaiah 57:6-10 *Your portion is among the smooth [stones] of the wadi; indeed, they are your lot. You have even poured out a drink offering to them; you have offered a grain offering; should I be satisfied with these? You have placed your bed on a high and lofty mountain; you also went up there to offer sacrifice. You have set up your memorial behind the door and doorpost. For away from Me, you stripped, went up, and made your bed wide, and you have made a bargain for yourself with them. You have loved their bed; you have gazed on their genitals. You went to the king with oil and multiplied your perfumes; you sent your couriers far away and sent [them] down even to Sheol. You became weary on your many journeys, [but] you did not say, "I give up!" You found a renewal of your strength; therefore you did not grow weak.*

YHWH posits 5 accusations against the wicked, as each of these verses start with an accusatorial "YOU" or "YOUR". Now the wages of sin are revealed. Those who murdered children in the wadi will face death there, as their blood will be poured out as they poured out offerings to their demons. They have sacrificed and made their homes at the high places - recall how many times Israel was told to take down the high places. The presence of the high places became an indication of Israel's morality; showing the lack of fear of God and the embrace of demons (see 2 Kings 17:7-23).

The wicked think they are far removed from God as they pursue their demon gods - sex is in view in verse 8. The wide bed refers to the pagan prostitutes' practice, Israel made a deal with them as they lusted after these strange women. The wicked lust after wealth and power as well, seeking to cushion their lives with luxury, no matter the cost. They renewed their strength in the pursuit of their lusts - so powerful are the desires of the wicked heart of the natural man.

Isaiah 57:11-13 *Who was it you dreaded and feared, so that you lied and didn't remember Me or take it to heart? Have I not kept silent for such a long time and you do not fear Me?*

I will expose your righteousness, and your works—they will not profit you. When you cry out, let your collection [of idols] deliver you! The wind will carry all of them off, a breath will take them away. But whoever takes refuge in Me will inherit the land and possess My holy mountain.

We know from the Scriptures that the carnal man never tires of hearing something new, always seeks after a sign that what he pursues is right for him. When carnal man does not see God (he suppresses his knowledge by his unrighteousness - Rom 1:18) he tells himself God is not real, he forgets what he knows about YHWH and hardens his heart against truth - fearing poverty in any form more than fearing God.

God IS NOT mocked; He will expose all the deeds and thoughts of the wicked - their righteousness is no more than menstrual rags, their deeds will not profit them. They devote themselves to dumb gods with no speech or sight or hearing; worthless idols that will be blown away and destroyed. BUT those who take refuge in YHWH will be taken care of. Note this: do not worry yourselves about what you eat or drink or wear, for your Father in heaven knows you have need of these things. But seek first His kingdom and all these lesser things will be given to you! Trust in God and He will provide bounty and peace and rest on His holy mountain - Zion.

Isaiah 57:14-16 *He said, "Build it up, build it up, prepare the way, remove [every] obstacle from My people's way." For the High and Exalted One who lives forever, whose name is Holy says this: "I live in a high and holy place, and with the oppressed and lowly of spirit, to revive the spirit of the lowly and revive the heart of the oppressed. For I will not accuse [you] forever, and I will not always be angry; for then the spirit would grow weak before Me, even the breath [of man], which I have made.*

God tells His people to prepare the way - foretelling the mission of John the Baptizer. Rather than put stumbling blocks of man's traditions in the way of people, we are to remove obstacles and proclaim the peace that comes with faith in Christ! There is peace with God, rest for weary souls who find their way to Mount Zion, the high and holy place where God's Spirit is. Those who are oppressed by the world, who hunger after righteousness will be revived, for God will not accuse and be angry with His people forever - for fragile man would grow too weary to continue on.

Isaiah 57:17-19 *Because of his sinful greed I was angry, so I struck him; I was angry and hid; but he went on turning back to the desires of his heart. I have seen his ways, but I will heal him; I will lead him and restore comfort to him and his mourners, creating words of praise." The LORD says, "Peace, peace to the one who is far or near, and I will heal him.*

Before being raised up in Christ, we were children of wrath like the rest (Eph 2:1-3). Because of our sin and selfishness God was angry and punished His people, in our times of rebellion. With His restrain removed, we turned back to the sinful desires of our hearts. But because He had set us apart from before the foundation of the world, there was never any possibility that He would abandon us to ourselves - God will heal, God will lead His people and restore us, comfort us and put words of praise into our mouths. For the promised Messiah proclaims peace, peace to those who are near (ethnic Israel, who had the oracles of God) and those who are far off (Gentiles, who were excluded from citizenship in Israel and foreigners to the covenants of the promise, without hope and without God in the world). To these, the wounds of Christ bring healing.

Isaiah 57:20-21 *But the wicked are like the storm-tossed sea, for it cannot be still, and its waters churn up mire and muck. There is no peace for the wicked," says my God.*

The wicked are in constant state of excitement as they accuse every one of the very things they do. They churn up the vile underbelly of the culture and declare it be virtue. They cannot live in peace with those who not agree with them, because own consciences accuse them of their sin. When you see the vile behavior and hear the vile speech of the popular and powerful in our world right now, it ought to cause you and me to vomit. But we need to take note of this: these wicked people have no peace with God and their souls are tormented by what they know about Him from the world He created. The wicked have no peace, says their Creator.

If you are raised up in Christ, you are an ambassador of peace; a messenger of reconciliation with God. All the more now we need to understand that the message the wicked consider foolishness is the only message that can bring life that is at peace with God.

Preach Christ to the wicked - whether they be at your place of work, school, home, of fellowship. There is no road to peace except the road of repentance and faith in Christ. Preach grace found in Christ as the only salve for what causes the souls of the wicked to wear themselves as they try to drown out their knowledge of Him. They will have no peace unless He gives it. His message of reconciliation is the only gospel we've been given - it is was brought us peace; it will bring peace to all of His people.

Isaiah 58 - Hypocrisy Exposed and Rebuked.

Having revealed the ways and the doom of the wicked in chapter 57, the prophet was inspired to reveal and rebuke the hypocrisy that was rampant in national Israel in this chapter.

Isaiah 58:1 Cry out loudly, don't hold back! Raise your voice like a trumpet. Tell My people their transgression and the house of Jacob their sins.

Isaiah is told by God to trumpet national Israel's sins to them - make it know widely to all. This is similar in intensity to the prior command to proclaim the good news, make it known to all (chapter 52). The balance of this short chapter is just that.

Isaiah 58:2-3a *"They seek Me day after day and delight to know My ways, like a nation that does what is right and does not abandon the justice of their God. They ask Me for righteous judgments; they delight in the nearness of God."* *"Why have we fasted, but You have not seen? We have denied ourselves, but You haven't noticed!"*

YHWH taunts Israel, acknowledging they APPEAR to seek Him, like a nation that does right in the eyes of God. They ask for righteous judgment and delight (this word is used several times in this chapter) in being close to Him. And yet - their actions speak louder than their words, as we shall see. Israel pointed to their pious actions and complain that God has not noticed. When Moses pleaded with God to NOT destroy the Hebrew nation, He did not tout their pious acts - He pleaded for God to remember His promise and act to keep His name from being profaned among the pagans. When people brag on their deeds of piety they are waving a flag of self-righteousness. Our desires to be close to God MUST be based on His righteousness for His glory and NEVER on our acts of piety.

Isaiah 58:3b-7 *Look, you do as you please on the day of your fast, and oppress all your workers. You fast [with] contention and strife to strike viciously with [your] fist. You cannot fast as [you do] today, [hoping] to make your voice heard on high. Will the fast I choose be like this: A day for a person to deny himself, to bow his head like a reed, and to spread out sackcloth and ashes? Will you call this a fast and a day acceptable to the LORD? Isn't the fast I choose: To break the chains of wickedness, to untie the ropes of the yoke, to set the oppressed free, and to tear off every yoke? Is it not to share your bread with the hungry, to bring the poor and homeless into your house, to clothe the naked when you see him, and not to ignore your own flesh [and blood]?*

Here is YHWH's response. He exposes their hypocrisy, as they treat the fast as a trifle while dealing wickedly with their workers and others. The fast respected by YHWH is one where a person denies himself in true humility and thanksgiving; when he breaks the chains of oppression rather than forges them, when he frees workers from the heavy yoke and shares bread with the hungry and his home and clothing with the poor. We see here a preview into the kingdom that Christ would bring to His people - where bearing one another's burden fulfills the law of Christ (Gal 6:2; James 2:1, 8-9; Matt 25:31-46)

Isaiah 58:8-12 *Then your light will appear like the dawn, and your recovery will come quickly. Your righteousness will go before you, and the LORD's glory will be your rear guard. At that time, when you call, the LORD will answer; when you cry out, He will say, 'Here I am.' If you get rid of the yoke among you, the finger-pointing and malicious speaking, and if you offer yourself to the hungry, and satisfy the afflicted one, then your light will shine in the darkness, and your night will be like noonday. The LORD will always lead you, satisfy you in a parched land, and strengthen your bones. You will be like a watered garden and like a spring whose waters never run dry. Some of you will rebuild the ancient ruins; you will restore the foundations laid long ago; you will be called the repairer of broken walls, the restorer of streets where people live.*

IF the people of Israel would truly humble themselves they would see a great light dawning and be healed. They would be clothed with His righteousness and the glory of YHWH would guard them. At that time, if they called upon Him, YHWH would answer - He would be near.

IF they got rid of the heavy yokes of oppression, the blaming, sharp tongues; IF they bore one another's burdens (Gal 6:2), poured themselves out as a drink offering their light would shine (Matt 5:14-16). YHWH would lead them, heal them, satisfy them - they would be like tree near the water (Psalms 1:3). The ruins and walls would be rebuilt upon the ancient foundation and the city would habitable again. When blessings depend on man's faithfulness, they are hard to come by. That was the nature of the Mosaic Covenant, called "Old" in the apostolic record describing the New Covenant.

Isaiah 58:13-14 *"If you keep from desecrating the Sabbath, from doing whatever you want on My holy day; if you call the Sabbath a delight, and the holy [day] of the LORD honorable; if you honor it, not going your own ways, seeking your own pleasure, or talking too much; then you will delight yourself in the LORD, and I will make you ride over the heights of the land, and let you enjoy the heritage of your father Jacob." For the mouth of the LORD has spoken.*

Israel profaned their Sabbath as they had their fasts. Rather than resting in the providential care of God, they did what they pleased. Upon their return from exile, while rebuilding the wall and town of Jerusalem, the Hebrews demonstrated their disdain for the Sabbath - the very sign and testimony of the covenant YHWH had made with Israel (Exodus 34:27 & 28; Deuteronomy 4:13; Nehemiah 13:15-22). They went their own way, seeking their own pleasure, talking endlessly. But IF they kept it, IF they honored it - THEN they would delight in seeing how wonderfully God had been providing for them. THEN God would cause them be victorious over the land, enjoying what was promised to Jacob (this was the land promise made to Abraham, Isaac, and Jacob). This is what YHWH has spoken - it is sure.

The sum of the matter is simple: no man has pure devotion, true piety, true humility that he can parade before God in a demand or plea for His favor. Not to us, not to us, but to thee be the glory! The only plea we have - for we can never be in position to demand ANYTHING from God - is to cry out for mercy. The work of Christ on our behalf is the only work that is pure, the only work acceptable to God. His righteousness is the only cover that can shield is from His wrath.

> Venture on Him, venture wholly
> Let no other trust intrude
> None but Jesus, none but Jesus
> Can do helpless sinners good

Isaiah 59 - Sin is SO hideous it takes an act of God to pay for it.

This chapter begins with a short reminder that the problem is not with God; He is not limited in His ability to hear His people and save them. The bulk of this chapter is a rather thorough description of sin with closure provided by getting back to salvation being of the Lord.

Isaiah 59:1 *Indeed, the LORD's hand is not too short to save, and His ear is not too deaf to hear.*

National Israel continued in the walk of Moses, complaining in trials and accusing God of not caring. On several occasions He reminded them of Whose strong arm delivered them from Egypt, the same made all things and rules all things - dried up the sea for Moses and his people to walk on. YHWH always hears His people, though we may not be aware - as Daniel wasn't for the 21 days Michael was delayed in getting word to him. The system of Sabbaths was to teach Israel to trust God - He would provide. The message to the women at the tomb, when they didn't see Jesus therein, was to "remember His words." This is our counsel today for the saints as well: trust God, remember His words. Pray to Him and trust nothing else.

Isaiah 59:2-3 *But your iniquities have built barriers between you and your God, and your sins have made Him hide [His] face from you so that He does not listen. For your hands are defiled with blood and your fingers, with iniquity; your lips have spoken lies, and your tongues mutter injustice.*

The sins of unregenerate people build impassible barriers between them and God, causing Him to turn from and not hear them. He lists their most egregious sins, which characterize people world-wide in every generation: they shed innocent blood, speak lies, and embrace injustice. In our day, those who "shout their abortions," who demand punishment for speaking truth, who declare falsehoods to be truth - all are storing up wrath for that great day of judgment.

God is not wooing these reprobates to repent. There may some elect therein that have yet to be called out, but as a group they have built barriers between them and Him and He does not hear them.

Verses 4 - 6 rehearse more of what characterizes these people, being those who speaks worthless words, gives birth to evil, set traps for any and all, yet they cannot hide behind their deeds, worthless and sinful deeds, and their hands are full of violence.

I am amazed whenever I hear someone claim man is basically good and just needs education and good role models. Our technology and other tools have merely given us as a people more ways to speak worthless words and fill our hands with violence, all the while thinking we are unseen - or that it's OK unless we get caught. Man in his natural state is depraved, totally wrecked in every function of his being and unable to do or even want anything good. This part of the chapter is the story of that person.

Isaiah 59:7-8 *Their feet run after evil, and they rush to shed innocent blood. Their thoughts are sinful thoughts; ruin and wretchedness are in their paths. They have not known the path of peace, and there is no justice in their ways. They have made their roads crooked; no one who walks on them will know peace.*

People who run after evil, not those who fall into it because they're sleep walking. People whose thoughts are only evil continually leaving ruin in their wakes. Here's the end: these have not known the path of peace, they know not justice. Like the river following the path of least resistance, the man who does so will have a crooked path and none who follow them find peace. This is the reason the promised Messiah came - to bring rest and peace to wretched sinners. None can know peace unless they are given new life and are brought near to Him.

238

Isaiah 59:9-11 *Therefore justice is far from us, and righteousness does not reach us. We hope for light, but there is darkness; for brightness, but we live in the night. We grope along a wall like the blind; we grope like those without eyes. We stumble at noon as though it were twilight; [we are] like the dead among those who are healthy. We all growl like bears and moan like doves. We hope for justice, but there is none; for salvation, [but] it is far from us.*

Isaiah speaks for Israel - justice and righteousness they know not. They live in the dark and grope like those in Rev 8 when the fourth trumpet sounds and a third of them wandered in the dark as if they were blind. They stumble in broad daylight, seeing not - as dead among the living. This ought to put Eph 2 in your mind, where the saints are described as those who WERE dead in sins but NOW made alive in Christ; we also should think of Romans 14:99ff and be careful to not cause a brother to stumble by our exercise of Christian liberty. These who rage against their Creator are like beasts who hope for what think justice is (overlooking their sins) but they cannot find it. Nor can salvation be found by them - as far as God has turned His face, further still is salvation for those who cannot hear His voice.

Isaiah 59:12-15a *For our transgressions have multiplied before You, and our sins testify against us. For our transgressions are with us, and we know our iniquities: transgression and deception against the LORD, turning away from following our God, speaking oppression and revolt, conceiving and uttering lying words from the heart. Justice is turned back, and righteousness stands far off. For truth has stumbled in the public square, and honesty cannot enter. Truth is missing, and whoever turns from evil is plundered.*

The prophet leads them to see how their rebellion has multiplied before God, testifying against them. They have lived and worked AGAINST God, turned from following Him; they sought to oppress others, revolting against

239

YHWH's covenant and lying to all. Just like the politicians who hold the high offices in the US of A these days. Justice is not to be found, not our Congress nor in our "Supreme Court." Truth is missing and honesty is barred from entry. Only those who try to keep themselves from evil are plundered. Our nation looks just like national Israel in this passage. God have mercy on us.

Isaiah 59:15b-20 *The LORD saw that there was no justice, and He was offended. He saw that there was no man— He was amazed that there was no one interceding; so His own arm brought salvation, and His own righteousness supported Him. He put on righteousness like a breastplate, and a helmet of salvation on His head; He put on garments of vengeance for clothing, and He wrapped Himself in zeal as in a cloak. So He will repay according to [their] deeds: fury to His enemies, retribution to His foes, and He will repay the coastlands. They will fear the name of Yahweh in the west and His glory in the east; for He will come like a rushing stream driven by the wind of the LORD. "The Redeemer will come to Zion, and to those in Jacob who turn from transgression." [This is] the LORD's declaration.*

When YHWH looks down on carnal man, He sees no justice, for natural man perverts every good thing God gives him. No man looking out for his neighbor, pleading for justice in place of the corruption that was normal. This is a stench in His nose.

Note the response to all this wickedness: God decides to intervene, using His own arm to bring salvation, His own righteousness as a breastplate with a helmet of salvation on His head. Did you ever see the connection between Eph 6 and Isaiah 59 before? He wore garments of vengeance, reminding me of the scene in Rev 19 with Jesus on a white horse, His eyes like a fiery flame, and He wore a robe stained with blood; and He will trample the winepress of the fierce anger of God, the Almighty. Isaiah says He will repay according to their deeds, fury to His enemies - from the islands and coastlands all will fear His name. His glory will spread from east and He will come like a rushing steam driven by YHWH. In the midst of all this judgment and fury against His enemies, God declares, *The Redeemer will come to Zion, to those in Jacob (Israel) who turn from their sin.* He will gather every one of His chosen ones to Himself, safe on Zion, where His righteousness protects them. This is YHWH's declaration - it is certain!

Isaiah 59:21 *"As for Me, this is My covenant with them," says the LORD: "My Spirit who is on you, and My words that I have put in your mouth, will not depart from your mouth, or from the mouth of your children, or from the mouth of your children's children, from now on and forever," says the LORD.*

This last verse confirms that the talk of bringing people to Zion speaks of eternal redemption and not merely a return to earthly Jerusalem. YHWH's language here is very reminiscent of what He spoke through Jeremiah: Jeremiah 31:31-34 *"Look, the days are coming"—[this is] the LORD's declaration—"when I will make a new covenant with the house of Israel and with the house of Judah. [This one will] not be like the covenant I made with their ancestors when I took them by the hand to bring them out of the land of Egypt— a covenant they broke even though I had married them"—the LORD's declaration. "Instead, this is the covenant I will make with the house of Israel after those days"—the LORD's declaration. "I will put My teaching within them and write it on their hearts. I will be their God, and they will be My people. No longer will one teach his neighbor or his brother, saying, 'Know the LORD,' for they will all know Me, from the least to the greatest of them"—[this is] the LORD's declaration. "For I will forgive their wrongdoing and never again remember their sin."*

Isaiah's account covers similar territory: His words would be in the mouths of His people and would not depart - which means they would not drift away. This is not like the covenant made with Moses and those people who wandered off more than they sought reconciliation. Isaiah's account says this constant presence would be with Jacob and his children on to countless generations. Rather than think this describes fleshly relationships as the Jews of Jesus' day rested on, it's far safer and more accurate to think this describes what Paul mentioned, calling Timothy his son in the faith (1 Tim 1:2) and told everyone that those who believe are children of Abraham according to the promise (Gal 3:29; Romans 4:16).

Dear reader, please carefully consider what God spoke here. Sin - yours, mine, everyone's - is hideous and is worthy of God's fiery wrath. Man cannot resolve this problem, it's his nature to continue in this grotesque rebellion against the Creator. God Himself has provided the only answer to this horrible situation - Christ the Son has come to give Himself as a redeemer, to pay the price for the wayward sheep called to come the great Shepherd of their souls. Believe on Him, repent of your sins - recognize they are wicked and you are responsible. Cry out to Jesus, the Redeemer has come to Zion and He calls all His people to come to Him.

Isaiah 60 - God's Glory in Zion.

This chapter is another example of what is called dual or double reference prophecy, where the Scripture gives word pictures of what will happen soon on this earth (near) and what will happen at the end of the age, on the new earth (far). As in the Olivet Discourse, references to near and far are mixed together in Hebrew fashion, making it difficult for our linear western minds to make sense of it. Hence, many think this chapter is ONLY near, lending false support for a dispensational view.

Isaiah 60:1-3 *Arise, shine, for your light has come, and the glory of the LORD shines over you. For look, darkness covers the earth, and total darkness the peoples; but the LORD will*

242

shine over you, and His glory will appear over you. Nations will come to your light, and kings to the brightness of your radiance.

In 59:9 the people of Israel cried for light, even as they refused the light God had given them; so it is in our current chapter. Isaiah used similar language in 9:2, 29:19, 30:26, 51:17, and 52:2. In this context, his words are reminiscent of the creation account, wherein darkness covered the earth and God created light. The opening of John's gospel conveys this very same message, which begins and ends this chapter: *A great light has come in the midst of the sin-darkened world. And His own knew Him not.* Lastly, we see in verse 3 a foretelling of the end of the age: Revelation 21:23-25 *The city does not need the sun or the moon to shine on it, because God's glory illuminates it, and its lamp is the Lamb. The nations will walk in its light, and the kings of the earth will bring their glory into it. Each day its gates will never close because it will never be night there.*

Isaiah 60:4-5 *Raise your eyes and look around: they all gather and come to you; your sons will come from far away, and your daughters will be carried on the hip. Then you will see and be radiant, and your heart will tremble and rejoice, because the riches of the sea will become yours and the wealth of the nations will come to you.*

Sons and daughters (young ones - being carried on the hip) were signs of wealth in the ancient near east. Having these children would cause the Jewish people to rejoice and be satisfied. But I think we ought to look back to the promise to Abram and how it is being fulfilled in the New Covenant - Abraham would be the father to many and all who believe on Christ are children of Abraham, according to promise, not according to fleshly lineage. This will cause all indwelt by the Holy Spirit to tremble and rejoice, as all the riches of the earth will be ours when Jesus returns to make all things new.

Verses 6 - 9 describe the wealth that will be brought to Israel, including camels carrying gold and frankincense; flocks of sheep and goats for sacrifice to glorify God's house; ships from Spain bringing children with silver and gold; all for the honor and glory of YHWH - the Holy One of Israel!

Isaiah 60:10-12 *Foreigners will build up your walls, and their kings will serve you. Although I struck you in My wrath, yet I will show mercy to you with My favor. Your gates will always be open; they will never be shut day or night so that the wealth of the nations may be brought into you, with their kings being led [in procession]. For the nation and the kingdom that will not serve you will perish; those nations will be annihilated.*

Perhaps God speaks of when Artaxerxes paid for Nehemiah to rebuild the wall of earthly Jerusalem - they were served by that king. He reminds Israel that they have been punished for their rebellion, yet He will have mercy on them, bestowing His favor upon them. Here is a look at prophecy fulfilled in our past, in national Israel's time. What comes next, I believe, is a look at prophecy fulfilled at the end of time, as recorded in Revelation 21:25-26 *Each day its gates will never close because it will never be night there. They will bring the glory and honor of the nations into it.* For until then, wars and rumors of war will fill our ears and wicked men and their governments will not be eliminated until the Lamb returns to judge them.

Isaiah 60:13-14 *The glory of Lebanon will come to you— [its] pine, fir, and cypress together— to beautify the place of My sanctuary, and I will glorify My dwelling place. The sons of your oppressors will come and bow down to you; all who reviled you will fall facedown at your feet. They will call you the City of the LORD, Zion of the Holy One of Israel.*

Lebanon coming to Israel reflects the restoration of that land as we read about in 35:2, with images of wealth (healthy trees flourishing) bringing beauty to the dwelling place of God.

This was accomplished with the rebuilding of the temple in Jerusalem, but God's glory never dominated that place as it had previous ones. His temple on the new earth will fulfill this prophecy, as the oppressors who have plagued God's covenant people will bow down and fall on their faces before us, as Christ noted in Revelation 3:9 *Take note! I will make those from the synagogue of Satan, who claim to be Jews and are not, but are lying—note this—I will make them come and bow down at your feet, and they will know that I have loved you.* God's people are now known as His temple; since we belong to the Holy One of Israel, even Christ, we are on Zion, not Sanai - the city of YHWH!

Isaiah 60:15-17 *Instead of your being deserted and hated, with no one passing through, I will make you an object of eternal pride, a joy from age to age. You will nurse on the milk of nations, and nurse at the breast of kings; you will know that I, Yahweh, am your Savior and Redeemer, the Mighty One of Jacob. I will bring gold instead of bronze; I will bring silver instead of iron, bronze instead of wood, and iron instead of stones. I will appoint peace as your guard and righteousness as your ruler.*

This short paragraph lists 6 different contrasts between Israel's treatment by the world and YHWH's treatment of His people, with a statement in the middle showing why He does these things. These 6 contrasts deal with temporal things, dealing with the wealth symbols of the era: prideful, served by kings, having gold, silver, bronze, and iron instead of lesser materials. All these are promised so His people *will know that I, Yahweh, am your Savior and Redeemer, the Mighty One of Jacob.* Saints, we need to keep this in mind - the primary, over-arching reason anything and everything was created is to bring glory and honor to God. Our salvation is not primarily about us - it is so God will be glorified in justifying sinners; the angels will continuously marvel at this! And YHWH will appoint peace as our guard and righteousness as our ruler - something that was begun at His first advent and will be complete upon His second and last advent.

Isaiah 60:18-20 *Violence will never again be heard of in your land; devastation and destruction [will be gone from] your borders. But you will name your walls salvation and your gates, praise. The sun will no longer be your light by day, and the brightness of the moon will not shine on you; but the LORD will be your everlasting light, and your God will be your splendor. Your sun will no longer set, and your moon will not fade; for the LORD will be your everlasting light, and the days of your sorrow will be over.*

Another series of contrasts, but all of these compare the fading glory and constant warfare of this age with the peace and rest of the age to come. No more violence, devastation, or destruction - things which plagued Israel and plague us this day. The walls that protect us will be called "salvation" and the gates called "praise" because the salvation Christ has earned for us keeps us secure for eternity, filling our mouths with praise!

Providing imagery for John's Apocalypse, Isaiah tells us no more sun and moon for light because YHWH will be our eternal light, God will be our splendor. YHWH will be our everlasting light - mentioned twice so we don't miss it - and sorrow will be gone. All that effects of the curse will be gone. See how God describes it: Revelation 21:1-4 *Then I saw a new heaven and a new earth, for the first heaven and the first earth had passed away, and the sea no longer existed. I also saw the Holy City, new Jerusalem, coming down out of heaven from God, prepared like a bride adorned for her husband. Then I heard a loud voice from the throne: Look! God's dwelling is with humanity, and He will live with them. They will be His people, and God Himself will be with them and be their God. He will wipe away every tear from their eyes. Death will no longer exist; grief, crying, and pain will exist no longer, because the previous things have passed away.*

Eternal light and the glory of God - that's what Isaiah is painting for us. Same as we read in Revelation 22:1-5 *Then he showed me the river of living water, sparkling like crystal, flowing from the throne of God and of the Lamb down the middle of the broad street [of the city]. The tree of life was on both sides of the river, bearing 12 kinds of fruit, producing its fruit every month. The leaves of the tree are for healing the nations, and there will no longer be any curse. The throne of God and of the Lamb will be in the city, and His slaves will serve Him. They will see His face, and His name will be on their foreheads. Night will no longer exist, and people will not need lamplight or sunlight, because the Lord God will give them light. And they will reign forever and ever.*

Note the parallels between John's account and Isaiah's and see that both speak the same language, describing the same scene. And this is how our chapter finishes.

Isaiah 60:21-22 *Then all your people will be righteous; they will possess the land forever; they are the branch I planted, the work of My hands, so that I may be glorified. The least will become a thousand, the smallest a mighty nation. I am Yahweh; I will accomplish it quickly in its time.*

In the New Covenant alone are ALL the members righteous, because each has been purchased by Christ and His righteousness imputed to them. We will possess the new earth forever because God has done this! Done this SO HE MAY BE GLORIFIED! He who would be great in the kingdom must be a servant of the least; whoever wants to be first in the kingdom must be slave of all (Matt 20:26-27). This reflects the means by which the Lord Jesus came into the world, the least of us from a nowhere town; a servant to His own creatures to the point of death on the cross. Brothers and sisters, let none of us think we He is fortunate to have us; let none of us think we are better than those who know Him not. All is done by God for His glory and we have no reason to boast except in Him. We are no better than the worst reprobate, we are better OFF because the Lamb of God has given Himself for us.

Isaiah 61 - Jubilee!

It's as if the prophet anticipated the climax of his work and saw the promise of the Messiah more and more clearly. It was most certainly a burden on his soul to have his kinsmen of the flesh come to see Him as well. That ought to be our desire!

Isaiah 61:1-3 *The Spirit of the Lord GOD is on Me, because the LORD has anointed Me to bring good news to the poor. He has sent Me to heal the brokenhearted, to proclaim liberty to the captives and freedom to the prisoners; to proclaim the year of the LORD's favor, and the day of our God's vengeance; to comfort all who mourn, to provide for those who mourn in Zion; to give them a crown of beauty instead of ashes, festive oil instead of mourning, and splendid clothes instead of despair. And they will be called righteous trees, planted by the LORD to glorify Him.*

This language has peeked out in various passages in Isaiah's gospel, all of which are based on the Levitical teaching about the year of Jubilee in Lev 25, which came every 50 years and was the basis for debt cancellation, release of slaves, return of property, and redemption and atonement.

When Jesus came back from His time of temptation in the dessert, He was teaching in their synagogues, being acclaimed by everyone (Luke 4:15). Then He entered into the synagogue, as was His custom, in Nazareth - the city of His birth. He walked in and stood up, indicating He was ready to read. (Luke 4:17) The scroll of the prophet Isaiah was given to Him, and unrolling the scroll, He found the place where it was written, in Isaiah 61, which details these Jubilee blessings and declared that His coming had fulfilled those promises! Jesus stopped quoting Isaiah at the point wherein prophecy was fulfilled at that time. The latter part of verse 2 will be fulfilled when He returns to judge the nations, gather His people, and make all things new: and the day of our God's vengeance; to comfort all who mourn.

When John's disciples asked if Jesus was the promised one (while John was in jail), Luke 7:22-23 *He replied to them, "Go and report to John the things you have seen and heard: The blind receive their sight, the lame walk, those with skin diseases are healed, the deaf hear, the dead are raised, and the poor are told the good news. And anyone who is not offended because of Me is blessed."*

Jesus did send John reassurance but not in the way we might expect, not with words of fleshly comfort. He declared Himself as Lord of the Sabbath as His witness. He brought the age of the true Sabbath, the day of the Lord's favor! This is true Jubilee!

Isaiah 61:4-7 *They will rebuild the ancient ruins; they will restore the former devastations; they will renew the ruined cities, the devastations of many generations. Strangers will stand and feed your flocks, and foreigners will be your plowmen and vinedressers. But you will be called the LORD's priests; they will speak of you as ministers of our God; you will eat the wealth of the nations, and you will boast in their riches. Because your shame was double, and they cried out, "Disgrace is their portion," therefore, they will possess double in their land, and eternal joy will be theirs.*

The first part of this passage points to the rebuilding of Jerusalem, which was the object of most Jews. Israel did have foreigners provide for them and trade with them, but did not have them as servants throughout the land. In Exodus 19, the infant Jewish nation was told they would be His kingdom of priests and a holy nation, IF they listened to Him and kept the covenant He gave them on Mount Horeb. Peter also used this language in declaring that all who had faith in Christ Jesus *are living stones being built into a spiritual house for a holy priesthood ... you are a chosen race, a royal priesthood, a holy nation, a people for His possession* (1 Peter 2:5, 9). The blessings promised in the Mosaic Covenant were temporal and dependent upon the obedience of those in that covenant; those promised in the New Covenant are spiritual (many with temporal aspects) and dependent on the faithfulness of the Messiah, in whom is the fullness of God. One is secure, like building on rock; the other is tenuous, like building on sand.

The last sentence in this passage shows how devoted God is protecting and rewarding His people. Those who were not His people but have now been made His people receive mercy (1 Peter 2:10) - the "double land" refers to the new earth that Peter also wrote about. All the inhabitants of that land, the royal priesthood, will have eternal joy, based on the unbounded blessedness and bliss of fully realizing what Christ has done for us. We see through a glass dimly now, but will see Him face-to-face one day!

Isaiah 61:8-9 *For I Yahweh love justice; I hate robbery and injustice; I will faithfully reward them and make an everlasting covenant with them. Their descendants will be known among the nations, and their posterity among the peoples. All who see them will recognize that they are a people the LORD has blessed.*

When YHWH announces He loves justice and hates theft and injustice, He is reminding national Israel of their consistent failure to be just, as they fell into oppression on a routine basis. Zechariah 7:8-14 is one such time when God spells out Israel's failures to do justice, Micah reminded them that to *do justice, love mercy, and walk humbly before your God* was the sum of obedience pleasing to YHWH. Since man is unable, in his natural condition, to do these things, God Himself has made a covenant by His Son, and His reward is in His hand, to give to every son and daughter He has purchased with His death. All the nations will be in awe of the glories of God poured out on His people and then all the nations will be judged and swept away as He descends upon the new earth with His spiritual house.

Isaiah 61:10-11 *I greatly rejoice in the LORD, I exult in my God; for He has clothed me with the garments of salvation and wrapped me in a robe of righteousness, as a groom wears a turban and as a bride adorns herself with her jewels. For as the earth produces its growth, and as a garden enables what is sown to spring up, so the Lord GOD will cause righteousness and praise to spring up before all the nations.*

The response to one who has been raised up by the Spirit is to GREATLY rejoice in YHWH, to exult in God! He has clothed us in His righteousness - that of the highest royalty! Garments of salvation are necessary - recall the parable of the wedding feast and the one at the end who had no proper clothes. These are not the ostentatious robes of the Levitical priesthood but the humble yet glorious robes of the eternal righteousness of the glorious Creator and Judge of all flesh! No amount of increase in the bounty of this world can truly compare with the amazing transformation of a sinner being raised up and clothed in Christ!

Saints - are you in AWE at being in Christ? Look deeply into His Word, seeking to see Him more clearly, more gloriously and mighty! Let your soul be swept up to the heavenlies, wherein we are seated with Him, to rejoice with all the saints because the Lamb has conquered and ransomed us from master sin!

People of the world: time is short, the Judge is coming. You will find no refuge, no hiding place anywhere on this world. He who created the world sees all and judges righteously. Cry out for mercy and plead for the Judge to pardon you and cleans you and give you a new heart.

Jesus is coming again. This time, not to deal with sin but to gather those who eagerly await Him. His reward is in His hand - and so is His sword.

Isaiah 62 - The Glory of Zion; God with us.

This chapter confronts the reader with a decision as to who is speaking here, is it the prophet or is it the promised seed - the Servant of God? I think throughout this chapter, we have words from Christ.

Isaiah 62:1-2a *I will not keep silent because of Zion, and I will not keep still because of Jerusalem, until her righteousness shines like a bright light and her salvation, like a flaming torch. Nations will see your righteousness and all kings, your glory.*

Throughout the Hebrew Scriptures, Zion refers to a fortified city prized by national Israel. In the New Covenant passages and in several Old Covenant prophets, Zion refers to the spiritual reality of God's people being present with Him. In Hebrews 12:18-29 we see this most clearly as earthly Israel is contrasted with spiritual Israel. Rather than gathering at Mt Sinai, with the blazing fire, gloom, and storm which was to terrifying that Moses was afraid; we who His people have come to Mount Zion, the living city of God (heavenly Jerusalem), wherein angels celebrate.

Isaiah refers to this in this passage, where he reports that Zion, also termed Jerusalem, will have righteousness that shines like heaven. She is marked by her salvation. Nations will see this glory and nothing is able to compare to it.

Recall the light of the world that John wrote of, John 1:1-5 *In the beginning was the Word, and the Word was with God, and the Word was God. He was with God in the beginning. All things were created through Him, and apart from Him not one thing was created that has been created. Life was in Him, and that life was the light of men. That light shines in the darkness, yet the darkness did not overcome it.* So intimately connected are the three-in-one that nothing happens apart from each being active, though the Spirit is often not mentioned, as in this passage from John. But Moses made note of the Spirit of God moving over the waters. The connection of John with Isaiah 62 is the light of the world that shines, which darkness cannot overcome. The shining light of the saints' righteousness is that of Christ Himself, and it brings salvation to sinners. This light overcomes the darkness of our unregenerate souls and brings life to that which was dead.

Isaiah 62:2b-5 *You will be called by a new name that the LORD's mouth will announce. You will be a glorious crown in the LORD's hand, and a royal diadem in the palm of your God. You will no longer be called Deserted, and your land will not be called Desolate; instead, you will be called My Delight is in Her, and your land Married; for the LORD delights in you, and your land will be married. For as a young man marries a young woman, so your sons will marry you; and as a groom rejoices over [his] bride, so your God will rejoice over you.*

Seven statements as to what Jerusalem will be, none of it contingent upon national Israel's performance under their covenant. Unilateral actions of God in redeeming and purifying His people, declaring they will have a new name (see Rev 3:12), will be a glorious crown (see Rev 4:10, 11). His people decorate the One who redeemed them, no longer barren but married to God, who delights in those He chose and ransomed. National Israel never had this fatherly relationship with God; heavenly Jerusalem, the spiritual house Peter spoke of - these are those who call Him Abba, Father. They are the ones described as Hs bride (2 Cor 11:2; Rev 19:7; 21:2, 9), the one to whom He is bound.

The first half of verse 5 is obscure: who are the sons marrying? John Gill thought this phrase was more properly interpreted, "as a young man dwells with a virgin, so thy sons shall dwell in thee" - which is how he says the Septuagint and Latin Vulgate render it. The last half of this verse is clear and is alluded to in the New Covenant passages, highlighted in Rev 19 and 21. In Rev 19 the marriage of the Lamb is announced, His bride has prepared herself and was given fine linen, bright and pure, to wear. This linen is the righteousness of Christ; the bride has prepared for this by being diligent in her walk in this wicked world, looking for the return of her Lord. In Rev 21, God's dwelling is with mankind as He makes all things new and the bride is revealed to be New Jerusalem, coming down out of heaven from God. There is no sanctuary because God almighty and the Lamb are such; there is no sun or moon because God's glory shines thereon and the lamp/light of the new world is the Lamb of God, who takes away the sin of this world.

Isaiah 62:6-7 *Jerusalem, I have appointed watchmen on your walls; they will never be silent, day or night. There is no rest for you, who remind the LORD. Do not give Him rest until He establishes and makes Jerusalem the praise of the earth.*

Here we have a double or dual application. Earthly Jerusalem did have watchmen - Ezekiel spends some time describing their function (chapter 34). In the kingdom of God inaugurated, present within the saints in this age, elders function in this role - warning of wolves and announcing the glories of the gospel of Christ. There will be rest for these watchmen when the New Jerusalem comes down out of heaven.

Isaiah 62:8-9 *The LORD has sworn with His right hand and His strong arm: I will no longer give your grain to your enemies for food, and foreigners will not drink your new wine you have labored for. For those who gather grain will eat it and praise the LORD, and those who harvest the grapes will drink [the wine] in My holy courts.*

Throughout Isaiah we've seen references to YHWH's raised arm, His strong arm. These refer to His might and power over all creation and alluded to His deliverance of Israel from Egypt. For generations, pagan nations raided Israel and took her produce - usually as judgment for their sin, as seen in Lev 26:16; Deut 28:31-33; and Judges 6:3-6. YHWH will put a stop to this, meaning Israel would retain more of her wealth and be very prosperous. National Israel never saw this prosperity. As long as people focus on kingdoms of this world, they will have difficulty seeing the kingdom of God. Unless one is born from above, he cannot see the kingdom of God!

Isaiah 62:10-12 *Go out, go out through the gates; prepare a way for the people! Build it up, build up the highway; clear away the stones! Raise a banner for the peoples. Look, the LORD has proclaimed to the ends of the earth, "Say to Daughter Zion: Look, your salvation is coming, His reward is with Him, and His gifts accompany Him." And they will be called the Holy People, the LORD's Redeemed; and you will be called Cared For, A City Not Deserted.*

Once more we see reference to clearing the way, preparing the way for the people to come to the Lord, raising His banner so all can see. John the Baptizer prepared the way, announcing the Lamb of God, awakening Israel to the consummation of their standing and the announcing of the new way, by faith and not by physical procreation. This is the gospel proclamation that we are charged with, heralding Christ Jesus as the savior of sinners, announcing peace that comes apart from the law and prophet even as it was foretold therein.

As promised to Abraham, salvation is proclaimed throughout the earth, as God will redeem His people from every nation, tongue, and tribe. The Lamb is coming to Zion, bringing salvation and His reward and gifts to those will be called "the Holy People, YHWH's redeemed" - which Peter alludes to: 1 Peter 2:9-10 *But you are a chosen race, a royal priesthood, a holy nation, a people for His possession, so that you may proclaim the praises of the One who called you out of darkness into His marvelous light. Once you were not a people, but now you are God's people; you had not received mercy, but now you have received mercy.* This is how all the ransomed souls are seen in the eyes of God.

Since this new city, made of spiritual stones, is the dwelling place of God, it will be cared for like none other; it will never be deserted for God is with us! That is why He was called Immanuel. He is not only **with** us, but He is **for** us - a **refuge** in every storm. Ponder that saints - God is with us and He preserves and protects us! I dare say this is something we do not meditate on enough - even though it is a wonderful truth that bring great comfort in times of trials. Carefully consider how this concept is put into song, this from Matthew Smith's rendition of "Hiding Place:"

> Should seven storms of vengeance roll
> And shake this earth from pole to pole
> No thunderbolt shall daunt my face
> While Jesus is my hiding place
> While Jesus is my hiding place
>
> On Him almighty vengeance fell
> Which would have sunk this world to Hell
> He bore it for a sinful race
> To make Himself our hiding place

Praise the Lord who gave Himself for us! Make His mercies known, proclaim His glorious gospel far and wide. He will gain the full reward for His work. He is worthy of our worship. God with us.

Isaiah 63 - The Revelation of Christ.

John's Revelation of Christ was not the first; it was the most complete. Even so, he leaned on several OT prophets, mainly Isaiah. We see in chapter 63 some striking connections, showing us this vision given to Isaiah was as much an apocalyptical work as is John's. This chapter has very descriptive pictures of Christ Jesus as the judge of creation

Who metes out punishment. Once more, we cannot keep from seeing John Apocalypse in our minds as we read Isaiah's words. The first part of this chapter has Isaiah asking questions of Christ, getting answers that reveal it is He.

Isaiah 63:1 *Who is this coming from Edom in crimson-stained garments from Bozrah— this One who is splendid in His apparel, rising up proudly in His great might? It is I, proclaiming vindication, powerful to save.*

In chapter 34 we read of YHWH's judgment on Edom (verses 4 & 5 speak of the sword used therein) as well as in Ezekiel 24:12-14. When this One comes from Edom in crimson-stained garments, this judgment is in view. Amos 1 tells of the judgment that fell on Bozrah (verses 11 &12). In Rev 19:13 we read, *And he was clothed with a vesture dipped in blood: and his name is called The Word of God.* None but Christ Jesus is this warrior, in garments that are splendid, representing the righteous judgement of the One Who created all things. No man other than Christ can be proud of His accomplishments and His might, because only His works are free from sin.

So when Isaiah asks, "Who is this?" Jesus answers, "It is I, proclaiming vindication, powerful to save." In the New Covenant passages we read, *Who are kept by the power of God through faith unto salvation ready to be revealed in the last time.* (1 Peter 1:5); *Now unto him that is able to keep you from falling, and to present you faultless before the presence of his glory with exceeding joy* (Jude 1:4); and *This [Jesus] is the stone rejected by you builders, which has become the cornerstone. There is salvation in no one else, for there is no other name under heaven given to people, and we must be saved by it.* (Acts 4:11-12). He is the answer to the only question that really matters: how can mortal man be reconciled to eternal God?

Isaiah 63:2-4 *Why are Your clothes red, and Your garments like one who treads a winepress? I trampled the winepress*

257

alone, and no one from the nations was with Me. I trampled them in My anger and ground them underfoot in My fury; their blood spattered My garments, and all My clothes were stained. For I planned the day of vengeance, and the year of My redemption came.

Isaiah can't seem to comprehend why the conquering One has red-stained clothes; white is the color of victory. Jesus' answer echoes again from what was later written (Rev 19:13-15): *He wore a robe stained with blood, and His name is the Word of God. The armies that were in heaven followed Him on white horses, wearing pure white linen. A sharp sword came from His mouth, so that He might strike the nations with it. He will shepherd them with an iron scepter. He will also trample the winepress of the fierce anger of God, the Almighty.* His robe is red because He has trampled the winepress of God's fierce anger. Note that His armies wear white. This trampling of the winepress is spoken of in Lamentations 1:15; Malachi 4:3; and Revelation 14, where we read (verse 20), *the press was trampled outside the city, and blood flowed out of the press up to the horses' bridles for about 180 miles.* As when the number of goats and bulls that the Levitical religion required to be sacrificed each year was astounding, so is the residue of the wicked on that great and terrible day when the Lord of Glory has His vengeance. This is what the rest of the answer in our passage reveals. The garments of Christ Jesus are stained by the blood of those who would not repent, could not believe. And their doom was sealed long ago as His day of vengeance was planned - as was the time of His redemption of His people. This we read in the jubilee chapter, 61 and verse 2: He came *to proclaim the year of the LORD's favor, and the day of our God's vengeance; to comfort all who mourn.*

Isaiah 63:5-6 *I looked, but there was no one to help, and I was amazed that no one assisted; so My arm accomplished victory for Me, and My wrath assisted Me. I crushed nations in My anger; I made them drunk with My wrath and poured out their blood on the ground.*

258

The victor, the judge of all flesh laments that no one came to help Him - this was amazing! I think it was written for our benefit - as we can be of no help to Christ in our redemption, so we can be of no help to Him as He metes out judgment. What's amazing is that we would think we are worthy to participate in either! All of His help came from Himself, just as the Father and Spirit helped Him in His earthly ministry. He crushed the nations in anger, made them drunk with His wrath, and He poured out their blood on the ground. Recall the astounding volume of blood that flowed from His winepress. There is no hope at this point for anyone who has not found a refuge in Christ Jesus. And there is no help from man that can be provided (see Acts 17:24-25).

Isaiah 63:7-9 *I will make known the LORD's faithful love [and] the LORD's praiseworthy acts, because of all the LORD has done for us— even the many good things [He has done] for the house of Israel and has done for them based on His compassion and the abundance of His faithful love. He said, "They are indeed My people, children who will not be disloyal," and He became their Savior. In all their suffering, He suffered, and the Angel of His Presence saved them. He redeemed them because of His love and compassion; He lifted them up and carried them all the days of the past.*

The prophet responds to His Lord. He will declare the faithful love and powerful acts that YHWH has done for them - his kinsmen of the flesh. A detailed review of how the Lord God had been compassionate to national Israel is found in several places, including Psalms 78:11-72 and 105:5-45. It was not due to their status as a nation or their moral character that God had compassion on them. His compassion on them was due entirely to His covenant to keep them as a unique people to Himself - until the appointed time, when the promised seed would come. In our passage here, the language of YHWH as Savior points us to the New Covenant, wherein He saved us according to the covenant He cut, not because of our status as a people apart from Him or any goodness He saw in us.

We are redeemed because of His love - read Ephesians 1:3-10 and 2:4-7 to see the eternal nature of the love God has poured out upon His elect people. We are lifted up and carried by the One Who cannot fail!

Isaiah 63:10-14 *But they rebelled and grieved His Holy Spirit. So He became their enemy [and] fought against them. Then He remembered the days of the past, [the days] of Moses [and] his people. Where is He who brought them out of the sea with the shepherds of His flock? Where is He who put His Holy Spirit among the flock? He sent His glorious arm to be at Moses' right hand, divided the waters before them to obtain eternal fame for Himself, and led them through the depths like a horse in the wilderness, so that they did not stumble. Like cattle that go down into the valley, the Spirit of the LORD gave them rest. You led Your people this way to make a glorious name for Yourself.*

We switch back to the covenant people led by Moses. Even in that covenant, rebellion against God grieved the Holy Spirit, for He is always attending to the people of God. Here is one difference between the Old and New Covenants: Rebellion against God by those in the New Covenant do not become enemies of God; He does not fight against us but for us. Rebellion against God by those in the Mosaic Covenant became enemies of God, against whom He fought. For a time. For then He thought about the covenant He made with them, as we read in Exodus 32:11-13 and Lev 26:40-45. He brings them back to their land, the substance of their covenantal blessing.

In our passage, we read of YHWH's glorious triumph over the Egyptians, with several word pictures to show His kindness towards them, giving them rest from their enemies on every side (Josh 21:44). All of this was done by God for the sake of His glorious name. Not for our sake did He sacrifice Himself for us, but for the sake of the Father's name.

Isaiah 63:15-19 *Look down from heaven and see from Your lofty home—holy and beautiful. Where is Your zeal and Your might? Your yearning and Your compassion are withheld from me. Yet You are our Father, even though Abraham does not know us and Israel doesn't recognize us. You, Yahweh, are our Father; from ancient times, Your name is our Redeemer. Why, Yahweh, do You make us stray from Your ways? You harden our hearts so we do not fear You. Return, because of Your servants, the tribes of Your heritage. Your holy people had a possession for a little while, [but] our enemies have trampled down Your sanctuary. We have become like those You never ruled over, like those not called by Your name.*

This passage begins a prayer of lament by ethnic Israel which stretches through chapter 64. It begins with a petition for God to look down from heaven and see them, wanting pity and compassion (see Deut 26:15; Psalms 33:14; and 102:19). They realized His habitation was holy and beautiful; they yearned to see His zeal and might in defending and lifting them up. Their appeal is partially based on Psalms 25:6 - *Remember, LORD, Your compassion and Your faithful love, for they [have existed] from antiquity.* His Word is the surest guide to what pleases Him; our emotions are not, our circumstances are not.

Notice in this passage that everything is of and from God - 17 times "You" and "Your" is used, reflecting the basis of the appeal is YHWH: His character, His might, His name. As God hardened Pharaoh's heart when he rebelled, so He has done so with national Israel when they rebelled. They realize this and know He must act if they are to repent and enjoy His compassion again. Without His active, positive engagement with them, Israel knows they will cease being His possession - trampled down and no different from those who were not His people, those not called by His name.

Saints - we have much in common with these souls that were in national Israel so long ago. If God pulled back from holding us up, we would fall. If we live in and enjoy our sin, He will harden our hearts. There is a line that cannot be crossed: those who were made His people and reconciled to the Father by the death of Christ CANNOT become "no longer His people." If you are in Christ, do not harden your heart like they did in the wilderness. When you and I grow weak and burdened by sin, the only effective recourse is to cry out God, draw close the Christ, plead for renewed love, repentance, humility, and joy. There is no other course that can restore us. There is nothing else that would please God.

Isaiah 64 - the Lament continues.

In chapter 63, the Spirit revealed the glory of Christ in the day of judgment. This scene prompted national Israel to cry out to God for mercy; this lament goes on to occupy all of chapter 64. If we fail to join in and seek mercy from God, even though our circumstances are different, we are in danger.

Isaiah 64:1-4 *If only You would tear the heavens open [and] come down, so that mountains would quake at Your presence— as fire kindles the brushwood, and fire causes water to boil— to make Your name known to Your enemies, so that nations will tremble at Your presence! When You did awesome works that we did not expect, You came down, and the mountains quaked at Your presence. From ancient times no one has heard, no one has listened, no eye has seen any God except You, who acts on behalf of the one who waits for Him.*

Chapter 63 ended with God's covenant people asking Him to remember them as such, despite their rebellion. This chapter opens with Israel asking YHWH to reveal Himself to the nations in a similar way He revealed Himself to them on My Sinai - with blazing fire, darkness, gloom, and storm (Heb 12:18) - so they would tremble before Him. As they had done - Hebrews 12:20-21 *for they could not bear what was commanded: And if even an animal touches the mountain, it must be stoned! The appearance was so terrifying that Moses said, I am terrified and trembling.)*

Israel might well have had this passage in mind: Judges 5:3-5 *Listen, kings! Pay attention, princes! I will sing to the LORD; I will sing praise to the LORD God of Israel. LORD, when You came from Seir, when You marched from the fields of Edom, the earth trembled, the heavens poured [rain], and the clouds poured water. The mountains melted before the LORD, even Sinai before the LORD, the God of Israel.* There is no god made by man that can hear, see, speak, or think; much less such a god that has or can make all things from nothing; can cause men to fear greatly and wish for death. And yet, men stop up their ears and minds to what creation tells them of this Creator-Judge God. The Son, alone, can look upon Him and not be consumed.

And this God is the one Paul testified of in front of the Oprah Winfry crowd of his day: Acts 17:24-26 *The God who made the world and everything in it—He is Lord of heaven and earth and does not live in shrines made by hands. Neither is He served by human hands, as though He needed anything, since He Himself gives everyone life and breath and all things. From one man He has made every nationality to live over the whole earth and has determined their appointed times and the boundaries of where they live.* This is the only God and He demands worship and is, alone, worthy of worship.

Isaiah 64:5-7 *You welcome the one who joyfully does what is right; they remember You in Your ways. But we have sinned, and You were angry. How can we be saved if we remain in our sins? All of us have become like something unclean, and all our righteous acts are like a polluted garment; all of us wither like a leaf, and our iniquities carry us away like the wind. No one calls on Your name, striving to take hold of You. For You have hidden Your face from us and made us melt because of our iniquity.*

God's character never changes: He welcomes those joyfully do what is right and remember His way and obey Him. But natural man can do nothing except sin and redeemed man is not capable of perfect obedience; while sin is no longer our master, we are still weak. Isaiah, on behalf of his people, asks the question that rings through history: "*How can we be saved if we remain in our sins?*" The wrong answer is to rely on self - because all are unclean and even the "good deeds" of the unregenerate man are polluted by his sinful nature. The sins of natural man are his master and they carry him about like a leaf on the ocean. Isaiah leaned on the ancient preacher: Ecclesiastes 7:20 *There is certainly no righteous man on the earth who does good and never sins.* God does not reveal Himself to non-elect sinners; His wrath against those who are not in the Son is unquenchable, hot, fierce anger against sin.

Isaiah 64:8-12 *Yet LORD, You are our Father; we are the clay, and You are our potter; we all are the work of Your hands. LORD, do not be terribly angry or remember [our] iniquity forever. Please look—all of us are Your people! Your holy cities have become a wilderness; Zion has become a wilderness, Jerusalem a desolation. Our holy and beautiful temple, where our fathers praised You, has been burned with fire, and all that was dear to us lies in ruins. LORD, after all this, will You restrain Yourself? Will You keep silent and afflict severely?*

This passage is also filled with statements about YHWH, 8 times You and Your are used to denote YHWH must act if sinners are to be reconciled to Him. The imagery of the clay and potter have been used before by Isaiah and was picked by Paul - there is no way to brush this aside because it is offensive to our flesh. While some are made for honorable use and other made for dishonorable use, the point is man is in no way qualified to participate in his redemption. The only hope man has is to be remade into something honorable, so the potter will look kindly upon him, to call "His people" those who were not His people. If He doesn't, their iniquity will be remembered forever. Contrast this with the redeemed, whose iniquity God promises never to remember! Without His hand of redemption, all things valued by man - cities, gardens, temples - become useless, burned down, ruined by fire. The people will be consumed if He does not relent and pour out mercy.

Saints - do not, I beg you, grow complacent about your walk. We should plead with God to guard us against drifting into mere rote religion, wherein the living faith of Christianity is traded out for something tame, manageable - traditions developed by men that are acceptable to the flesh. Daily we should ask YHWH to stir our hearts, wake us up to the truth of who we are IN HIM! How can one which has died to sin live therein any longer? Joyful obedience to what Christ calls us to is what is pleasing to Him - and this He gives us, as He wills and equips us to do that. Do not grieve the Holy Spirit but submit to Him with joy unspeakable, for He will abide in those the great Shepherd has brought into the sheepfold of God.

Isaiah 65 - Two Categories of People.

This is a relatively long chapter, with much of it describing the differences between the wicked and the godly. One main point the first part brings to us is that God has wrath for the wicked which cannot be escaped; many who are wicked are, as then, people who claim to be His people. Let those who have ears, hear what the Spirit says.

Isaiah 65:1-4 *I was sought by those who did not ask; I was found by those who did not seek Me. I said: Here I am, here I am, to a nation that was not called by My name. I spread out My hands all day long to a rebellious people who walk in the wrong path, following their own thoughts. These people continually provoke Me to My face, sacrificing in gardens, burning incense on bricks, sitting among the graves, spending nights in secret places, eating the meat of pigs, and putting polluted broth in their bowls.*

This chapter opens up with YHWH declaring that someone other than His covenant people had been called to Himself and found Him - though they were not looking for Him, did not ask for Him. In contrast, His covenant people, to whom He was known, rebel and follow the wrong path, their own wisdom. This provokes the Lord, as does their pagan religious practice. Their law said don't speak with the dead, don't eat pork - and they did these things and much more. Law against sin provokes sin. This is why those who say the Decalogue is the rule for the saints or for society miss the mark. Laws against things give the state the authority to punish evil doers, but they do not give the members of society the ability to obey them. These laws can only provoke sin - which is what Paul wrote in Romans 5:20, the law came in to INCREASE the transgressions! This to refute the Jews who had grown to believe they could obey the law and merit God's favor. Highlighting the difference between law-keeping and walking in the Spirit, Paul wrote, *But the fruit of the Spirit is love, joy, peace, patience, kindness, goodness, faith, gentleness, self-control.* ***Against such things there is no law.*** (Galatians 5:22-23) Unregenerate man needs laws against sin to be in place so he can be punished for his evil. 8 of the 10 words in the Decalogue are laws against sin. When the Spirit gives life, His people know that evil is wrong and they have new desires to please God, not rebel against Him.

Isaiah 65:5-7 *They say, 'Keep to yourself, don't come near me, for I am too holy for you!' These practices are smoke in My nostrils, a fire that burns all day long. It is written before Me: I will not keep silent, but I will repay; I will repay them fully [for] your iniquities and the iniquities of your fathers together," says the LORD. "Because they burned incense on the mountains and reproached Me on the hills, I will reward them fully for their former deeds."*

Self-righteous people of all stripes believe they are good and do not want anyone to confront them. This is a stench in the nose of the One Who created them and gives them breath. These people think that because judgment is delayed that either God is asleep or that they have escaped His notice or that He doesn't judge anyone. But there is coming a day - Isaiah has revealed this time and time again in this gospel vision. On that day, all who are not in Christ will suffer His wrath - each will be rewarded FULLY for their sinful deeds.

Isaiah 65:8-12 *The LORD says this: As the new wine is found in a bunch of grapes, and one says, 'Don't destroy it, for there's some good in it,' so I will act because of My servants and not destroy them all. I will produce descendants from Jacob, and heirs to My mountains from Judah; My chosen ones will possess it, and My servants will dwell there. Sharon will be a pasture for flocks, and the Valley of Achor a place for cattle to lie down, for My people who have sought Me.*

But you who abandon the LORD, who forget My holy mountain, who prepare a table for Fortune and fill bowls of mixed wine for Destiny, I will destine you for the sword, and all of you will kneel down to be slaughtered, because I called and you did not answer, I spoke and you did not hear; you did what was evil in My sight and chose what I did not delight in.

Using something familiar to the agrarian community, YHWH tells them that there are a few of His people in that community, servants of His - such as Isaiah. Perhaps Peter was thinking of this when he said, *The Lord does not delay His promise, as some understand delay, but is patient with you, not wanting any to perish but all to come to repentance* (2 Peter 3:9). In both places, the elect are the object of His mercy - God does not wait for those who hate Him to change their minds and come to Him. It's abundantly clear throughout the Scriptures what Jesus said, *No one can come to Me unless the Father who sent me draws him.* From Jacob - called Israel - God will deliver children that are His; and it's these chosen ones who will dwell with Him in places Isaiah describes in terms that would delight those who made their living off the land but have deeper meaning for those who know Him spiritually.

Those who abandon YHWH and live for their best life now are heaping up wrath for the day of judgment, destined for the sword because they did not have ears to hear. They are evil in His sight - the only visage that matters - and they will be slaughtered eternally.

Isaiah 65:13-16 *Therefore, this is what the Lord GOD says: My servants will eat, but you will be hungry; My servants will drink, but you will be thirsty; My servants will rejoice, but you will be put to shame. My servants will shout for joy from a glad heart, but you will cry out from an anguished heart, and you will lament out of a broken spirit. You will leave your name behind as a curse for My chosen ones, and the Lord*

GOD will kill you; but He will give His servants another name. Whoever is blessed in the land will be blessed by the God of truth, and whoever swears in the land will swear by the God of truth. For the former troubles will be forgotten and hidden from My sight.

The Word of God is that His people will be well cared for but the wicked will be ever hungry and ever thirsty. These terms brought up memories in their ranks of the promised land - the land of milk and honey God promised His people; they thought that was the end-game; but this description means something heavenly to those with eyes to see it.

Note this back and forth contrast between those who are called His people and those who are not His people. It carries through the Scriptures and Isaiah's gospel. The wrath poured out on the wicked is dire - they will cry out from a broken spirit and be put to death by God for their concern is for self. Let those who think God is nothing BUT love read that passage over again, slowly. God loves His people, His spiritual people; He has NO LOVE for those not in Christ. Yet for all who trust in Jesus, believe on Him and His finished work - God will put their deeds out of His sight and mind. This is blessedness by the God of truth! Every other message is from the god of lies.

The final section in this chapter is rightly titled in HCSB as A New Creation! I see a literary feature in this next section that helps our understanding: the basic building block of Hebrew poetry - the couplet.

Isaiah 65:17-20 *For I will create a new heaven and a new earth; the past events will not be remembered or come to mind. Then be glad and rejoice forever in what I am creating; for I will create Jerusalem to be a joy and its people to be a delight. I will rejoice in Jerusalem and be glad in My people. The sound of weeping and crying will no longer be heard in*

269

her. In her, a nursing infant will no longer live only a few days, or an old man not live out his days. Indeed, the youth will die at a hundred years, and the one who misses a hundred years will be cursed.

These four verses are said to be two poems, with the first part being YHWH describing and rejoicing over His new creation and the second part Him describing what life thereon will be like for those who are His people. When we consider what the rest of relevant Scripture says about the New Jerusalem, streets of clear gold, pearls as big as large doors, walls 200 feet think and 1,400 miles long! This is John's description from Rev 21, alluding to Ezekiel's vision of this city in Ezek 40-41. It is beyond description in human language. The life in that city as described by John is pure bliss - no more sorrow, sin, pain, or death! Isaiah described this in words he and his kinsmen could comprehend. The present cursed age is full of sorrow, sin, pain, and death. Isaiah said life in the New Jerusalem would be empty of weeping and full of long life. The one who dies young is cursed - yet this is life in the New Jerusalem and death is not known, so no one CAN BE cursed. This colorful, poetic language is not meant to taken literally; but are meant to paint a picture of what God has in store for His people.

Another thing to think on: In verse 17 God declares He will create a new heaven and new earth and a new Jerusalem. When He redeems His people He gives them a new name (Rev 2:17) as He makes ALL THINGS NEW! (Rev 21:5)

Isaiah 65:21-22 *People will build houses and live [in them]; they will plant vineyards and eat their fruit. They will not build and others live [in them]; they will not plant and others eat. For My people's lives will be like the lifetime of a tree. My chosen ones will fully enjoy the work of their hands.*

Note the first two sentences above - a couplet that repeats the idea that their work will be rewarded and not taken from them. People will build houses and live in them; they will not build and have others live in them. They will plant and eat; they will not plant for other to eat. And the reason for this goodness is that they are God's people and He insures their needs are taken care and their good works are rewarded. Another reference to long life (the man in Psalm 1 - like a tree planted next to a river) and enjoyment in the work YHWH provides. Work now isn't always enjoyable, even though every honest job is a gift from God. In the age to come, all work will be honorable and enjoyable.

Isaiah 65:23-25 *"They will not labor without success or bear children [destined] for disaster, for they will be a people blessed by the LORD along with their descendants. Even before they call, I will answer; while they are still speaking, I will hear. The wolf and the lamb will feed together, and the lion will eat straw like the ox, but the serpent's food will be dust! They will not do what is evil or destroy on My entire holy mountain, " says the LORD.*

Another aspect of life in New Jerusalem - all labor will be successful. Though we have no giving in marriage and, therefore, no child-bearing there, this is simply another metaphor for life without the sorrow and pain of this life. This will be on account of YHWH blessing all His people and being attentive to them - before we call, He hears. Unlike in this age, wherein it took 21 days for Michael to get back to Daniel. The wild animals will be at peace as well - but no rest or peace for the serpent! Nothing and no one that does evil with be allowed on the holy mountain of God, where His New Jerusalem resides.

Saints - hear this: We have peace with God through faith in Christ Jesus. No other way. His way, His name, His grace -

is the only way. This is the gospel and it's all we have for those who are perishing. Be faithful with His gospel and trust Him to redeem every lost sheep.

Isaiah 66 - Judgment and Redemption.

As we come to the end of Isaiah's vision of judgment and redemption as it's been laid out in virtually every chapter, it's fitting that it ends with the same contrast and a focus on the One who makes a difference.

Isaiah 66:1-2 *This is what the LORD says: Heaven is My throne, and earth is My footstool. What house could you possibly build for Me? And what place could be My home? My hand made all these things, and so they all came into being. [This is] the LORD's declaration. I will look favorably on this kind of person: one who is humble, submissive in spirit, and trembles at My word.*

Make no mistake, YHWH is speaking; the One who created all things and will judge all flesh. He inhabits the entirety of His creation, using known celestial bodies to represent His kingdom. "Throne" and "footstool" represent royalty and power. Considering Who He is and what He is, He asks His people two rhetorical questions, revealing that nothing man can do is fit for Him to dwell in. This is what Paul alluded to when he told the Oprah Winfry (she is useful as an example!) crowd of his day, *The God who made the world and everything in it—He is Lord of heaven and earth and does not live in shrines made by hands. Neither is He served by human hands, as though He needed anything, since He Himself gives everyone life and breath and all things* (Acts 17:24-25). Nothing came into existent apart from His will and word. The only think He will look favorably upon is what

He has made - humble, submissive people who revere His Word.

Look back 2 Samuel 7 and other place and see if God ever asked David or Solomon to build Him the temple that was built. What God had promised David, and what David misunderstood because of his fleshly outlook, was that YHWH Himself would make a house for David! In 2 Samuel 7:4-7, God reminds David of His faithfulness and reminds him (verse 7) that He never asked for a house of cedar. The verse 11b through 16 is what David got wrong, thinking Solomon would do this. The beginning of this passage is clear: God would build the house through a Son, descended (according to the flesh) from David. This Son would be charged with the wrong-doing of others and take their punishment from God on their account - but He would rule and that house will endure forever! Read Peter talk about the spiritual stones being built up into a house; read John's description of Jerusalem from heaven; and read Paul's allegory of the two Jerusalems, with the note about our mother being the heavenly Jerusalem. Spiritual Jerusalem is the city for spiritual Israel!

Isaiah 66:3-4 *One slaughters an ox, one kills a man; one sacrifices a lamb, one breaks a dog's neck; one offers a grain offering, one offers pig's blood; one offers incense, one praises an idol— all these have chosen their ways and delight in their detestable practices. So I will choose their punishment, and I will bring on them what they dread because I called and no one answered; I spoke and they didn't hear; they did what was evil in My sight and chose what I didn't delight in.*

In verse 2 we read about those God approves; in these verses we see composites of those who are evil. These wicked people see no difference between killing a beast and killing a man. In our day, it's worse to kill a beast than a man, according to the voices that dominate our society! But evil people will deal cruelly with one for no reason; he will offer up pig's blood! A beast forbidden and the blood - which was forbidden; a vivid picture for the Hebrew nation of the extreme wickedness of these enemies of His - some of whom were their own kinsmen of the flesh. These idol worshipers delight in their detestable practices - just as people in our day parade for "gay rights" and celebrate the murder of babies.

These people, who have suppressed their knowledge of the truth by their unrighteousness, will be punished by God, according to the evil they have done. Dread beyond their ability to comprehend will come on them - this is what John wrote about with the plagues where people asked for death but it would not come; where they cried out for mountains to fall on them, but they could not hide them from the wrath of the Lamb. The terrors of being naked before God on that Day are beyond words; we ought to be filled with sorrow for those who are perishing, witnessing to them and praying God would give them a new heart.

Isaiah 66:5-6 *You who tremble at His word, hear the word of the LORD: "Your brothers who hate and exclude you because of Me have said, 'Let the LORD be glorified so that we can see your joy!' But they will be put to shame." A sound of uproar from the city! A voice from the temple— the voice of the LORD, paying back His enemies what they deserve!*

This contrast continues as those who are His people are to hear Him, just as His people were told, *This is my beloved Son, LISTEN to HIM!* (Luke 9:35). Jesus is the living Word of God - HEAR HIM! Those who are His people have brothers in the flesh who hate them, as Peter taught: 1 Peter 4:1-5 *Therefore, since Christ suffered in the flesh, equip yourselves also with the same resolve—because the one who*
274

suffered in the flesh has finished with sin—in order to live the remaining time in the flesh, no longer for human desires, but for God's will. For there has already been enough time spent in doing what the pagans choose to do: carrying on in unrestrained behavior, evil desires, drunkenness, orgies, carousing, and lawless idolatry. So they are surprised that you don't plunge with them into the same flood of wild living—and they slander you. They will give an account to the One who stands ready to judge the living and the dead.

Our joy at being in Christ is not dependent on the approval of people who do not know Him! The Creator of all things will resound from His temple - His people - as He pays His enemies their wages.

Isaiah 66:7-11 *Before Zion was in labor, she gave birth; before she was in pain, she delivered a boy. Who has heard of such a thing? Who has seen such things? Can a land be born in one day or a nation be delivered in an instant? Yet as soon as Zion was in labor, she gave birth to her sons. "Will I bring a baby to the point of birth and not deliver [it]?" says the LORD; "or will I who deliver, close [the womb]?" says your God. Be glad for Jerusalem and rejoice over her, all who love her. Rejoice greatly with her, all who mourn over her—so that you may nurse and be satisfied from her comforting breast and drink deeply and delight yourselves from her glorious breasts.*

Zion gave birth before labor, delivered before pain. Who has heard of or seen such things? The next question shows us the line of thought - this is a nation He is speaking of; alluded to in Gal 4:26; Acts 2:41; 21:20; and Rom 15:18-21. From the beginning, God's plan for His people to come from every nation - Gen 15:4-5. Nothing can stop His people from being given new life - this ought to be cause for us to rejoice as we are part of New Jerusalem! As new born babes desire their mother's milk, we ought to be content with being found in Christ as His people. Rom 15:9-12: *and so that Gentiles may glorify God for His mercy. As it is written: Therefore I will praise You among the Gentiles, and I will sing psalms to Your name. Again it says: Rejoice, you Gentiles, with His people! And again: Praise the Lord, all you Gentiles; all the peoples should praise Him! And again, Isaiah says: The root of Jesse will appear, the One who rises to rule the Gentiles; the Gentiles will hope in Him.* As there is no Jew or Gentile IN Christ, we who were such rejoice TOGETHER as ONE!

Isaiah 66:12-13 *For this is what the LORD says: I will make peace flow to her like a river, and the wealth of nations like a flood; you will nurse and be carried on [her] hip and bounced on [her] lap. As a mother comforts her son, so I will comfort you, and you will be comforted in Jerusalem.*

YHWH gives peace like a river to our souls - hear the old hymn? As when Egypt gave up her riches to the Hebrew people when God rescued them by His strong arm, He will provide all we need in this life - though we be buffeted by trails. He will carry us as a mother carries her infants, He will comfort us as a mother comforts her infants; we will be comforted in New Jerusalem - the dwelling place of the Lamb.

Isaiah 66:14-17 *You will see, you will rejoice, and you will flourish like grass; then the LORD's power will be revealed to His servants, but He will show His wrath against His enemies. Look, the LORD will come with fire— His chariots are like the whirlwind— to execute His anger with fury and His rebuke with flames of fire. For the LORD will execute judgment on all flesh with His fiery sword, and many will be slain by the LORD. "Those who dedicate and purify themselves to [enter] the groves following their leader, eating meat from pigs, vermin, and rats, will perish together." [This is] the LORD's declaration.*

This contrast between worlds continues, as YHWH declares He will reveal His power to His people, as the means to cause them to flourish; this will be reason for them to rejoice. To His enemies, His power will be revealed as wrath, fire that cannot be withstood; to bring His fury and rebuke upon them with flames that will never die out. Again, YHWH declares He will execute judgment on all flesh - those not born of the Spirit - and they will suffer the second death, which does not end. And yet, YHWH declares that there will be false brothers who go through religious rituals yet continue to show their disdain for His instructions and covenant. All who do these things, following those wicked men who lead the way, will all perish. This is YHWH's declaration, built upon what He said in Isaiah 65:3 & 4.

Isaiah 66:18-21 *"Knowing their works and their thoughts, I have come to gather all nations and languages; they will come and see My glory. I will establish a sign among them, and I will send survivors from them to the nations—to Tarshish, Put, Lud (who are archers), Tubal, Javan, and the islands far away—who have not heard of My fame or seen My glory. And they will proclaim My glory among the nations. They will bring all your brothers from all the nations as a gift to the LORD on horses and chariots, in litters, and on mules and camels, to My holy mountain Jerusalem," says the LORD, "just as the Israelites bring an offering in a clean vessel to the house of the LORD. I will also take some of them as priests and Levites," says the LORD.*

This passage is devoted to the good news for those who are His people. The deeds and thoughts of those indwelt by His

Spirit are pleasing to God. He will call to Himself people from every nation and tongue - they will come to Him, as none called by YHWH can refuse. They will be given eyes to behold His glory and be amazed and rejoicing. He will give them a sign, as He gave the Sabbath to national Israel - the sign of this New Covenant is the fulfillment of the Jewish Passover and by it His death and victorious return will proclaimed to all, near and far, as a means to bring them to the Great Shepherd; they will, in return, proclaim His glory to the world. All the redeemed will be presented as gifts, from the Father to the Son and from the Son to the Father. All the trappings of worldly wealth can only hint at the glory of God's presence with His people in New Jerusalem. In what I believe to be a preview of the apostles and prophets of the inaugurated kingdom of the first century, YHWH declares He will call some of His elect to serve as priests and Levites - offices of import in Isaiah's day. Signs and shadows portrayed in familiar terms to partially reveal the spiritual reality that would be made clear in the fullness of time.

Isaiah 66:22-24 *For just as the new heavens and the new earth, which I will make, will endure before Me"— [this is] the LORD's declaration— "so your offspring and your name will endure. All mankind will come to worship Me from one New Moon to another and from one Sabbath to another," says the LORD. "As they leave, they will see the dead bodies of the men who have rebelled against Me; for their worm will never die, their fire will never go out, and they will be a horror to all mankind.*

The final 3 verses in Isaiah's vision bring us back to the contrast between those who are His people and those who are not. When Jesus returns, He will judge the nations, gather His people, and make all things new. That's what we see here, but not in that order.

YHWH declares that the new heavens and the new earth that He will make shall endure and so will His people. All who are His will worship Him with faithful devotion national Israel was unable to perform, even with a clear order to follow. Those New Moons (monthly events) and weekly Sabbaths were a type and shadow of the spiritual things (Col 2:16 & 17; Heb 8:1-6). We saw in Isaiah 1:13 & 14 that national Israel's religious performance was a stench in God's nose. That covenant community was not given the Spirit to guide them in truth, to give them spiritual understanding. They grew comfortable living in religion that demanded outward compliance and gave false assurance to those who thought their birth connection and appearance of godliness was sufficient. Those in the spiritual covenant each have the Spirit and know the Lord, growing in the grace and knowledge of Christ Jesus (2 Pet 3:18). They will grow in confidence in Him and His work, seeing all their false goodness as rubbish. This is preparation for the saints to worship God rightly - in spirit and in truth. The spiritual fulfillment of the Jewish religion.

As these people run to Christ, leaving this world and its system behind, they will see the bodies of those who did not find peace. These people will not be annihilated - their worm (inner man) never dies, the fire that burns them will never go out; they will be a horror to everyone. This is seen in Revelation 19:17-21 and 14:10-11. These passages teach us that our joy at being secure in Christ is not held hostage to being ignorant of His judgment on the wicked. If you cannot love the Lord Jesus because you have loved ones who belong to the devil, you have a seriously wrong view of justice and mercy. None of us deserve anything less than the endless, unrelenting, terrifying wrath of God. Isaiah's gospel has pointed out in many ways that natural man is an enemy of God; that God has chosen a remnant that He will save for and to Himself. And that ALL who find peace in Him will be filled with joy.

True faith in Christ brings peace and joy that no amount of world news or sorrow over departed family who died in their sins can take from us. Having an accurate picture of Jesus, as the suffering Servant and the victorious Savior, is essential for His people to having the joy He promises. This is the gospel Isaiah proclaimed, this is the gospel Jesus gave to us to proclaim. You and I may not get a vision from God as Isaiah and John did, but we have a more sure word, we benefit from faithful men who have gone before us. Let us encourage one another while it is today and may none of us harden our hearts as they did in the wilderness. All things were written for us so we won't sin like they did. He has given Himself to us and given us to one another - this is His plan, His work, to build His people until He comes the second time.

FINIS

Bibliography

1. Hal Brunson, The Rickety Bridge and the Broken Mirror, (New York, iUniverse, 2007), page 60

Made in the USA
Las Vegas, NV
18 June 2021

24979704R00160